LAND INTO LANDSCAPE

LAND into LANDSCAPE

J O H N   M I C H A E L   H U N T E R

George Godwin
London and New York

George Godwin
an imprint of:
Longman Group Limited
Longman House, Burnt Mill, Harlow
Essex CM20 2JE, England
Associated companies throughout the world

*Published in the United States of America
by Longman Inc., New York*

First published 1985

British Library Cataloguing in Publication Data

Hunter, J.M.
  Land into landscape.
  1. Landscape – History
  I. Title
  719'.09   GF50

  ISBN 0-7114-5625-9

Library of Congress Cataloging in Publication Data

Hunter, John Michael, 1932–
  Land into landscape.

  Bibliography: p.
  Includes index.
  1. Landscape assessment—History. 2. Landscape
architecture—History. 3. Landscape
assessment—Great Britain—History. 4. Landscape
architecture—Great Britain—History. I. Title.
GF90.H86   1985   712'.09   84–6016
ISBN 0–7114–5625–9

Set in 10/11 pt Linotron 202 Baskerville
Printed in Great Britain at The Pitman Press, Bath

Contents

Foreword

In the late 1970s changes in the countryside and the loss of sites important for wildlife conservation became political issues. Concern was also voiced at the decay and loss of historic parks and gardens. This late development in Britain – the North Americans were a century ahead of us in this respect – reflected an attitude. While the need for protection for historic buildings and settlements was accepted earlier, the former by the Town and Country Planning Act of 1947 and the latter by the Civic Amenities Act 1967, the rural hinterlands of these buildings and towns remained neglected, possibly because the countryside had for long been taken for granted and its antiquity unappreciated. Yet Professor Hoskins had demonstrated the great age and interest of many features of the countryside in *The Making of the English Landscape*, first published in 1955 and running subsequently into many editions. While his book must have been read by many, I suspect that it was digested by few. Fortunately these few included historian geographers, archaeologists and historian biologists whose work has confirmed Hoskins's dictum that 'everything is older than we think'.

Appreciation and dissemination of the knowledge gained has come late. The lowland landscape of Britain has altered, although not as drastically as some would have us believe. If information had been available earlier at the local level, I do not doubt that many farmers and their ministry advisers would have devised their farm improvement schemes to take account of valuable archaeological and biological features. Now that the information is there the speed of change has slackened in our productive landscapes, although marginal land remains another matter.

In 1972 I became involved in advising Essex farmers on tree planting in the wake of Dutch Elm disease and I soon found that the most important part of my job was to evaluate existing landscape features and to give advice on how they could be retained and managed as part of the farm plan. Those days were exciting; Dr Oliver Rackham's studies of Essex woods were coming through to us, we were applying biological dating techniques recently pioneered at Monk's Wood to hedgerows and archaeologists had begun to specialise in the study of early field and settlement patterns. Most importantly, we found that many farmers welcomed us on to their land and were interested in what we had to say.

One thing of course leads to another. The preservation of important features such as ancient woodlands or historic parks requires an understanding of their traditional management and this leads to the field of landscape history, a delightful subject in itself, but also of practical value in providing clues to beneficial management. History leads us to inquire into our forebears' attitudes to nature and landscape, and into their beliefs and their concepts; and to ask whether these have a value for us today. This is what this book is about; the ecological ethic extolled by Aldo Leopold and Frank Fraser Darling has something in common with the world of Cato, Varro and Virgil and, indeed, that of the ancient Persians.

The study of Essex hedgerows and woods has led me back, inevitably it seems and perhaps extraordinarily, to the earliest written records, and this book begins in ancient Sumeria and goes on to embrace the early Near East and Mediterranean. Like a zoom lens the field narrows to Britain, and ultimately to the Essex of the early 1980s. This may be a limitation, but I make no apology for this approach; it is best that an author deals only with subjects he has studied or has direct knowledge of. No one could now write a comprehensive history of landscape for there is too much information available.

A disadvantage of this 'zoom' approach is the relative speed of change. In ancient Rome it is slow, depending on new discoveries by archaeologists, but in contemporary Britain and America the scene may change in a matter of months: the narrower the lens, the more fluid the subject. Already I have amended the final text of this book to omit criticism of the management of rivers; the engineers I now meet professionally are sensitive men, very different from those of a year or two ago. By the time this book is published I may have certain regrets for what is written in *Modern Landscapes*, but this is inevitable – if one is to say anything about the present, some of it may soon appear ephemeral.

Professor Hoskins, in his great work, included many quotations from contemporary poets. Taking this cue, I have examined the works of poets, writers and painters in Antiquity, the Middle Ages and the Renaissance. Oddly I have found a marked lack of communication between different fields of study; for example, writers on Flemish landscape paintings appear to give no thought to the factual value of what they were depicting and conversely, students of landscape and technology do not appear to have considered the information some of these paintings contain.

I am personally impressed by the emotive power of symbols and their long survival and recurrence. The problem is that of corroborative evidence. We have written accounts of the symbolism of every flower and tree in a Persian garden and the medieval cloister, but none to substantiate Lethaby and Spenglers' view of Gothic architecture which I personally accept but cannot prove. So we come down to opinion, and I have woken in the night considering the awful prospect that some poor student will receive a black mark for quoting me on the origin of the crown post. I hope that I have given sufficient disclaimers to avoid such a pitfall.

Another problem in landscape history, as in the history of architecture, is that of exemplars. Most books still depict the garden of the

Generalife as the exemplar of Saracenic garden design. We now know that the planting, garden levels and jets belong to a later age and that there is little that is Saracenic to see. Instead we now have the excavated gardens described by Mr Dickie. But are these representative of their time? We must assume that they are, but there is no abundance of evidence to prove that this is so. I have discussed the early medieval cloister garden of the Quattro Coronati as an exemplar. This may be shaky ground and I take refuge in the disclaimer: 'to the best of our present knowledge'.

Finally, I recall the words of my tutor, the late David Roberts, who on concluding a superb course of lectures on the history of architecture declared that his sole purpose was to persuade his students to visit the buildings he had described. I cannot equal his skill, but I do hope that some who may read this book will visit, if they have not done so already, the great planned landscapes of Tivoli, Lante, Villandry, Rousham, Stowe and Sissinghurst, and also look with interest at the parks, hedgerows, moats, ponds, grass roads and woodlands of their familiar countryside where perhaps they will discover features of interest that have been missed or neglected, for these are many.

Acknowledgements

I wish to record my gratitude to Mr P. Aynsley-Smith and Mr K. Peake-Jones who respectively introduced me to the history of art and the Roman authors when at school; to Dr M. Evans, Mr A. Horn, Miss A. Ness and Mr I. Robinson for their help in the course of writing this book and to Mrs M. Batey for leading me to a better understanding of the English achievement of the early 18th century. I am particularly indebted to Miss M. O'Donnell for her considerable guidance and to Mr P. Selman for his comments before undertaking final editing.

I thank my employers, Essex County Council, whose concern for countryside conservation has enabled me to write about today's countryside from direct experience of its problems and opportunities. Also the many Essex farmers I have met and worked with, in particular Mr J. Tabor, Mr E. Tabor and Mr J. Padfield.

I wish also to thank Mr P. Rogers for help with reprographics.

To Julia, Richard, Caroline and Simon

Chapter 1

Concepts

Land and landscape

Land is defined as earth, the solid portion of the surface of the globe; *landscape* is the appearance of that portion of land which the eye can view; the aspect of a country, or a picture representing it [1]. The land is primeval, shaped and reshaped by geophysical forces and climatic change eons before man's arrival. Land becomes landscape when seen by man, revealing the record of his activities on the surface of the earth and his relationship with his environment. The perception of landscape reveals his attitude towards it and generates emotions ranging from distrust and fear to reassurance and delight. These may arise from the view of a real landscape or from the imagery of a poet, painter or writer.

For long, mankind seems to have achieved a symbiosis with nature and respect for the environment. The conservation ethic was often disguised within religious beliefs, and calamities which occurred such as drought, famine and flood were usually outside man's control and not brought about by his actions. Real problems began as technology developed and populations grew with demands on resources and consequent spoliation of the land, waste and pollution, and destruction of wildlife. These problems are now recognised, but solutions often founder because although a complex problem may be reduced to its components and each component understood, their reassembly and comprehension as a whole prove far more difficult, for there are many specialists but few synthesisers. This is termed *reductionism* and is a besetting problem in our attitudes to land and landscape in the late twentieth century.

The effect of reductionism in Britain is unhappily apparent in many redevelopment schemes for the inner areas of cities and the centres of towns which result too often in an assemblage of parts that fails to achieve a coherent whole. The concept of an urban unity of parts related to the whole has been lost and instead we often find social and visual cacophony.

Similar problems are evident in our use of rural land in Britain and are reflected in the landscape. The traditional fabric of the countryside, a rich and complex pattern often evolved over many centuries, has been subjected to swift and sweeping changes, usually for a single

1. Chambers Twentieth Century Dictionary.

purpose. As with urban redevelopment, major changes in the landscape are often the result of intervention by government departments
and agencies pursuing their own sectional aims with small regard for
the aims of other parties, for there is no overall strategy that could
provide a synthesis. Spending power lies with 'improving' rather than
conserving interests, resulting in the ploughing up of moorlands, the
draining of wetlands, the conversion of uplands and woodlands to conifer plantations, and the canalisation of rivers and streams, all of
which activities receive attractive subsidies from central government
and are usually contrary to amenity interests and nature conservation.
These instances mostly concern marginal land where government intervention in itself is not wrong, rather it is the method and approach
which are unbalanced due to reductionist thinking and lack of
synthesis.

On productive land, changes as a whole have been less drastic due
perhaps to a certain conservatism and traditional distrust of specialists
on the part of landowners and farmers. Even so, the trend to single
aims and uses may give cause for concern; a complex system is inherently more stable than a simple one, and the countryside looked
at as a system, has become progressively more simple.

This process is not new. Parliamentary enclosures (c. 1740 onwards)
of common lands and open fields conformed to a trend away from the
complex manorial system of multi-use and customary rights, with forward planning governed by manorial court or village council towards
the private ownership and exclusive use of land for a single purpose.
The Highland clearances of that time were extreme examples of this
trend, accompanied by human suffering and resulting in the ultimate
degradation of the land; grouse moors often now cover former fields
and woodlands which sustained a considerable population. The landscaped parks of the later eighteenth century, so admired today, served
a single use: to provide picturesque settings for country houses; other
uses such as grazing and timber growing were incidental, cows or deer
were there for their appearance and trees planted for their effect in
the landscape. Earlier parks were often richer in social and economic
terms and this was reflected in the management and variety of their
landscape. Similarly with woodland, one can compare the complex
and careful management of a self-renewing resource in the Middle
Ages in which everything was used and nothing wasted with the commercial plantations of today whose sole function is the production of
timber, raised by methods that make them vulnerable to diseases and
pests.

The same trend is evident in the history of garden design. Productivity and delight were both indivisible elements of the paradise
tradition and the separation of functions would appear inexplicable
to a designer of gardens before the seventeenth century. Both medieval
gardens and the Islamic char-bagh, rooted in the traditions of ancient
Persia and Mesopotamia, combined the growing of fruits and useful
herbs with the beauty, colour and scent of flowers; the garden itself
was both a microcosm of a wider order and an analogue of the Eden
man had lost in his Fall and of the celestial Paradise which might be
his reward. This symbolism within a framework of belief was also a
fundamental element in the design. Productivity was hidden within
the gardens of Versailles and a century later this element was treated
as an embarrassment by Capability Brown and kept from view in the

many schemes he was called on to devise. This schism has persisted down to the gardens of today which mostly appear bereft of any guidelines or principles; the art that enhanced our villages, towns and country houses in the past appears dormant. If this comment appears harsh, compare the traditional cottage garden with its subtle combination of function and amenity, with the new gardens of most housing estates today.

Reductionism, fragmentation and lack of guiding principles characterise our attitudes to land and the activities which affect and alter the landscape. The optimist may look to the conservation movement, the knowledge gained from ecology and to recent practical studies to achieve a synthesis of aims in the productive countryside. This points to a holistic view, which may indeed be necessary for our survival. It is unrealistic as well as hypocritical to expect Third World countries to preserve landscapes of global importance if richer nations allow their own landscape resources to be destroyed, even if these are only of regional or local significance. In Britain, for example, it is hypocrisy to lament the loss of tropical rain forest while ancient woodlands are still degraded or destroyed.

The holistic approach demands that all factors are taken into account and this requires an understanding of the past if a full evaluation is to be made of the components which form the landscape of today. The study of history may illumine the present, revealing the source of conflicts, the consequence of past actions and may even point to solutions, and this is true of landscape. It is not suggested that we seek to re-create the landscapes of the past, but by understanding the context in which they were formed, the concepts and beliefs which governed them, we may be better equipped to approach the problems of the present. The historic dimension is essential if a coherent and creative philosophy is to form the framework for preservation, conservation or change. A true understanding of the past is the key to the quality of our future landscapes.

The pursuit of understanding leads us to consider concepts which historically lay behind attitudes to landscape and the planning of landscapes in Europe, and this in turn leads us far back to the mythologies of Antiquity (ancient Greece and Rome) and the Near East (Mesopotamia, Palestine and Persia) which describe events thought to have occurred before early civilisations arose. These concepts had remarkable persistence, and together with others which appeared later, can be followed through subsequent centuries to our own time when they are still not wholly forgotten.

Before examining these early concepts, some broad definition of types of landscape is useful, here termed the *functional*, the *ideal* and *wilderness*. This is for convenience and it must be borne in mind that the distinctions implied are by no means always exclusive.

Definitions

The functional landscape is the community's source of food and until recent times supplied its fuel, materials for clothing, and clay, stone and timber for building. Its appearance has been determined by these functions and by the underlying factors of soil quality, topography and climate. It has been affected over the ages by economic development, social and political organisation, and the expansion and decline of populations; the structures of defence and war have left their imprint, and the monuments of former peoples, their purpose often long forgotten, are a visible reminder of the antiquity of a landscape which may have first been altered and adapted to meet the needs of farmers in Britain some 6,000 years ago. No doubt this landscape has always delighted countrymen in their leisure time (it is a townman's myth that the countryman is oblivious to his surroundings), and occasionally the sporting or aesthetic interests of landowners have left their mark with spinneys and groves, but functional considerations have been paramount and if a landscape has evolved that is deemed beautiful by the observer, this is by way of a bonus.

Ideal landscapes include the garden, cloister, park and pleasure ground; they were planned for a variety of reasons, ceremony, pleasure, relaxation, contemplation and spiritual peace and, sometimes, prestige; they range in size from tiny cloisters to planned landscapes of many square kilometres. They sprang from a delight and respect for the forms of nature rather than from functional needs for food and other products, although they sometimes supplied them, particularly in pre-Renaissance times. Medieval hunting parks and forests combined a multiplicity of uses in addition to recreation and delight and in these cases the 'functional' and 'ideal' overlap and defy generalisations that over-simplify, for management would depend essentially on local need and custom. Attitudes to the wider landscape, beyond the pale or wall surrounding the planned and ideal have varied over the centuries. Views over the *paessagio* were planned into the formal hillside gardens of Italy and, similarly, by the designers of the Alhambra. By contrast, in the later eighteenth century in England the wooded pale tended to exclude the functional countryside; the productive landscape which produced the wealth to support mansion and park was screened from view. Certain concepts and symbols stemming from ancient beliefs, religions or philosophies, often underlay the design of these landscapes, whether small cloisters or vast parks [2]. The variety of these landscapes and the forms evolved since an enclosed park was first described in the *Epic of Gilgamesh* perhaps 5,000 years ago is extraordinary, but certain themes recur and their history, evolution and progeny can be followed.

A third landscape is that of wilderness, the realm of untamed Nature, traditionally feared as unpredictable, alien and full of hidden menace. In later centuries the remaining areas of wilderness came to be admired for their qualities of remoteness, solitude and sense of natural order, free from the imposed order and interference of man. But this is a relatively modern attitude; few would have understood it in Antiquity, or in succeeding centuries in the West until painters of the Flemish school began to study and depict the fantastic shapes of rock formations [3]. At much the same time in Persia, the development of landscape painting enabled artists to depict scenes of wild and rocky country with a loving humility and respect for nature. But it was only in the later eighteenth century with the cult of the Sublime that mountain and moorland scenery became generally admired and later still that it became popular as an escape from towns and cities, an antidote to crowded and often degraded urban life [4].

Concepts which underly both planned landscapes and appreciation of the wider landscapes beyond are a theme of this book. Two are of paramount importance in Western Europe and concern man's origin

2. W. R. Lethaby, writing at the beginning of the century, explored the concepts that underlay the temples and palaces of the ancient world and how often forms which appear to us purely architectural or decorative were used to reflect a belief in the basic order of the world and cosmos. The building was a microcosm. Written records of Islamic gardens reveal a wider order and symbolism expressed in their layouts and planting, and since these gardens stood in a tradition long preceding the rise of Islam, it seems likely that they reflect the gardens of ancient Babylonia and Persia.

3. In Antiquity the Younger Pliny could admire the summits of mountains crowning the view from his Tuscan villa, but more generally it was the gentler slopes such as those of Mounts Ida and Parnassus which were regarded as benevolent, the latter sacred to Apollo and the Muses. In Byzantine and medieval paintings mountains are depicted without interest by symbolic forms deriving from the late Hellenistic. Petrarch was thought to be unique in climbing a mountain to enjoy the prospects, but even he was then seized by an attack of bad conscience for admiring earthly things.

4. The term *wilderness* is used here in a European sense. For natural wilderness one must travel to other continents, for example to North America, where Amerindian traditions of a hunting economy and respect for nature preserved superb landscapes which were appreciated, fought for, and in part ultimately saved from exploitation by the American conservation movement. European wilderness is largely the work of man, although climatic change has also played its part. A case might be made in Britain that many foreshores and rocky heights above the snowline represent natural wilderness areas, but even here the effects of pollution and human activity are generally evident.

and early life in a primal state of innocence and harmony with the natural order, followed by a fall from grace. With the general acceptance of Darwinian theory these concepts were demoted to the level of myths, explained away as symbolic analogies or treated simply as fairy-tales, and it is difficult for us now to comprehend their former strength and persistence; yet from Antiquity until the nineteenth century they influenced philosophers, poets and painters in their attitudes to the landscape and the natural world, and took form in the creation of planned landscapes and gardens where an ideal landscape, reflecting a lost world of order and innocence often underlies the more immediate and functional factors of design. In considering the landscapes of the Ancient World, the Middle Ages and, to some extent, more recent times, it is useful to begin with a description of these concepts and the traditions which belong to them. The first is the belief of the Greeks and Romans in a former Golden Age, the second, from the East, is the concept of Paradise.

The golden age

In the classical world the belief existed in a former age when men were newcomers on a world already peopled with the attendant spirits of natural features and strange creatures, half human and half animal. Men lived in peace on the fruits of a bountiful earth, unaware of the arts of agriculture. Virgil describes this happy time in the 'pastoral' eighth book of the *Aeneid* [5] through the words of Evander as he shows Aeneas the landscape that will one day be the site of Rome:

These woods were once the home of indigenous fauns and
    nymphs,
And of men who has sprung from hard-wood oaks, who had no
    settled
Way of life, no civilisation; ploughing, the forming of
Communal reserves, and economy were unknown they lived on
    the produce of trees and the hard-won fare of the hunter [6].

Fig. 1.1 Claude Lorraine: a nostalgic pastoral landscape in the spirit of Virgil and Ovid. The Genius Loci, a river god, reclines in the foreground and a shrine crowns the hill. The dimension of time is evident in the eroded rock formations and crags, and in the distant ruins.

5. The *Aeneid*, written by Virgil but uncompleted at his death in 19 BC, is a twelve-book epic honouring Rome's past and the new era of peace and prosperity he hoped would come under the Emperor Augustus. Aeneas, the central figure, escapes from burning Troy with his family and followers, arrives at the mouth of the Tiber and becomes embroiled in local wars. He seeks alliance with Evander, a Greek from Arcadia who has founded Pallantium, a town at the foot of the Palatine, one of the seven hills to be enclosed within the future walls of Rome.
6. Virgil: *The Eclogues, Georgics and Aeneid*. Trans. C. Day Lewis. Oxford (1966). Subsequent quotations are taken from this text.

Saturn arrives, an exile from Olympus, he unites these scattered folk
and gives them laws [7]:

> His reign was the period called in legend the Golden Age,
> So peacefully serene were the lives of his subjects. It lasted
> Till, little by little, the time grew tarnished, an age of baser
> Metal came in, of mad aggression and lust for gain.

The reign of Saturn is described to Aeneas in an age no longer golden,
men are now often bloodthirsty and violent, but many attributes of
the Golden Age remain and it is directly remembered. This is usually
called the Heroic Age and the description of it, together with its
golden predecessor, by the classical poets have fascinated Europe ever
since [8]. Its landscapes are pastoral in what we might term a state
of ecological repose; trees, groves, springs and streams have their attendant spirits in a world not yet anthropocentric – man must tread
warily, he is one species among many and Nature must be propitiated;
fearful retribution might follow the unwitting felling of a sacred grove.
Aeneas has encountered one such guardian spirit on his journey up
the Tiber to meet Evander:

> . . . rising amidst the leaves of
> The poplars out of that pleasant river, its deity, old
> Tiberinus: a veil of grey and gauzy stuff was draped
> About him, a coronal of reeds shadowed his brow.

Sometimes a sterner, more awe-inspiring deity may haunt the place:

> . . . This wood, this hill with its leafy crest
> Some god inhabits; though which, we cannot be sure. The
>   Arcadians
> Believe they have witnessed great Jove himself, seen him
>   repeatedly
> Shaking his dark aegis and summoning up the storm clouds.

The Genius Loci, the spirit of the place, is everywhere, guarding his
or her part of the natural order – the earth is not to be sullied or despoiled by man [9].

Already a historic dimension is apparent as Evander guides Aeneas
around the future site of Rome. Ruined walls, the monuments of a past
age, are the relics of citadels built by the gods Janus and Saturn: the
Janiculum and Saturnian [10]. On the Palatine are the relics of a
wilder and more sinister landscape:

> Look at that scarp up there, that overhanging rock face!
> See the wide scatter of boulders! How desolate stands the
>   mountain
> Abode, with the crags that have toppled down, gigantic debris!
> Once a cavern was there, deeply recessed in the hillside,
> Impervious to the sun's rays: its occupant was a half human,
> Horrible creature, Cacus; its floor was forever warm with
> New spilt blood, and nailed to its insolent doors you could see
> Men's heads hung up, their faces pallid, ghastly, decaying.

Even in translation the imagery is compelling. Virgil had a first-hand
knowledge of the countryside and his *Georgics* give detailed and practical advice on the management of farms, woodlands and vineyards.
This realism gives a quality of consistency and conviction to his de-

7. Saturn was originally an early Italian god of agriculture afterwards identified with Cronos, King of the
Titans, defeated by Jupiter and the Olympian gods.
The Romans celebrated his festival, the Saturnalia,
during which slaves changed places with their masters
and there was much jollity. The festival was taken over
by the Christians in the fourth century AD to become
New Year's Day.

8. The Heroic Age is the setting for Homer's *Iliad* and
Odyssey written c. 700 BC in which former wars between Greeks and Trojans, and the subsequent wanderings of Odysseus are recounted. The actions
concern heroes, most of whom are second- or third-
generation descendants of gods and goddesses who
still influence or control events and are occasionally
seen.

9. Punishments following violation of natural features
occur in many legends, notably that of Erysichthon
who fells a huge and venerable oak sacred to Demeter,
its branches thickly hung with votive tablets and gar-
lands in sign of gratitude to the beneficent goddess.
Following his impious act he is seized with a ravenous
hunger, and having sold all to buy food, ends consuming his own flesh and perishes miserably.

10. The mood of pastoral simplicity and ecological repose appealed to painters of the seventeenth and
eighteenth centuries and is most perfectly reflected in
the works of Claude Lorraine, who also captured Virgil's mood of nostalgia for the ruins of the former age
expressed in this passage. The actual ruins of Imperial
Rome, seen and drawn by Claude, are transported to
this distant time, long before Rome was founded and
pursued her imperial destiny.

scription of the legendary world; his landscapes are kindly and pastoral with valleys, hills and groves attended by rustic spirits and divinities, while heroes and demi-gods ponder the crumbling ruins of the Golden Age. All seem suffused with the light of the former age, the landscape is fruitful, balanced and in repose. In contrast, certain dramatic rocky areas are haunted by gods – or monsters such as Cacus; Mount Etna houses the smithies of Vulcan, the seas are unpredictable and fraught with dangers: Scylla, Charybdis and the Isles of the Cyclops.

The Latin poets were latecomers in the classical world; Virgil and Ovid were writing 700 years after Homer and 300 after Theocritus. They inherited the rich Greek tradition and view of nature and grafted it on to their own. The landscapes that Virgil described are those of Italy, but much of their mythological content comes from the Greek Arcadia. His earliest work, the *Eclogues*, is modelled on the *Idylls* of Theocritus, a pastoral poet from Syracuse, who described the scenery and rural life of Sicily and southern Italy to which he transposed the idealised landscapes and inhabitants of Arcadia.

Arcadia is a wild and mountainous region in the centre of the Peloponnese which, in legend, was peopled by nymphs and satyrs, shepherds and herdsmen, living and loving in a life of innocent simplicity. Arcadia was the home of Pan to whom Mount Maenalus was sacred, and who became the patron of pastoral poets, a god of idealised wild nature. Pan also had his darker side and could be dangerous if disturbed, creating 'panic'. No doubt he originated as a primitive fertility god, later evolving into a powerful but benevolent rustic deity of the classical world; subsequently the Christians disliked his cult and when the saints succeeded to the roles and attributes of many familiar deities, Pan's physiognomy was inherited by the Devil. Arcadia, like Latium, also had its monsters; savage bronze-beaked, man-eating birds inhabited Lake Stymphalus and were expelled by Heracles as his Sixth Labour.

Greek tradition also told of the Garden of the Hesperides, the 'daughters of the evening', situated at the world's end beyond the Pillars of Heracles, and guarded by a dragon. The Hesperides were custodians of a tree bearing golden apples. The Greek tradition was carried to Greater Greece in southern Italy and Sicily where it fused with the native tradition and was given expression by the Latin poets. Virgil described an Arcadian Age of Gold as a remote legendary era, whose echoes could still be glimpsed in the rustic simplicity of the countryside in his own time. But he was optimistic that in the cycle of centuries Justice and the Golden Age would one day return:

> Goats shall walk home, their udders taut with milk and nobody
> Herding them: the ox will have no fear of the lion . . . .
> . . . Traders will retire from the sea, from the pine-built vessels
> They used for commerce: every land will be self supporting.
> The soil will need no harrowing, the vine no pruning knife;
> And the tough ploughman may at last unyoke his oxen [11].

Thus all is not lost for ever; Virgil's vision of the Mesolithic, when hunters and gatherers lived in peace under the tutelage of a benign deity on a boundlessly fruitful earth may yet return.

This vision, the subject of the *Fourth Eclogue*, recalls the passage in which Isaiah describes the New Jerusalem:

11. *Eclogues No. IV.*

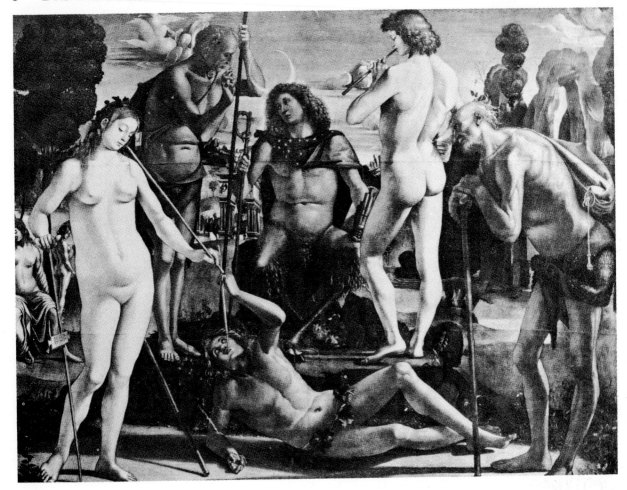

Fig. 1.2 Luca Signorelli: *Pan and other Gods.* (Destroyed, formerly Kaiser Friedrich Museum, Berlin.) A joyful early Renaissance interpretation of Arcadia which, while rocky, is no longer seen as wild or dangerous. The painter's interest lies in the figures, their symbolism and mythology, rather than the landscape which has a second-hand appearance.

The Wolf and the lamb shall feed together, and the lion shall eat straw like the bullock: and dust shall be the serpent's meat. They shall not destroy in all my holy mountain, saith the Lord.

The similarity did not pass unobserved by Christian writers. Moreover the poem is addressed to an unknown boy, shortly to be born, and subsequently Christians, including St Augustine, believed it to be a prophecy foretelling the birth of Christ. In the Middle Ages it became known as the *Messianic Eclogue* and the pagan Virgil came to be venerated as a prophet.

Paradise

The belief in Paradise, man's expulsion and hope of return, is a concept similar to the Golden Age, but far more powerful in its effect on Western civilisation, for all Christians believed the account in Genesis to be the literal truth until serious doubts were cast in the nineteenth century.

Muslims regarded the account similarly, for Muhammad respected the Judaeo-Christian tradition, and as the last of the prophets absorbed much of its teaching into Islam. Return to a heavenly Paradise would be the reward of loyal and devout followers, and the Quaran contains many references and descriptions of the ultimate garden of contemplation and delight. In the centuries of Islamic pre-eminence in culture and learning this ancient concept of the East again influenced the imagination of the West. The imagery of both cloister and paradise garden was similar in the Middle Ages, with a vision of Eden re-created beyond the Apocalypse, as the abode of blessed souls.

The Genesis description is as follows (II. 8–10):

> And the Lord God planted a garden eastward in Eden; and there he put the man whom he had formed. And out of the ground made the Lord God to grow every tree that is pleasant to the sight, and good for food; the tree of life also in the midst of the garden, and the tree of knowledge of good and evil. And a river went out of Eden to water the garden, and from thence it was parted, and became into four heads.

God takes Adam and puts him in the garden to dress it and keep it. Every fowl of the air and beast of the field is created and brought to to Adam to name; finally woman is created. The serpent, 'more subtile than any beast of the field' tempts Eve, and she Adam, to eat the fruit of the Tree of Knowledge which has been expressly forbidden by God. The transgression is discovered and they are expelled from the garden for 'the man has become as one of us, to know good from evil: and

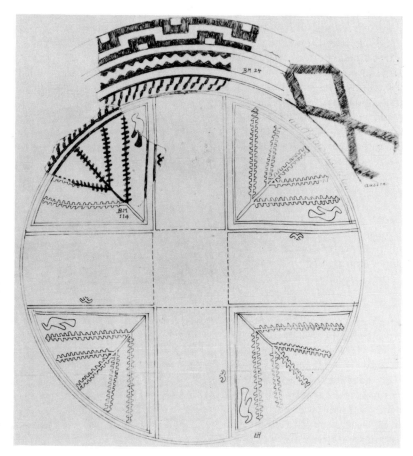

Fig. 1.3 Bowl reconstructed from a fragment found at Samarra and dating to *c*. 2000 BC (E. Hertzfeld: *Die Ausgrabungen der Samarra*, Band V, Plate XVI (1923)). This was interpreted as a quadripartite garden with central spring and crossed canals by Arthur Upham Pope in *An Introduction to Persian Art* (1930). A formally planted tree with attendant songbird stands in each quadrant.

now, lest he put forth his hand, and take also of the tree of life, and
eat, and live forever', cherubims are set as guards and a flaming sword
'which turned every way, to keep the way of the tree of life' (II, 22–).
The serpent is condemned henceforward to move on his belly; presumably he previously had legs and was, in effect, a dragon.

It seems likely that the description of the garden dates from the exile
of the Jewish people in Babylon. Here they would have seen royal
parks with their lush planting and water, and in the heat of the Mesopotamian summer these must have seemed the most blissful landscape man could conceive. The term *paradise* which became
synonymous with the Garden of Eden derives from the Persian word
pairidaeza, meaning an enclosed park [12]. In Babylon two traditions
seem to have fused to create these parks: the enclosed hunting parks
of the Sumerian and Assyrian kings and the oasis gardens, where
water was the source of life and flowed from its source in four channels. It seems that this was an extremely ancient form, as a quadripartite garden with central spring and crossed canals is depicted on
a pot dated to *c.* 2000 BC.

The Genesis description, however, contains elements that occur in
many ancient mythologies and which are by no means limited to the
Near East. The concept of a heaven tree giving life or knowledge appears to have been a universal idea [13], and at its grandest a great
tree standing at the centre of the world, its branches spreading to support the revolving heavens and its roots descending into the under-
world, the tree both supporting and uniting the cosmos. At its feet is
a well of all waters. In Norse mythology the ash Yggdrasil is 'the best
and greatest of all trees, its branches spread out over the whole world
and reach up over heaven'; the gods daily hold court nearby, and
beneath a root lies the spring of Mimir, the source of hidden wisdom and understanding. Harts and birds of prey live in its branches,
and below the ground, the serpent Nidhogg gnaws at its roots [14].

Images of the great tree occur in many places. In India the *Mansara*,
a book of coronation procedures written about AD 500, describes a
'wishing tree' made with leaves of jewels and pearls which grants all
wishes and is all-productive. Divinities stand among its branches and
a seven-headed serpent is coiled around its stem. A similar tree is recorded at the court of the Byzantine emperors. Engraved gems and
seals from Minoan Crete depict sacred trees within enclosures. These
and other examples of the heaven tree are described by Lethaby who
points out that the Celtic crosses which survive in northern England
stand firmly in this tradition [15]. The tree, water source and enclosure of the Genesis account are elements common to the beliefs of
early peoples 'fixed' in the context of the Mesopotamian paradise
garden.

Persia and the East were to influence Europe first through the
Greeks, and the Hellenistic kingdoms, later through contacts in Spain,
Sicily and the Kingdom of Outremer, but above all through trade, for
the caravan routes bringing silks and spices crossed Persia. The cultural benefits to the Western kingdoms, sunk in semi-barbarism following the invasions of the Northmen, were considerable; architecture
and applied design revived under the stimulus of Eastern influence,
example and technology, and also attitudes to landscape and the design of gardens and parks. But the concise description of the garden
in Genesis remained the ideal for gardens in monasteries, where civi-

12. The Persian term *pairidaeza* was used in the *Sep-
tuagint* to translate Garden of Eden. It passed into ec-
clesiastical Latin and from thence to common usage.
  Eden: 'traditionally derived from Heb. Eden, delight,
pleasure, probably connected with Babylonian *edina*,
field or park'. *The Century Encyclopaedia of Names*,
The Times (1894).
13. An account of the Heaven Tree as it occurs in traditions and mythologies is given in R. Cook: *Tree of
Life*, Thames and Hudson (1974).
14. *The Prose Edda of Snorri Sturlason*. Trans. J.
Young. Bowes and Bowes (1954).
15. *Architecture, Nature and Magic*. W. R. Lethaby.
Duckworth (1956).

Fig. 1.4 The Limbourg brothers: *The Fall and Expulsion from Eden* from the *Très Riches Heures du Duc de Berry* (Musée Condé, Chantilly, MS 65). The medieval concept of Eden as remote and inaccessible, surrounded by a high wall and guarded by Cherubim. Magnificient Gothic structures adorn the portal and the source of rivers in the centre of the garden, flowers bloom in the turf and the trees have the clean browsed trunks of parkland.

lisation was preserved in the darkest years of the West, and later in secular gardens as the ruling caste became literate and conscious of a fuller life than that dictated by war and survival.

Chapter 2

Antiquity

Mesopotamia

The oasis garden, designed around four 'rivers' flowing from a water source, has been studied from surviving examples in India, Persia and southern Spain. These, however, are medieval or later in date. It seems logical that in the arid climate of the East water should be seen as the source of fertility and basis of garden design, but the evidence for the use of a cruciform plan in ancient Babylonia rests on the Genesis account. The description states that Eden contained all species of fowl and beast, and all trees that are edible or good to see; moreover, the Persian term *paradise* came to be applied to Eden. This suggests the fusion of the oasis garden with the formalised and planted royal hunting parks. For these parks we have little physical evidence; the archaeologists of the past sought structures, sculptures and tablets and in the course of excavations valuable information on planned landscapes may have been ignored or destroyed. Fortunately, there remains documentary evidence, the descriptions of Greek travellers and historians, and some pictorial evidence survives in late Assyrian bas-reliefs.

The hunting park occurs throughout history, the preserve of kings and rich men, and the form it takes tends to vary between two extremes, one forming a part of the functional landscape, the other essentially a created, ideal landscape. In its functional form the park is a tract of wild country enclosed within a pale for the dual purpose of the sport of hunting and a consequent supply of fresh meat. The pale prevented illicit hunting and predation and the escape of game, and allowed planned management of the stock as a resource which otherwise could be lost through wholesale destruction.

The first records of planned parks come from the Assyrians, a people who lived along the upper reaches of the Tigris in the hill country of northern Mesopotamia. To the south, in the fertile plain formed by the rivers Tigris and Euphrates, lay the ancient civilisation of Sumeria, which the Assyrians conquered. The last great King of Assyria was Assurbanipal, a formidable soldier, but also an antiquary and a man who loved learning. He collected texts from the archives of the Sumerian cities, which were then translated and preserved in the library of his palace at Nineveh. This vast collection, dealing with sci-

Fig. 2.1 Pavilion and artificial hill in a park at Khorsabad (Paul Emile Botha: *Monuments de Ninive* (1849)) from the palace of Sargon. The pavilion, set on a platform to catch cool breezes and overlook the park anticipates a building type which occurs throughout Persian history. Wildfowl inhabit the hill which is crowned with an altar.

ence, history, medicine and religion, was discovered in the mid-nineteenth century and among them was a translation of the *Epic of Gilgamesh*, a Sumerian poem probably dating from the third millennium. This epic contains the earliest known description of the Flood; it also gives the earliest description of a park. The two heroes, Gilgamesh and Enkidu, journey through wild and hilly country to seek a mountain covered by a forest of great cedar trees. This is entered through a gateway, which presumes a pale, and within, the custodian of the forest lives in a house of cedar wood. The forest has its terrors, the custodian himself is a monster, yet the heroes are dumbfounded by its beauty, the hugeness of the cedars, the comfort of the shade and greenery of the brushwood [1].

This forest appears a prototype of the functional hunting park; doubtless areas of wild hill country were emparked by the Sumerian kings and the Assyrians afterwards. The Assyrian kings, with wealth and vast resources of slave labour obtained from their conquests, created the formal park – an 'ideal' landscape sited close to their palaces and cities [2]. Tiglath-Pileser I (*c.* 1100 BC) boasted of a park in his capital Assur. He transplanted thither the trees of countries he had conquered – cedar and box – and rejoiced that none of his forefathers had possessed them. He also brought wild oxen and goats, elephants and dromedaries. Foreign kings sent him 'beasts of the sea' as gifts, for which he constructed vast fish-ponds. The flora and fauna of the hunting park were now exotic and no longer those of the enclosed wilderness – the pendulum had swung to its opposite; this landscape has affinities with the zoological garden and arboretum.

Subsequently, further parks were constructed by his successors, with similar exotic planting and beasts. A characteristic was earth-moulding, creating terraces and artificial hills crowned with temples or pavilions. These foreshadow the mounts of late medieval and Tudor gardens some 2,000 years later, raised to give a view over the park or a glimpse of the outside world over the pale.

King Sennacherib (9th century BC) gave the land outside Nineveh to the men of the city, laying it out as an extensive complex of gardens,

1. N. K. Sanders: *Epic of Gilgamesh* (1960).
2. For the best summary of Assyrian and other early garden achievements see M. L. Gothein: *A History of Garden Art* (from the German), Dent (1928).

irrigated by canal from the distant river Chursur, and planted with vines, fruit trees, palms and cypresses. Extensive lakes were constructed, their margins planted with reeds. This is the first known example of an 'urban park', or pleasure ground, laid out for the benefit of the populace.

Sculpted reliefs which survive from Assurbanipal's palace at Nineveh (7th century BC) show the King and Queen banqueting in a vine arbour in the royal park. The planting is formal – pines alternate with palms; below them are lilies, and vines growing up into the lower branches. Lions, huntsmen and hounds are depicted in a scene of general tranquillity, the only jarring note a severed head hanging from a tree near the royal couple. It is fortunate that these reliefs have survived, they are refined and more developed than most Assyrian sculptures, and the trees and plants are delineated with care.

The Assyrians, to our present knowledge, were the inventors of the formal park and the first to create ideal landscapes on a grand scale. This involved extensive earth-moulding, irrigation and the formal planting of exotic trees. The purpose of the parks was for hunting amid spectacular and magnificent surroundings, and also for social functions such as feasts, assemblies, and royal audiences to princes and ambassadors. Parks were also created for enjoyment by the people and reflect the love of trees and flowers which was a characteristic of the ancient East. The parks also embody the desire of powerful rulers to shape the wild landscape into an ordered form, reflecting their ability to conquer climate and natural conditions as surely as they conquered other races and civilisations. The garnering of the knowledge of former cultures into the library at Nineveh was complemented by the gathering of exotic trees, animals and birds into the royal parks.

Nineveh was sacked in 612 BC, and the Assyrian empire collapsed. Briefly, for 70 years, Babylon was the capital city of Mesopotamia and the surrounding lands. One of its principal ornaments was an artificial wooded hill, known in Antiquity as the 'Hanging Gardens' and considered one of the Seven Wonders of the Ancient World. Two descriptions have come down to us, both at second-hand, written by the later geographer-historians Strabo and Diodorus of Sicily [3]. They agree on the main points, but disagree on who built the gardens, and it is possible that structures of this kind were widespread in Meso-

Fig. 2.2 Assurbanipal dining in a park (Victor Place: *Ninive et l'Assyrie* (1867) from the palace of Assurbanipal at Nineveh. The planting is formal with pine trees alternating with date-palms.

3. Neither writer could have seen the gardens except as a ruin. Pausanius relates that Babylon was depopulated following the foundation of Seleucea around 300 BC. In his own day (*2nd century* AD), of 'the greatest city of its time under the Sun nothing now remains except the wall and Sanctuary of Belus' (VIII.33).

potamia, the Hanging Gardens being the most spectacular. The term 'hanging' is misleading as the descriptions make clear that the gardens were constructed in the form of a ziggurat. These were stepped towers that were built to great dramatic effect in the flat plain of Mesopotamia; they are usually regarded as artificial mountains built to commune with the gods. The Sumerians came from hill country before they settled on the fertile plain and the shrines on the summits of the ziggurats enabled them to worship their mountain gods in the manner of their forefathers. No doubt also, the desire of powerful kings to build monumentally played its part.

The origin of the Hanging Gardens, according to Diodorus, was a princely gift. The King (probably Nebuchadrezzar, 605–562 BC) created them for one of his concubines, a Median princess, who longed for the wooded mountains of her own land. Diodorus calls the gardens a *paradise* and agrees with Strabo that each side was four plethra long (480 metres). The structure consisted of stepped terraces supported on stone beams spanning between walls 6.7 metres thick, presumably of brick. This created a cool gallery beneath each planted terrace which would look out on to its own terrace.

> The roof had first a layer of reeds laid in great quantities of bitumen, over this two courses of baked brick bonded by cement, and as a third layer a covering of lead, to the end that the moisture from the soil might not penetrate beneath. On all this again earth had been piled to a depth sufficient for the roots of the largest trees; and the ground, when levelled off, was thickly planted with trees of every kind that, by their great size could give pleasure to the beholder. And since the galleries, each projecting beyond another, all received the light, they contained many royal lodgings of every description; and there was one gallery which contained openings leading from the topmost surface and machines for supplying the garden with water in great abundance from the river, although no outsider could see it being done [4].

The Hanging Gardens were regarded as a wonder in Antiquity and

Fig. 2.3 A relief from the palace of Assurbanipal depicting a temple on a wooded hill and what appears to be a hanging garden with formally planted trees and bushes on its roof (Rawlinson: *Five Great Monarchies* I (1862)).

4. Diodorus Siculus: Book 11.10, Loeb translation.

have remained a powerful image to architects and landscape designers. The planting of stepped, formal terraces was a feature of Italian landscape gardens and at Isola Bella achieves a form which must owe something to the memory of Babylon. This rocky island in Lake Maggiore was cut and levelled into terraces from 1630 onwards, the topmost four forming a stepped pyramid rising some 30 metres above the lake; the labour and expense to create it, and the enormous quantity of topsoil transported to render it fertile, make it a venture on a truly Babylonian or Assyrian scale. The paradox of the roof garden has also continued to fascinate, particularly in the designs and fantasies of twentieth-century architects.

The Achaemenians

Babylon fell in 538 BC. Its conquerors the Persians, formerly a pastoral and nomadic people, continued the tradition of planting great formal parks. All classes of society loved trees and regarded planting as a sacred occupation and an essential part of education. It is said that Xerxes was so impressed and enamoured of a plane tree at Sardis that he placed gold chains and amulets on its branches and set a guard. Plutarch describes Artaxerxes on campaign against the Cadusii in a barren plain. It was midwinter and very cold when the army encamped on a royal estate with gardens. The King ordered the felling of the trees to make fires, but the soldiers refused to cut the trees until the King himself took an axe and set an example. The story illustrates the veneration in which all Persians held trees, an attitude that has no parallel in later societies. When subject races rose against oppressive Persian tyrants they took immediate and hurtful revenge by laying waste their parks.

Much of our small knowledge of the Persians and their parks comes from the Greek writers. Xenophon – soldier, historian and pupil of Socrates – reflects the impression made on the Greeks by the Persian paradises (Xenophon is the first writer to use this term). 'In all the districts the Great King resides in and visits he takes care that there are paradises, as they call them, full of all the good and beautiful things that the soil will produce, and in this he spends most of his time, except when the season precludes it' [5]. He describes Cyrus the Younger, whom he served as a mercenary, showing the Spartan Lysander around his paradise at Sardis: 'Lysander admired the beauty of the trees in it, the accuracy of the spacing, the straightness of the rows, the regularity of the angles and the multitude of the sweet scents that clung around them as they walked.' The park was clearly very formal. Cyrus reviewed his army of mercenaries in his park at Celaenae, which extended on both banks of the river above the town; this was a further function of the Persian park, the mustering of armies in shade and security.

These references are tantalisingly brief. The Achaemenian was the first of successive empires and kingdoms based on the huge tract of land we now call Iran, but for convenience here termed by the ancient and more attractive name of Persia. European histories tend to place Persia on the periphery of events, the source of border wars that afflicted the Greeks, and later the Roman Empire, and for a brief period under the Seleucids brought into the Greek world of the Successors. But from the point of view of the historian of planned landscapes,

5. Xenophon: *Oecunomicos*, IV.20, Loeb translation.

Fig. 2.4 *The Gardens of Fidelity* (Bagh-i-vafa) 1504, Dhanu. A central fountain in a raised tank irrigating a garden through four water channels. Luxurious planting of palms, fruit trees and evergreens which appear to be holm-oaks (British Library, OR 3714 f.173v).

attitudes to landscapes and the design of fine artefacts there would be some justification in reversing this view over many of the centuries between the Fall of Babylon and the close of the Middle Ages [6]. Persian influence on the West was intermittent rather than continuous; during periods of invasion and foreign occupation, it lay dormant, to emerge renascent as the Persians time after time, re-established their traditions, always with respect for the past. Consequently, it is possible to see certain consistent cultural threads running through 2,000 years from the Achaemenians to the Safavids.

Terrain and geographical situation are keys to this culture. The land covers a wide variety of natural landscapes ranging to extremes. Persia is a triangular plateau, bounded by mountain ranges and hills and set between the Caspian Sea and Persian Gulf. The plateau con-

6. Higher education in Britain until recently requiring knowledge of the Classics, has perhaps given a Greek bias. The term 'barbarian' to describe Persians was not originally derogatory, but became so from the Renaissance, if not much earlier. It is difficult for the student to find books that give an overall view of the Achaemenian achievement and history, whereas books on ancient Greece could fill a library. An interesting view of Persian versus 'barbarian' is put in André Malraux's *Alexander the God* and also in Gore Vidal's *Creation*.

tains regions where true oases occur, but elsewhere is so arid and in-
hospitable that nothing will live or grow [7]. To the south-west, the
fertile plain of the Tigris and Euphrates that had cradled and sustained the civilisations of Mesopotamia, is separated from the plateau
by the Zagros range, formerly covered with forest of which relict
woodlands still remain containing oak, walnut, holm-oak, wild al-
mond and pistachio. To the north, the high Elburz chain divides the
plateau from the fertile slopes to the Caspian, clad with luxuriant vegetation and sustained by a virtually tropical climate.

The desert fostered an appreciation of the oasis with plentiful water
and shade, while the wooded hills and forests, with abundant wildlife
and game, the beauty of spring blossom and flowers, provided country
for hunting and showed the kinder and more verdant aspects of nature
– the antithesis of the desert and sheltered garden. V. Sackville-West
was astonished at the richness and variety of the wild Persian flora
with its roses, tulips, anemones and orchises. Appreciation of both
oasis and benevolent wilderness appear deep-rooted in Persian
tradition.

Geographically the land is the meeting point of East and West, the
bridge of communication for China, India and the steppes, with An-
atolia and Europe: the hub of trade routes including the Silk Road,
perhaps the oldest of all international communications, the source of
wealth and also the path for invaders. Under the Roman Empire,
silks, spices, ivories, perfumes and precious stones moved westward
while manufactured goods, wines, oils and gold moved east. Trade
must have influenced the traditional attitude of tolerance in Persia and
also fostered native skills in fine crafts and production of artefacts:
ceramics, fine textiles and rugs; as early as the fifth century BC, Plato
is reputed to have owned a magnificent set of Oriental rugs, they were
much in demand in Byzantium and we find them depicted in Western
paintings as late as the fifteenth and sixteenth centuries.

Cyrus, conqueror of Babylon and founder of the Achaemenian Empire, was one of the great rulers, a builder rather than destroyer.
Having conquered he sought the allegiance of the diverse nations and
tribes that peopled his huge empire, giving them humane government,
tolerance for their religious, cultural and social organisations, peace
and the benefits of trade [8].

Threads link the Achaemenians to later revivals of Persian culture
and tradition. The love of nature is a constant characteristic as is skill
in applied arts and decoration; the two may account for an element
of ambiguity between the natural and artificial in which the Persians
seemed to delight; Xerxes adorned his beloved plane tree and more
than 1,000 years later Chosroes I commissioned the fabulous gem-
studded carpet depicting spring flowers, that was a wonder of his time
[9]. In late medieval painting the same ambiguity is evident in patterns and figures worked into screens and rugs set in landscapes of
trees in blossom and flower-rich turf. This vision directly influenced
the West and can be seen in the fine series of French tapestries *La Dame
à la Licorne*, in which natural, artificial and fabulous elements are combined without conveying any sense of inconsistency to the observer.

Themes recur in Persian architecture, notably the pavilion with
high columns set on a platform, to catch cool breezes and enjoy the
garden or distant view. An early example built by Cyrus survives in
ruins in Pasargadae. At Persepolis, monumental columns are topped

7. R. Ghirshman: *Iran* (1978).

8. Later conquerors, notably the Arabs and Ottoman
Turks, were often to follow similar forms of governing
with tolerance within the limits of empire, to the benefit of both subjects and rulers, and to civilisation and
the arts. The Empire of Cyrus was to last for over two
centuries and when it collapsed before the Macedon-
ian advance, the weakness lay in dynastic strife; the rot
lay at the top, but the foundations laid by Cyrus remained sound.

9. The carpet was said to measure 450 by 90 feet, em-
eralds and rubies formed the flowered borders, pearls
laced with gold and silver thread, the streams. It was
sent to Medina when the Arabs captured Ctesiphon in
AD 637 (R. Payne: *The World of Art*. Doubleday (1972)).
It is tempting and not unreasonable to see in it the tradition of Persian garden carpets of which examples
súrvive only from recent centuries.

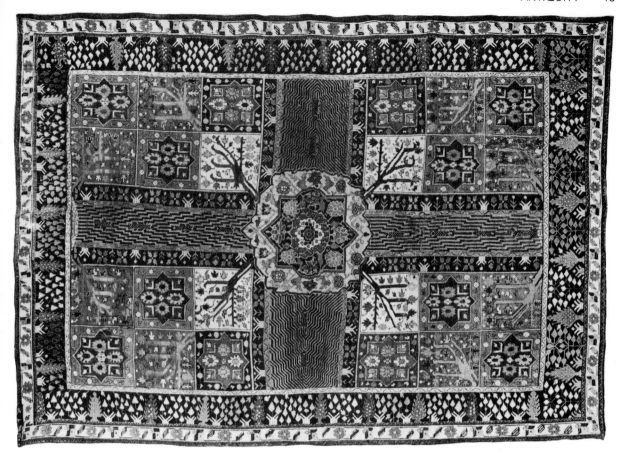

Fig. 2.5 A Persian garden carpet of the eighteenth or nineteenth century depicting a central water source with four rivers. Plane trees mark the intersection and the garden is protected by trees. Although late, the carpet stands in a tradition going back at least to the famous carpet of Chosroes I captured by the Arabs in the seventh century AD (Crown copyright Victoria and Albert Museum, T.10-1924).

by capitals with double heads of bulls and griffins giving an illusion of fruits hanging below the spreading branches of the roof beams — the effect evokes a grove of lofty date-palms and whether or not this was consciously intended, the image of the oasis would lie in the minds of the architects and their royal clients. The date-palm is a native to oases and the area around the Persian Gulf. Fifteen hundred years later we find similar imagery in the airy porticoes of the Chahil Sutun Palace at Isfahan, and the resemblance to Persepolis suggests continuity, although examples in Persia which would confirm this view are lacking. The extent of Mongol destruction could account for this and intermediate links must be sought elsewhere, for example in Saracenic Spain.

Most important of all and most lasting in influence, were the Achaemenian skills in hydraulics and irrigation. The huge network of subterranean canals (*qanats*) which brought water tapped from mountain foothills out into the plateau, appear to be an achievement of this period [10]. At Pasargadae the remains of an extensive water garden have been excavated, which consists of a rectilinear network of stone watercourses linking pools at regular intervals. The pavilion already referred to was sited to overlook the garden [11], a relationship similar to the Chahil Sutan and many other garden complexes constructed after the Mongol invasions. It is tragic that so few standing monu-

10. *Qanats* are surely the source for Quaranic imagery of the garden 'underneath which rivers flow'.
11. '*Excavations at Pasargadae: Third Preliminary Report, Iran*', *Journal of the British Institute of Persian Studies*, Vol. 3 (1965), p. 32, Fig. 9.

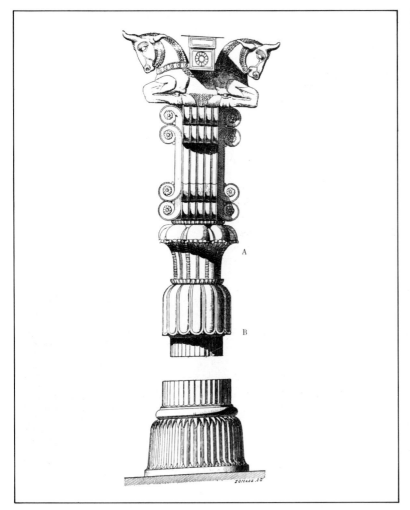

Fig. 2.6 Column from the Achaemenian capital at Persepolis (J. Ward: *Historic Ornament* (1897)).

Fig. 2.7 Diagram of a *qanat* (long section – not to scale).Subterranean tunnel-wells (*qanats* or *foggaras*) appear to have originated in ancient Persia and in Achaemenid times spread to the Levant, Arabia and Egypt. Under Arab rule they spread to North Africa and Spain, and have been found as far away as China and certain areas of Latin America. Their development was (and remains) a vital factor in the irrigation and settlement of arid landscapes, yet knowledge of their existence appears limited to specialists in Britain.

A *qanat* (Arabic for 'lance' or 'conduit') is a gently sloping tunnel which pierces an alluvial fan, tapping the water which emerges downslope as a surface stream supplying an oasis. Digging them is a perilous trade, usually a family occupation. Vertical shafts are sunk every 50 to 150 metres to supply air and allow the removal of spoil when the tunnel is dug or repaired. While there is considerable variation in length and depth, some *qanats* are triumphs of engineering, extending for more than 50 kilometres and with shafts up to 125 metres deep. The deepest reported mother-well has a depth of more than 300 metres.

Qanats supplying a town often terminate in the *suq* (bazaar), a mosque or the home of the owner. Summer living rooms may be built underground for coolness beside the flowing stream. The orthogonal plans of traditional Iranian cities is due to growth along parallel channels originally dug to supply orchards and fields, and following the slope of the land.

G. B. Cressy: 'Qanats, karez, and foggaras', *The Geographical Review*, Vol. 48 (1958); P. W. English: 'The origin and spread of qanats in the Old World', *Proceedings of the American Philosophical Society*, Vol. 112, No. 3 (1968); M. E. Bonine: 'The morphogenesis of Iranian cities', *Annals of the Association of American Geographers*, Vol. 69, No. 2 (1979).

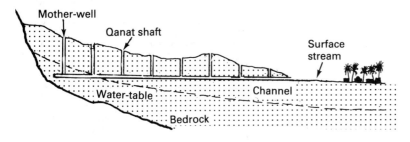

ments survive of early Persian civilisations and that descriptions are so brief. An account of a paradise garden does, however, survive from a later source, a novel of the Roman period [12]. It is four-sided with a central spring, tall trees with intertwining branches and fruit allow dappled light to reach the floor which is carpeted with flowers, and provide supports for vines and ivy. The account looks back to Assurbanipal's garden on the one hand, and on the other to pre-Mongol descriptions of gardens in medieval Persia.

The Greeks

Exiled from Athens, Xenophon settled at Scillus and there built a temple and sanctuary to Ephesian Artemis which he set in a park. Here on the soil of mainland Greece Xenophon united the traditions of the formal Eastern paradise with the native sacred grove. The Greeks had long venerated certain groves and trees, usually in association with a temple, hero-shrine or the tomb of the founder of a city; the trees being protected from cutting by custom or law and the fruit remaining untasted. Of all groves that of the Academy was to become the most famous, for here was born a specifically Greek concept, the Philosophers' Garden.

The Academy began as a sacred enclosure surrounding the shrine of Academus, a legendary hero – one of many such shrines in ancient Athens. In the late sixth century the tyrant Hipparchus founded a gymnasium in the precinct and subsequently the statesman Cimon, finding it dry and dusty, provided an abundant supply of water and planted planes and poplars, leaving it a garden of delight [13]. Gymnasia were established to provide young Athenians with physical training and exercise, but increasingly they became centres of moral education as philosophers adopted them as places to meet and instruct their pupils. Plato taught at the Academy, later retiring there and building a house and temple to the Muses. His enormous prestige, and the happy combination of garden and gymnasium, created an ideal that was to be emulated throughout the classical world. In time the emphasis on physical education was forgotten and in the villas of cultured Romans the 'Academy' was a place for intellectual discussion, shaded from the Mediterranean sun, by mature trees and adorned with colonnades, fountains and fine sculpture.

The graceless Sulla violated the sacred precinct, cutting down its trees to make engines of war, but it was speedily replanted. The Elder Pliny, writing in the first century AD, admired its elms and poplars, and in particular the famous planes whose roots stretched for 15 metres. Here too was a scion of the sacred olive which grew on the Acropolis, traditionally the gift of the goddess Athena, the patron of Athens. The Academy was to survive until the year 529 when it was closed by the Emperor Justinian. But by then the concept of the Philosophers' Garden had been adapted to the monastic ideal in the form of the cloistered garden, a sanctuary of learning and culture amid the turmoils of the Age of Migrations and feudalism. In its classical form it was to be revived by the Renaissance humanists and its shade lingers today in the grass courts and cobbles of our older academic centres.

Alexander the Great (356–343 BC) led the armies of Greece and Macedon to the conquest of Persia, and in his subsequent empire and the Successor kingdoms the two cultures, which had long grudgingly admired each other, fused to produce the Hellenistic civilisation. Historians predisposed to divide cultures into periods which ascend and descend, ending in decadence, have tended to place the Hellenistic in the latter category. Predictably, others have reacted to an opposite view. Whatever the truth of the matter, sculptors and architects had the unenviable task of working in the shadow of the achievements of classical Greece: the sculptures of Phidias and Praxiteles, the architecture of Ictinus. Landscape architects worked in the shade of the

12. *After the funeral I hurried to the girl, who was in our paradeisos. This paradise was a meadow, a thing of great delight to the eyes. A tall enough wall round it, and on each of the wall's four sides was a portico standing on a group of pillars, within which was the plantation of trees. The branches in full foliage intertwined with overlapping leaves and fruits conjoined. Some of the bigger trees had ivy and smilax attached, the smilax dropping from planes and filling all the spaces between the boughs with its soft leafage, the ivy twisting up the pines and embracing the trunks, so that the tree supplied its support while it supplied the tree with a garland. Beside each tree grew vines, creeping on reed props with luxuriant growths: now in full fruitage they hung from the reedjoints and formed as it were the tree's ringlets. The higher leaves were in gentle movement, and the sun's rays, coming through as the wind stirred them, gave the effect of a pale dappled shadow on the earth. Flowers too of various colours displayed each its own beauty, setting the ground aflame. Narcissus and rose with their blossoms (the cup of the flowers) were there, alike in shape but varying in hue, the rose being the colour of blood above and milk below, while the narcissus was wholly of the undercolour of the rose. There were violets too, with cupshaped blossoms you couldn't distinguish but their colour was that of a shining calm at sea. In the midst of all these flowers bubbled a spring with its waters caught in a square man-made basin. The water served as a mirror for the flowers, so that there seemed a double grove, a real one and a reflection. Birds were there too. Some, tame, sought for food in the grove, pampered and domesticated by the rearing of men. Others wild and winging, sported round the treetops, some chirping out in birdsong, others brilliant in gorgeous plumage. There were tame birds too, a peacock, a swan, a parrot. The swan fed round the sources of the spring, the parrot was hung in a cage from a branch, the peacock spread his tail among the flowers, and the brightness of the flowers shone up against the hues of the birds, whose wings were themselves flowers.*

Trans. from Achilleus Tatios in J. Lindsay, *Leisure and Pleasure in Roman Egypt*, Frederick Muller Ltd (1965).

13. Harrison and Verall: *Mythology and Monuments in Ancient Athens*, Macmillan (1890).

paradises. Sculptors came to explore the byways of complexity and realism, and with the wealth and resources available, the construction of colossi. In landscape, opulence and monumentality seem to have been the aims. At Antioch the main street followed a vast portico facing the famed gardens of the Seleucids which stretched to the foot of the mountain and contained bathing pavilions, summer houses, fountains and all manner of aromatic plants. The Ptolemies sought to emulate the gardens of Babylon, building stepped terraces with banqueting halls and courtyards, richly planted and hung with tapestries, and enlivened by ingenious mechanical toys: water organs, elaborate fountains and automata. All have vanished and in spite of their opulence, they were a backwater to the mainstream of landscape development. The Hellenistic forms which were to persist were on a humbler scale than these gardens of kings and evolved in the context of the town and city state. Through the Greek towns of Campania they were eagerly adopted and assimilated by the Romans and so passed into the European heritage to be revived at the Renaissance, thus continuing to form part of a living tradition until the nineteenth century. Of these forms, the peristyle or colonnaded garden court, the public pleasure garden and the nymphaeum were the most important and lasting.

Fig. 2.8 Wall-painting from Boscoreale of a grotto.

The colonnaded inner courtyard is an eminently functional form for houses set beneath a blazing sun, and can be seen at Delos in the Aegean Sea where many Hellenistic houses have been excavated and reconstructed. Their small deep courts are cool and sheltered from the noise of the streets, and the Mediterranean light illuminates the shady recesses of the colonnades which would be dark and gloomy beneath a northern sky. In the Greek cities of Italy, the native love of nature gave an added dimension. Traditionally, the Italian inner courtyard was the atrium which was hard surfaced with a central tank (*impluvium*) for storing rain-water from the inward sloping roofs; the garden lay behind the complex of the house, sometimes entered through a portico. The 'frozen' houses of Pompeii show the subsequent union of the Greek and Italian traditions; the atrium remains, but the garden has evolved into the peristyle in which trees [14], formal flower beds, aromatic shrubs and potted plants bring an echo of the distant countryside, against a background of elegant architecture and the murmur of water gushing from a central fountain – a sound the Romans loved, and which more than anything can give a sense of peace and seclusion by shutting off the hum of urban life beyond. Satisfying to the senses of sight, hearing, smell and touch, this delightful form persisted to become a feature of the Byzantine imperial palaces, where it was known as a paradise, and it can still be seen today in the surviving Moorish palaces of southern Spain. In Christian Europe the 'potted' paradise of the peristyle combined with the Philosophers' Garden to become the monastic cloister of the Middle Ages.

The Greeks of Asia Minor considered it important to adorn their cities with public gardens. These were essentially for pleasure and relaxation, providing shaded walks, cool springs and seats for informal conversation. This valuable element in civilised urban living disappeared at the close of Antiquity to be revived in relatively modern times. Essentially this concept originated in the Hellenistic world, although as we have seen, King Sennacherib had bestowed a similar amenity on the citizens of Nineveh many centuries before, and no

14. Recent work is beginning to show the species used in the lavish planting of these gardens. Evidence has been found for olives, lemons, soft fruits, pomegranates, walnuts, filberts, sweet chestnuts and vines grown on trellises. J. Ward-Perkins: *Pompeii* AD 79 (1976).

doubt there are forgotten links in a chain which joined Assyria with Greece in this respect through the intervening Babylonian and Persian cultures.

The nymphaeum is in essence a water source, usually taking the form of a fountain or spring issuing from a cave. Here one discerns the reverence for water as the source and sustainer of life, seen emerging mysteriously from the rocks or ground, and guarded by an attendant deity. This Mediterranean concept has obvious affinities with the water source of the oasis garden and also with the sacred wells of Celtic countries where a saint or holy man fulfils the role of guardian spirit, for even in the Welsh and Irish mountains droughts occur in the summer months. In the frescos of the Villa Boscoreale at Pompeii the water tumbles from the rocks of a cave into a fountain; ivy covers the rocks and above, the formal architecture of a pergola supports climbing roses. The nymph is pictorially absent yet her presence pervades the scene. Sometimes the nymphaeum was the entrance to a grotto – a natural, or more often, artificial cave with a mosaic floor and walls lined with pumice stone forming a cool retreat in the Italian summer months. A fine re-creation of the nymphaeum can be seen at the sixteen-century Villa Giulia in Rome (the Etruscan Museum).

The Greeks and Romans inherited the Persians' love of trees and sense of wonder at ancient and unusual examples. The Elder Pliny in his *Natural History* describes the famous planes of the Academy and also a specimen growing in Lycia, so vast that the governor, Licinius Mucianus, held a banquet for eighteen retainers in its hollow interior which resembled a grotto, being lined with mossy pumice stones beside a cool spring. Afterwards the governor slept within the tree, where shielded from every breath of wind he declared that he received more delight from the sound of the rain dropping through the trees

Fig. 2.9 Re-creation of a classical nymphaeum in the gardens of the Villa Giulia, Rome, constructed in the 1550s (Falda: *Giardini di Roma* (1676)).

than a man-made palace could afford with its marble walls, painted decorations and gilded panelling. Pliny reports that the branches were themselves as big as trees, and gave the impression of a grove rather than a single tree [15].

Funerary groves and mounds

The Greeks and Persians both planted groves and gardens around the tombs of famous men. Alexander the Great punished the Magi responsible for maintaining the grove around the tomb of Cyrus when he found them neglectful of their duty. The tradition of funerary planting has lasted to our own time, yews being appropriate to the churchyard in Britain and cypresses in warmer climates; but the origins of the custom are obscure and subject to all manner of unverifiable explanations. Descriptions survive of the two gigantic mausoleums of Imperial Rome; that of Augustus consisted of a concrete drum, 88 metres in diameter, faced with travertine and surmounted by an earthen tumulus planted with evergreens, the whole being enclosed within a wooded park. The later mausoleum of Hadrian was similar in form, the tumulus being planted with cypresses. It would seem unlikely that such planting was an invention of the time for both mausoleums belong firmly to an Etruscan tradition, varying from their predecessors in their colossal size. At Cerveteri (the Etruscan Caere) the cemetery is a haunting and beautiful sight; a multitude of tumuli of various sizes stand on carved stone plinths grouped informally beside 'streets' against a backcloth of noble cypresses and pines, planted relatively recently but so appropriately that they seem a response to an atavistic instinct. It would seem not unlikely that these tumuli were once planted with evergreens as were the imperial mausoleums. One wonders whether the tumuli of the British Isles were once planted in this manner; often they crown the summits of hills and it may be that the groves of beech or pine, of recent origin, that sometimes surround them, follow instinctively an ancient tradition.

The form itself of the tumulus – an artificial hill – may derive from the concept of the sacred mountain and if so relates to the ziggurats of Mesopotamia and mound structures in the temples and palaces of India and China. The idea of the plane of the heavens resting on mountain tops occurs in ancient mythologies, and also the idea that certain high peaks such as Olympus were so close to the heavens that they were inhabited or visited by gods. The concept of the world mountain either supporting the sky or forming a link, or soul-ladder, between earth and heaven is described with many examples by Lethaby [16].

Whatever their underlying symbolic purpose, the tumulus, ziggurat and pyramid have a quality as shapes in the landscape which derives from the basic simplicity of their geometry. To the figures of circle and square is added the dimension of height, modified by gravity, giving the stable forms of the cone and the stepped or sloping pyramid. The contrast of ideal man-made shapes with nature's softer forms can be deeply satisfying.

Republican Rome

Greek culture, influenced by the East, produced the Hellenistic. Soon

15. Pliny (the Elder): *Natural History*, X11.5, Loeb translation.
16. W. R. Lethaby: *Architecture, Nature and Magic*. Duckworth (1956).

this was to be absorbed by the robust civilisation of the Romans, a nation which had achieved dominance in Italy by the time of Alexander's death. The later Romans regarded their success historically as the due of stern republican virtues: duty to the state, frugality, seriousness (*gravitas*), obedience and austerity. Essentially they saw their origin as that of a race of hard-working, warrior farmers: a hero of their early days was Cincinnatus, a farmer called from his plough by a delegation of senators to lead his country in time of need. This attachment to the soil and love of the land was to persist, and when the influence of Greece and the East was assimilated it produced a complete attitude to landscape, combining the functional and ideal, that has possibly never been achieved since, at least in the West.

In the Italian tradition the world was not anthropocentric. A hierarchy of divinities descended from the twelve councillor-gods to the attendant spirits of grove, spring and field. Nature was animate and powerful, and farming had to be conducted with reverence to the guardians of the natural order; local spirits of the harvest and crops had to be propitiated. Above these local matters were the heavens, whose constellations and planets dictated the seasons, the sowing and ripening of crops. The Elder Cato (234–149 BC), who was regarded by later Romans as the embodiment of republican virtue, wrote a manual *On Agriculture*. His lack of humanity seems appalling – he recommended that old and sickly slaves should be sold without compunction – yet his humility before the natural world is intense. Precise prayers and sacrifices are specified before various estate and farming functions are performed. Before the thinning of a grove (where we would be considering the need for a Forestry Commission licence), Cato recommends the sacrifice of a pig and the following prayer:

> Whether thou be god or goddess to whom this grove is dedicated, as it is thy right to receive a sacrifice of a pig for the thinning of this sacred grove, and to this intent, whether I or one at my bidding do it, may it rightly be done. To this end, in offering this pig to thee I humbly beg that thou will be gracious and merciful to me, to my house and household, and to my children. Wilt thou deign to receive this pig which I offer thee to this end [17].

To some, this attitude may seem superstitious, to others an indication of a deeper awareness; certainly it illustrates a powerful respect for the unknown and unpredictable forces of the natural environment.

Cato hated the influence of the Greeks, which he regarded as leading to a lifestyle of luxury which would undermine the Roman state, and he opposed it bitterly. In this he was unsuccessful and also wrong, for Rome evolved to dominate the civilised world of the West for 600 years after his death. We have seen that the Greek cities of Italy developed the peristyle, and by the first century BC the Hellenistic culture had become a part of the Roman tradition. This fusion found expression in the design of the villas and surrounding farms and landscapes of leading Romans. The term 'villa' in Cato's day had meant a farmhouse; this use of the word continued, but it also came to embrace the country house, often palatial in size and construction and, in the later case of Hadrian's villa at Tivoli, a complex of buildings which virtually formed a small town. The villa as a country house had now become a synthesis of the old agricultural traditions and love of

17. Cato: *De Re Rustica*, CXXXVIII.

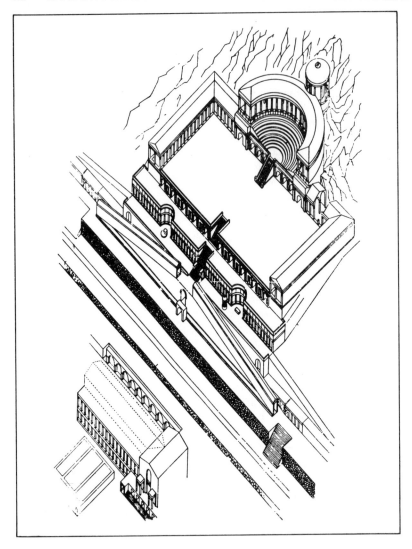

Fig. 2.10 Axonometric plan of the Temple of Fortuna Primogenia at Praenesta (Palestrina). Built *c.* 80 BC by Sulla, the temple is an outstanding example of the Roman's skill in fashioning hillsides into terraces linked by ramps and stairs; a landscape form to be revived at the Renaissance. (From *Etruscan and Roman Architecture* by A. Boethius and J. B. Ward-Perkins (The Pelican History of Art, 1970), p. 142. Reprinted by permission of Penguin Books Ltd. Copyright © the Estate of Axel Boethius, and J. B. Ward-Perkins, 1970.)

nature, with the Greek concept of the Philosophers' Garden, and the Hellenistic tradition of palatial architecture amid landscapes, which derived from the paradises. The villas of Lucullus (117–55 BC) made a great impression on his contemporaries and his name became a by-word for sybaritic luxury and grandeur. A successful general, enriched by his conquests in the East, he devoted himself in his retirement to the creation of villas and gardens, the most famous of which were in Rome on the slopes of the Quirinal and Pincian hills. The approach was on the present site of Santa Trinita del Monte, to which a series of terraces and stairs ascended the hill; their remains survived to be studied and drawn by Pirro Ligorio in the sixteenth century, and appear to have similarities with the Temple of Fortune at Praeneste (Palestrina), built earlier by Sulla, where a great series of terraces, ramps and stairs rise on the slopes of a hill to culminate in a semi-circular double portico. Sufficient elements of this temple survive today to give some impression of its composition and scale; the ruins of Lucullus' stair, however, have made way for a worthy successor,

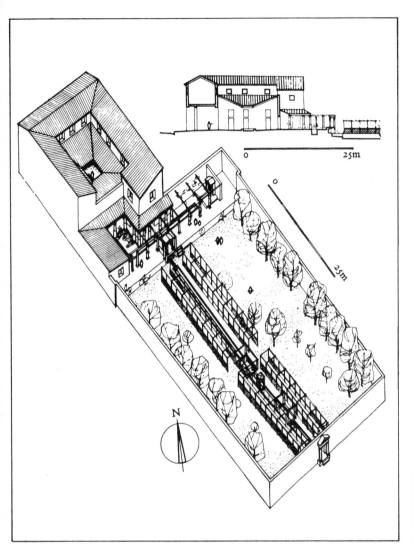

Fig. 2.11 The house and garden of Loreius Tiburtinus at Pompeii. (From *Etruscan and Roman Architecture* by A. Boethius and J. B. Ward-Perkins (The Pelican History of Art, 1970), p. 315 reproduced by courtesy of Miss Sheila Gibson and reprinted by permission of Penguin Books Ltd. Copyright © the Estate of Axel Boethius, and J. B. Ward-Perkins, 1970.)

the baroque Spanish Steps which stand firmly in the tradition of this specifically Roman contribution to the history of planned landscapes, the fashioning of a hillside into a series of ascending formal terraces linked by ramps and stairs. This form, revived at the Renaissance, was the base for many of the most successful landscape gardens of Italy; in particular, the renowned gardens of the Villa d'Este at Tivoli, brilliantly designed by the same Ligorio as an elaborate water garden in which fountains, water staircases, jets and cascades add a dynamic element to the formal structure of the Roman hillside landscape.

A hillside garden, termed that of 'Loreius Tiburtinus' has been excavated at Pompeii [18]. The house was set on a street, but the whole rear frontage opened on to a terrace with a marble-lined channel and trellised pergola. A central fountain flowed into a second channel running down to the hill for a length of the garden, with a pavilion sited over the channel at a point slightly beyond the centre point from the house. Parallel lines of trees carried the eye towards the distant mountains. The terrace and fountain were adorned with statuary. The

18. J. Ward-Perkins: *Pompeii* AD 79.

whole garden, its relationship to the house, and embrace of the functional and wild landscape in its view, is a striking precursor of Renaissance gardens. The pavilion is of particular interest as it is a feature one associates with Persian rather than Roman gardens.

Unfortunately, most of our knowledge of Lucullus' gardens is contained in references by writers of his time. Cicero (106-43 BC) has left more detailed descriptions of his villas in his letters, including that of one designed to display his collections of Greek sculptures and paintings, with the wings appropriately named Lyceum and Academy. Cicero's villas were probably typical of many belonging to rich and successful Romans in the late Republic. These were now being built on the Pincian and Janiculam hills outside the walls, and further afield in the Alban and Sabine hills which remained cool in the Roman summer and commanded magnificent views across the Campagna. Similar sites were to be favoured 1,600 years later in the Renaissance. By the end of the Republic, Rome was surrounded by these villas and gardens of the wealthy.

Varro and Virgil

Marcus Terentius Varro (116-27 BC) was the author of a manual on farm and estate management. As a personality he appears to us as attractive as Cato is repellent. A public servant, commander and greatest scholar of the Roman Republic (*Vir Romanorum eruditissimus*), he was interested in all branches of learning and wrote some 600 books of which only a few fragments survive and, fortunately, the three books which make up *De Re Rustica*. This work was written in his eightieth year (he lived another 10 years) for his young wife Fundania, who had bought a farm. Varro, warned 'that he must pack his baggage for departure', wished to leave her a practical book to refer to on all matters to do with farming. His humanity, humour and detailed knowledge of the subject are evident throughout the work and much of the technical detail was to reappear a century later in the voluminous treatise of Columella on agriculture and in Pliny's *Natural History*. It also probably influenced the *Georgics* of his younger comtemporary, Virgil.

De Re Rustica gives a full description of the functional landscape of his time, its economics and methods of husbandry. It also deals with farming in the wider context of religious belief and considers the social virtues of the countryman compared with the townsman. 'It was divine nature which gave us the country, and man's skill that built the cities', tilling of the fields is not only more ancient than the arts, it is also more noble, for in peace the country Romans feed the city and in time of war come to its aid. The ancestors of the Romans of Varro's time considered that the tillers lived a pious and useful life, and they were the only survivors of the stock of King Saturn. In fact, the hard work of the farm Varro describes was now done by slaves, as it was on Cato's farm. The example of Cincinnatus was revered but not followed – the owner had become an overseer, not a working farmer. However, in the case of Varro, and also Virgil, Pliny and Columella, the owner remained extremely well informed on all matters of husbandry, and the fact that these books of his survived suggests that they were widely read and were of considerable interest to many Romans. Essentially, Varro's work shows that the leading Romans at the end of the Republic and beginning of the Empire, retained their respect for their agricultural traditions and were still interested in the land and its management, even though they mostly lived in the towns and treated their estates as part-time country residences.

Varro begins his work by invoking the twelve councillor-gods; not the urban gods whose gilded images adorn the forum, but the special deities of husbandmen. Jupiter, 'the Father' or the sky, and Tellus 'Mother Earth', Sol and Luna, whose courses are watched in all maters of planting and harvesting. The other eight Olympians follow, also under the names by which they were known to the tillers of the soil. Later he describes at length the celestial calender, the heavenly bodies and constellations which govern the practice of farming – the signs of the zodiac, the Pleiades and Dog Star – their rising and setting with the solstices and equinoxes, which define the proper times to carry out the seasonal tasks of the farm. The waxing and waning of the moon also governs farming operations; grain and firewood should only be gathered and sheep sheared under a waning moon. The period for making cheese lies between the rising of the Pleiades in spring and the time in summer when they appear near midnight. This concept of a divine order governing celestial bodies and the seasons, which in turn govern the fruitfulness of the earth and the conduct of husbandry was later absorbed by Christianity. It appears in the calenders of the later Middle Ages and finds perhaps its most perfect expression in the Limbourg brothers' illustrations of the seasons in the *Très Riches Heures* of the Duc de Berry, where the chariot of the sun moves through the zodiac above fruitful landscapes.

In his third book, Varro considers the immediate environs of the villa, where fish-ponds, aviaries and enclosures for the animals of the chase – deer, wild boar, and hares – were sited. These now had ornamental value as well as the function of supplying the homestead with a variety of food. Specialised structures were built for rearing dormice and snails, which the Romans esteemed as delicacies. Varro comments that in the past there were two ways for keeping birds for the table: hens were fed in the barnyard and pigeons were kept either in cotes or on the roof of the villa. Now aviaries, called 'ornithones', were built, often larger than whole villas used to be. Similarly, the Leporarium which used to produce a single hare had grown to be a home park. Varro deals humorously with some of his contemporaries whose wealth and enthusiasms outstripped their sense of the practical; Lucullus for example, in his villa at Tusculum, had built his dining room within the aviary, thinking to dine luxuriously while seeing birds flying around and others cooked for the table; unfortunately, the pleasure to the eyes did not match the disagreeable odour to the nostrils. However, Varro was exceedingly proud of his own aviary at his villa near Cassino and describes it at length; a rotunda stands on an island surrounded by a netted colonnade through which an enclosing wood is visible – fish tanks and netted pavilions line the approach. Inside the dome of the rotunda the morning and evening stars revolved, reflecting the order of the heavens, and a compass of the eight winds, geared to a weather vane, indicated the direction of the prevailing wind. This aviary is one of the first examples of garden architecture for which we have a detailed description.

Some 10 years after *De Re Rustica* was written, Virgil composed his *Georgics*: four poems which deal with the growing of crops, trees and

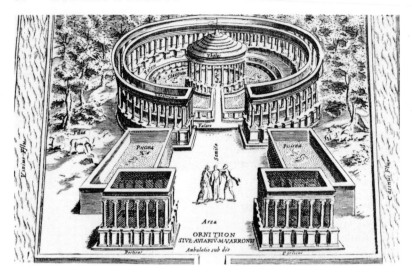

Fig. 2.12 Varro's ornithon reconstructed by Laurus in *Antiquae Urbis Splendor.*

vines, horses, herds and flocks, and bee-keeping. Virgil's knowledge of husbandry is as detailed as Varro's, but to this he adds an acute personal observation of the countryside, with its changing moods, hardships and rewards, and a profound sympathy for its inhabitants and, indeed, all living things. Wild creatures are as much a part of his landscape as domestic breeds; swallows, rooks, moles and toads engage Virgil's attention as does the bull, grunting as he pulls the ploughshare, and the 'tiny republic' of the hive. All is expressed in the medium of great poetry, and inevitably, Varro's fine work appears by comparison somewhat limited.

Virgil's observation is that of the true countryman: direct and never sentimental. Only one who has grown up in the countryside and knows it intimately can wholly take this view. He also experienced dispossession, as his modest family estate near Mantua was confiscated during the civil wars as part of a land settlement programme for retired veterans. It was later restored to him, but as a result of this experience he does not take the countryside for granted, as countrymen tend to do. Both his first and ninth *Eclogues* deal with the personal tragedy of eviction:

> But the rest of us must go from here and be dispersed –
> to Scythia, bone-dry Africa, the chalky spate of the Oxus,
> Even to Britain – that place cut off at the world's end.
> Ah, when shall I see my native land again? After long years,
> Or never? – see the turf dressed roof of my simple cottage,
> And wondering gaze at the ears of corn that were all my
>   kingdom?
> To think of some godless soldier owning my well-farmed fallow,
> A foreigner reaping the crops! To such a pass has civil
> Dissension brought us: for people like these we have sown our
>   fields [19].

The speaker, Maliboeus, could be a Highland crofter or Irishman of the eighteenth century, or an English cottager of the same years dispossessed of his smallholding by Act of Parliament and driven for employment to the towns. His companion, Tityrus, is more fortunate,

19. Virgil: *The Eclogues, Georgics and Aeneid.* Trans. C. Day Lewis. Oxford (1966).

having petitioned the young prince in Rome and had his land restored: 'pasture your cattle, breed from your bulls, as you did of old'.
It seems likely that Tityrus is Virgil himself and the poem expresses
his gratitude to the young prince, Octavian, who, as the Emperor
Augustus, reformed the Roman constitution, brought stability to the
state and secured the frontiers, to bring two centuries of internal
peace. The arts flourished under his patronage and clearly Virgil considered that he was living in an especially favoured age, a fulfilment
of the long hard struggle of the Roman nation through survival to
dominance and empire.

Like Varro, Virgil dwells on the virtues of the countryman who
lacks a mansion, wealth and imported luxuries, but has instead the
calm security of a life that will not cheat him:

> Rich in its own rewards, are here: the broad ease of the
>   farmlands.
> Caves, living lakes, and combes that are cool even at
>   midsummer,
> Mooing of herds, and slumber mild in the trees' shade.
> Here are glades game-haunted,
> Lads hardened to labour, inured to simple ways,
> Reverence for God, respect for the family. When Justice
> Left earth, her latest footprints were stamped on folk like these
>   [19].

The distant glow of the Golden Age and the rule of Saturn are per-
ceptible in the life of the countryman. Others will pile up wealth, fight
on sea and land, toady at royal courts, destroy whole towns and the
tenements of the poor in the lust for riches, shed their brothers' blood,
and barter their homes for countries lying under an alien sun.

> But still the farmer furrows the land with his curving plough:
> The land is his annual labour, it keeps his native country,
> His little grandsons and herds of cattle and trusty bullocks.
> Unresting the year teems with orchard fruit, or young
> Of cattle, or sheaves of corn,
> Brimming the furrows with plenty, overflowing the barns [19].

Varro saw husbandry governed by the celestial bodies and seasons,
themselves governed by divine order. Virgil brings an added dimension to this concept: the importance of well-ordered land to the well-
governed state, its harmony with the natural order and links with an
earlier world when Justice ruled. In the *Georgics* the functional landscape becomes divine – 'Such was the life that golden Saturn lived
upon earth.'

The *Georgics* are the work of a true countryman who was also a great
poet. Dryden called them the 'best poem of the best poet'. Virgil
makes the countryside ideal, whereas most poets idealise it. The distinction is important: as other artists and poets were to observe and
depict the countryside from outside, Virgil saw it from within, with
its toils, hardships, fruits and rewards. Linked to its origins in mythology, the divine order, and ordered state, Virgil's practical landscape achieves a fusion of the ideal and functional which had not been
achieved before and has not been equalled since.

The Roman Empire

The writings of Varro and Virgil reflect the respect of the cultivated Roman for his farming origins and his interest in the land. Inevitably, in the Republic and early Empire he had become separated by wealth and circumstances from the personal practice of husbandry and many landowners treated their villas as part-time country residences. Elsewhere, many of the old farms had passed into the ownership of absentee landlords and were cultivated by tenants and slaves. With cheap grain from Egypt and North Africa, good arable land went out of cultivation – a trend deplored by Varro – the great estates prospered on pasturage, bought out the small farmers and, in time, inevitably the rural population diminished. But in the first century AD many traditional farms and smallholdings still survived and could be admired as the rural context of the villa and be depicted in the wall-paintings of the urban dwellers of Pompeii and Herculaneum, preserved under pumice and ash by the disaster of AD 79.

These paintings record the Roman appreciation of the landscape as a totality: the functional landscape of farming in the plains and foothills, groves, temples and 'sacred sites', rocky mountains beyond, lakes and sea coast overlooked by portico villas, islands and ships. These were the views from favoured country villas; in town houses they were the creations of painters who used the device of dividing up the wall with pilasters, columns and architraves, with landscapes in between, to give the illusion of looking through a pierced wall or portico to the countryside beyond. Contemporary descriptions of this style are given by both Vitruvius and the Elder Pliny [20] and many actual examples survive showing all manner of landscapes, often romanticised with scenes from mythology – in particular the wanderings of Odysseus – but also the country pursuits of fishing, fowling, hunting, the tending of flocks and herds, and the gathering of the vintage. Frescos from the villa of Empress Livia in Rome show a different, more intimate, scene; a lush paradise garden of fruit trees, flowers and birds, painted naturalistically, but there immutable – a garden for all seasons.

While the paintings of Pompeii re-create the countryside for town-dwellers who could enjoy its fruits while living close to the luxuries of urban life, a more direct observation and understanding is preserved in that storehouse of information on Roman life, the letters of the Younger Pliny (AD 60–111), who combined a distinguished career in public service with an active and personal interest in his country estates. At some stage he decided to publish his correspondence and by good fortune it has survived. He shared with his uncle, the Elder Pliny, a love of nature and delighted in the planning and improvement of his villas and gardens, to which he devoted all the time and energy that his public duties would allow. The description of his gardens with their pavilions, colonnades, pergolas, topiary, clipped hedges of box and rosemary, cypresses and planes, marble seats and fountains, became a textbook for Renaissance designers and Pliny would probably have appreciated Italian gardens created 1,500 years after his time. Perhaps also he would feel their limitations, for he saw his own formal gardens as an element in the total landscape which contained them, rather than as an end in themselves:

20. *Painting walls with pictures of country houses and porticoes and landscape gardens, groves, woods, hills, fish-ponds, canals, rivers, coasts, and whatever anybody could desire, together with various sketches of people going for a stroll or sailing in a boat or on land going to country houses riding on asses or in carriages, and also people fishing or fowling or hunting or even gathering the vintage.*
Pliny (the Elder): *Natural History*, XXXV.116, Loeb translation.

The whole garden is enclosed by a dry-stone wall which is hidden from sight by a box hedge planted in tiers; outside is a meadow, as well worth seeing for its natural beauty as the formal garden I have described; then fields and many more meadows and woods.

Pliny accepts the landscape on its own terms and admires its contrasts, intricacies and variety as the work of nature and husbandry. His villa near Ostia is 27 kilometres from Rome and can be reached after the day's work. The by-road to it is sandy and narrows as it passes through woods and broadens through meadows where sheep, cattle and horses are brought to fatten on the spring pasture. It is a scene full of variety. The villa itself lies beside the beach, artificially designed to take advantage of the moods of the sea and to exploit the heat of the sun, shutters control through-draughts, the effects of shade are worked into the design, and the description appears startlingly contemporary in terms of today's environmental engineering and search for climatic control. The garden, consisting mainly of fruit trees, lies sheltered from the salt spray, an intimate and functional adjunct, subordinate to the maritime landscape for which the site was chosen.

The garden of Pliny's Tuscan villa was a far grander affair, but here too it is the landscape setting which is of primary importance and his description of the site leaves no doubt that for him the observation of nature outweighed the enjoyment of the planned gardens which formed the immediate setting of the villa [21]. His description is objective and direct, full of wonder and free of preconceptions and the urge to tamper and improve. Such acceptance of the natural world is rare, even in Antiquity, and has much in common with the freshness and precision of Flemish landscape painting.

Elsewhere Pliny describes his visit to the source of the River Clitumnus which has greatly impressed him. The spring gushes out below a hill covered with ancient cypresses, and the water collects in a pool, so clear that coins thrown in and pebbles shine on the bottom. From the pool the water becomes a broad river, the banks clothed with ash trees and poplars whose green reflections are so clear, they seem as if planted in the stream. The water is as cold and as sparkling as snow. Nearby is the temple of the guardian spirit, the god Clitumnus, and written tablets around his image bear witness to his living presence and prophetic powers. The scene recalls sacred sites depicted in Pompeian paintings of temples beside tree-clad rocks and springs, and the renowned 'Temple of the Sibyl' at Tivoli, standing dramatically above cascades and best admired in Piranesi's engravings, for today the waters have been diverted.

The directness of Pliny's vision may have been a family trait: the spirit of inquiry linked to the precision of the scientist that had led his uncle to write the *Natural History*. Natural phenomena, such as the floating islands of Lake Vadimon, fascinated him as did the technicalities of designing buildings and their environment. His appreciation of landscape was founded on a practical knowledge of husbandry and, although largely absent from his estates, he took a detailed interest in their management and the welfare of his tenants.

Wall-painting brought an illusion of the countryside into the town; the Emperor Nero sought to make it a reality in the remarkable grounds of his Golden House. Following the great fire of AD 64, which destroyed a wide area of the old city, he took advantage of the disaster

21. *The countryside is very beautiful. Picture to yourself a vast amphitheatre such as could only be a work of nature; the great spreading plain is ringed by mountains, their summits crowned by ancient woods of tall trees, where there is a good deal of mixed hunting to be had. Down the mountain slopes are timber woods interspersed with small hills of soil so rich that there is scarcely a rocky outcrop to be found; these hills are fully as fertile as the level plain and yield quite as rich a harvest, though it ripens rather later in the season. Below them the vineyards spreading down every slope weave their uniform pattern far and wide, their lower limit bordered by a belt of shrubs. Then come the meadows and cornfields, where the land can be broken up only by heavy oxen and the strongest ploughs, for the soil is so stiff that it is thrown up in great clods at the first ploughing and is not thoroughly broken until it has been gone over nine times. The meadows are bright with flowers, covered with trefoil and other delicate plants which always seem soft and fresh, for everything is fed by streams which never run dry; though the ground is not marshy where the water collects, because of its downward slope, so that any surplus water it cannot absorb is drained off into the River Tiber flowing through the fields.*
Pliny (the Younger): *Letters*. Trans. B. Radice. Penguin (1963).

to create a royal palace and park which effectively covered the three hills of the Palatine, Esqueline and Caelian and in the low-lying ground between he created a lake. The fullest contemporary description is by Suetonius, who would have seen the Golden House in his boyhood [22]. The wonder of the Golden House to Nero's contemporaries was that here, in the heart of Rome, he had realised 'Rus in urbe' – the solitude of the countryside. Yet the achievement was short-lived; Nero's successors dismantled the palace and park, the Colosseum rose on the site of the lake and the Baths of Titus near by. The Romans accepted the ostentatious display of wealth and luxury, but the ruthless expropriation of land in the centre of Rome was a crime.

The Golden House was to be a potent memory. In the extensive gardens of the Villa Borghese at Rome (early 17th century) pavilions, statuary, fountains, lakes and island temples echo the great parks of Imperial Rome; at the Villa d'Este a model of ancient Rome revived the 'Cities' of Nero's shore. Probably the landscapes nearest in spirit to Nero's highly artificial creation are those of eighteenth-century England, where temple pavilions, shrines, grottoes and contrived lakes are set in the informal fabric of the traditional parks. But there is an essential difference: the boundary belt of the later English park forms an enclosing pale, shutting out the functional countryside, whereas Nero re-created the fields and vineyards of the working landscape within.

Half a century later, the Emperor Hadrian began the building of his great landscape villa in the Tivoli foothills. 'Villa' seems a modest term for a complex the size of a small town which combined a royal palace, accommodation for the Emperor's household, personal guard and the imperial administration. The villa reflects the personality of the Emperor – a superbly able and civilised man, who travelled widely through his dominions and was obsessed by building. He may well have been an architect himself – the buildings of his reign which include the Pantheon have the stamp of a guiding personality and the variety, idiosyncrasy and overall taste of the villa suggest the personal interest of Hadrian in all its details. Inevitably one compares it with other citadels of other times built by powerful rulers to govern their empires: Diocletian's palace at Spalato – a rectangular complex containing all the court functions, separated from the world outside; Philip II's somewhat similar Escorial, a vast, forbidding fortress defying, or ignoring, the barren hills around; and Louis XIV's Versailles forcing both town and landscape, on their respective sides of the palace, into a rigid geometrical framework.

Hadrian's villa, by contrast, respects the spirit of the place; its axes follow the natural topography of the land and along them, loosely grouped and built in magnificent and varied architecture, are the traditional buildings familiar from the Hellenistic and later Republic: baths, libraries, gymnasia, sculpture galleries, theatres, dining rooms and audience halls; each built in a style and manner befitting its function. Water pervaded the complex, from a great canal, the 'Canopus' which culminated in cascades surrounding the dining chamber, to the many fountains, nymphaea and watercourses which irrigated the garden courts and the so-called 'Marine Theatre' – a garden house in the centre of a pool, where movable bridges could ensure seclusion for the Emperor from the world. Water was a connecting element through the exuberance and variety of the architecture; so too would have been

Fig. 2.13 Piranesi's engraving of the Temple of Vesta at Tivoli – a sacred site with the temple overlooking the cascades of the River Aniene tumbling into the gorge below (unfortunately diverted in 1831).

22. The following details will give some notion of its size and magnificence. A huge statue of himself, 120 feet high, stood in the entrance hall; and the pillared arcade ran for a whole mile. An enormous pool, more like a sea than a pool, was surrounded by buildings made to resemble cities, and by a landscape garden consisting of ploughed fields, vineyards, pastures and woodlands – where every variety of domestic and wild animal roamed about. Parts of the house were overlaid with gold and studded with precious stones and nacre (mother of pearl) ... When the palace had been decorated throughout in this lavish style, Nero dedicated it, and condescended to remark: 'Good, now I can at last begin to live like a human being'.
Suetonius: The Twelve Caesars. Nero 31. Trans. E. V. Rieu. Penguin (1957).

the park in which the buildings were set, its trees clothing the steps below the main axes and linking the villa to the ordered agriculture of the plain and the wooded hills behind.

A miniature valley, named after the Vale of Tempe, lies beside the villa. The original vale, in Thessaly, was much admired in Antiquity for its natural beauty [23]. At Tivoli the valley was deepened by the excavation of stone for the villa and with its rocky sides reproduced the wilder landscape of Thessaly into the scheme of the park. A small open shrine to Venus overlooks it, silhouetted against the hills beyond and forming the abode of the guardian spirit of the place – essentially this was a god-haunted landscape, created in miniature.

There is no pale at Tivoli, in the sense of an enclosing barrier, shutting out the functional landscape from the 'ideal' landscape within, nor is there any attempt to force a contrived geometry on the villa's surroundings. The farming plain, the hills and distant rocky skyline were accepted as the total landscape in which the villa was sited, and the buildings and terraces were placed on high ground to take full advantage of the views. Privacy and enclosures were provided in the courts and water gardens behind.

Abandoned and forgotten in later centuries, the ruins of the great villa were to survive the turmoils of the Gothic wars and use as a ready source of building stone in the Middle Ages [24]. Acquisition by the state in the 1870s saved what was left and in recent years systematic excavation has been accompanied by the judicious reconstruction of buildings from their fallen elements, the replacement in replica of sculptures known to have been removed and the restoration of water to the Canopus and other great pools. Consequently, it is possible today to gain some impression of the villa's original appearance and extent, without undue recourse to the imagination. Italian conservers tolerate the coexistence of fine trees with monuments and the site has not been stripped to its bare archaeological essentials as tends to happen in Britain. It is indeed a romantic spot, highly evocative, to the visitor, of the age which produced this last and greatest of the Roman landscape villas.

Hadrian's villa was the personal creation of a brilliant ruler at a time when the creative power of Rome seemed at its zenith. Since the foundation of the Empire by Augustus, except for one brief year following Nero's death in AD 69, the Empire has known exactly 170 years of civil peace when Hadrian died in 138 [25]. In the reign of Marcus Aurelius, Hadrian's successor, the military situation on the frontiers grew sharply worse. The pressure of barbarian nations seeking to invade the peaceful provinces became almost overwhelming and henceforward the first object of the state was military survival; the Pax Romana was over for ever. In AD 192 the murder of Marcus' unworthy son Commodus plunged the Empire into civil war and during the next 100 years barbarian invasion, civil strife and economic and social chaos destroyed the world of the Antonines. The subsequent survival of the Roman state was perhaps its greatest achievement [26], but the cost was the metamorphosis of the benevolent state of the first and second centuries into a totalitarian, standardised, coercive police administration; personal freedom was almost extinguished, the towns and middle classes ruined and the peasantry forced into grinding serfdom to support a vast administration and an army nearly twice as large as it had been two centuries previously. Such was the price of

23. *Part of the course of the Peneus is called the Vale of Tempe, five miles long and nearly an acre and a half in breadth, with gently sloping hills rising beyond human sight on either hand, while the valley between is verdant with a grove of trees. Along it glides the Peneus, glittering with pebbles and adorned with grassy banks, melodius with the choral song of birds.*
Pliny (the Elder): *Natural History*, IV.8, Loeb translation.
24. Serious destruction began at the Renaissance, paradoxically at the hands of men dedicated to the revival of classical civilisation; the site became a place of pilgrimage both for humanists and treasure hunters, and popes, cardinals and princes looted it for sculptures and bronzes to fill their galleries; architectural details were removed, unrecorded, to adorn palaces and gardens.
25. Wars were limited to the defence of the frontiers, internally they had become a memory of the past and from the Clyde to the Euphrates, the Sahara to the Danube, Rome ruled with equity, restraint and humanity. Gibbon has said of Hadrian's successors, Antoninus Pius and Marcus Aurelius, 'their united reigns are possibly the only period of history in which the happiness of a great people was the sole object of government'.
26. M. Grant: *The Climax of Rome*. Weidenfeld and Nicholson (1968).

the postponement of the dissolution of the Empire. It is no wonder that men questioned the fundamental purpose of life and their thoughts turned to transcendental worlds, rather than the grim reality around them.

We may speculate that the great parks and villas of Italy survived intact until the final collapse of the Roman state in the sixth century with the subsequent destruction of the economy and civilised life brought about by the Gothic and Lombard wars. In North Africa the paradises were inherited by the Vandal conquerors who loved them too well according to Procopius, the historian of Justinian's wars of reconquest, for the life of luxury they symbolised made the Vandals an easy prey to the armies of Belisarius. But these Italian and North African planned landscapes were survivals of a creative movement and framework of thinking that had effectively died in the third century. Echoes of the landscape vision of the classical world would occur in poems of the fourth century, but the imagery seems contrived and second-hand, pale echoes of the great age of Virgil, Varro and Pliny that was now remote in time and irrelevant to the transcendental ideals of the Christian Church and the rigours of the Empire geared to the necessities of survival.

In Eastern Europe the Empire was to survive for many centuries, but its character was to be very difficult from that of the earlier Empire. The concept of embattled Byzantium as the New Jerusalem is one of the noblest ideals to have inspired European civilisation, with its slow but heroic decline, brought it seemed to its people by their failure to match their lives to their high ideals [27]. This lies outside landscape history and little is known of that side of Byzantine life, except that they termed their courtyard gardens 'paradises'. Possibly the archaeologists will provide new knowledge as they have of Islamic Spain. An early medieval account survives of the Emperor's park at Philopation:

> In front of the town is a beautiful, spacious, enclosed place with all sorts of animals for game, also canals and ponds and ditches and caves, so that instead of woodland the creatures have hiding places. At this delightful spot there are shining palaces, built by the Emperor for coolness in summer, all indescribably grand [28].

The brief description raises questions that must remain unanswered: whether this was an ancient park or one built in the ancient tradition; or whether it was built under the influence of the revived civilisation of Persia.

The Sassanians

During the great years of the late Roman Republic and early Empire, Persia was ruled by Parthian dynasties who looked westward cultur- ally rather than to Persian traditions. In AD 226 the family of Sassan overthrew them; 'five and a half centuries after the fall of the Achae- menians the Persian people had regained power, and the new dynasty, as the legitimate successor of the Achaemenians, ensured the con- tinuity of Iranian civilisation' [29]. While they looked back to the Kingdom of Cyrus, the traditional Persian regard for nature is ex- pressed in a new vitality and naturalism in depiction of animals in

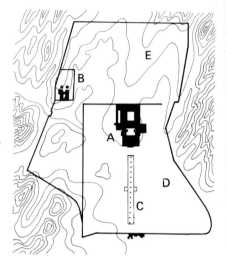

Fig. 2.14 Plan of Qasr-i-Shirin: (A) Main palace; (B) Smaller palace; (C) Formal canal; (D) Inner *paradeisos*; (E) Outer *paradeisos*.

27. R. Sherrard: *Constantinople. The Iconography of a Sacred City.* Oxford University Press (1965).
28. M. L. Gothein: *A History of Garden Art.*
29. R. Ghirshman: *Iran* (1978).

their rock carvings and the engraved silver salvers that are among the surviving achievements of Sassanian art. There is a tenderness and a realism that must stem from direct observation and sympathy, and although the context in which wild animals are shown is the hunt, there is no brutality or morbid delight in their deaths such as is evident in Assyrian bas-reliefs. Trees too, are shown with this new realism which looks forward to the art of the Safavids.

The outlines of a planned landscape have been found at Qasr-i-Shirin, sited below the Zagros, where the mountain wall meets the Mesopotamian plain. The remains of a palace survive built by Chosroes II for the beautiful Shirin. A wall bounds an extended paradise, enclosing the level ground between foothills, while a more formal rectangular space is enclosed to the south of the palace complex, traversed by an axial canal suggesting a formal arrangement of gardens within this area, viewed from a huge raised terrace which forms an extension of the palace and links its symmetry with that of the canal. Thus, the landscape is graded: formal gardens, viewed from above, give way to the controlled, semi-natural hunting park, which in turn is surrounded by the wild landscape of the hills beyond the pale, but ever in sight from the palace [30]. Qasr-i-Shirin is the link between Pasagardae and later Persian planned landscapes.

Sassanian Persia was seen as a heroic age in later centuries, just as they themselves looked back to the Achaemenians. Chosroes I became a legendary hero, remembered as Chosroes of the Immortal Soul, and today any peasant asked about ancient ruins will readily reply that it was the work of this mighty King [31]. He was a true reformer, in the mould of Cyrus, who cared for the common people and remade

Fig. 2.15 This floor mosaic in the baths of the palace of Khirbat-al-Mafjar in Jerusalem reflects the continuing influence of Persia in the Arab Empire (8th century) – a delight in the forms of nature and wild animals whose curvilinear shapes echo Sassanian rock carvings and salvers.

30. R. Pinder-Wilson: 'The Persian garden', *The Islamic Garden*. Dumbarton Oaks (1976).
31. G. Herrman: *The Iranian Revival*. Elsevier Phaidon (1977).

the state so that all might have land to till. But his victories, reforms and consolidation were short-lived and ultimately to the benefit of a succeeding empire. A few years before he died the Prophet Muhammad was born (AD 570). Seventy years later Arab armies utterly destroyed Sassanian power, weakened by incessant and fruitless warfare with Byzantium. After initial bloodshed the Arabs realised that they lacked the experience and machinery of government required to rule their vast and unexpected empire. Sassanian organisation and civil service were employed to govern, and even their noble class were allowed to continue in positions of power, provided that they were converted. Thus Persian civilisation survived, to renew itself like the phoenix in succeeding centuries, to the inestimable benefit of both Islam and the West.

Chapter 3

The Middle Ages

Monastic gardens

The classical world disintegrated in the social and economic chaos of the third century and Christianity emerged from persecution and harassment to assume the spiritual leadership of the Roman world. In the remaining years of the Western Empire the Church rapidly absorbed and synthesised classical culture, forming a new and vital framework of thinking and perception and an organisation strong enough to survive the final collapse of the state and to convert, civilise and lead the barbarian nations that were to succeed the Empire in the West. The new faith was essentially concerned with the inner and spiritual world to which the outer world seemed a distraction; consequently landscape appreciation and observation was considered an irrelevance. In the evolving figurative arts there was a conscious rejection of classical realism; deliberate distortion and flattened perspectives were used to project symbolic meaning and transcendental truths, separate from the day-to-day realities of the immediate world. Landscapes which occur as backgrounds or adjuncts to figures and themes are reduced to stylised symbols: the River Jordan for baptism, the rocky garden of Gethsemane and the Mount for the Transfiguration.

Transition to the new art was gradual and in the fourth century links with the past were still strong. Christian themes were often expressed in familiar classical imagery, the pastoral landscapes of the Golden Age becoming those of Paradise and the figure of Orpheus, Christ the Good Shepherd. On a sarcophagus in the Lateran Museum Christ/Bacchus carries a lamb amid a complex and luxuriant pattern of vines among which rustic figures disport themselves, gathering grapes and trampling them in vats: 'I am the vine, ye are the branches.' In striking contrast, a mosaic in the church of the Saints Cosmos and Damien illustrates the severe and uncompromising nature of the new iconography, in which realism is excluded and the essence of the subject directly expressed. A lamb stands on a mound from which flow four streams, the waters of Paradise; above is the inscription 'Jordanes'. The symbolism combines the traditional concept of the waters of life with the sacrament of baptism, the washing away of sins and initiation into eternal life; the guardian deity of the

Fig. 3.1 A fresco in the Catacombs depicting Christ the Good Shepherd (A. N. Didron: *Christian Iconography*).

water source has become the Lamb of God. The imagery is direct and moving in its simplicity. There are numerous examples of the use of similar symbolism [1].

The rivers of Paradise and garden of Eden are analysed by St Augustine in *The City of God against the Pagans* [2]. Augustine did not question the Genesis account of Eden as a truthful record, but saw its purpose in his own time as a description to be interpreted and understood allegorically. Paradise can be seen as the life of a blessed man; its four rivers are the four virtues: prudence, courage, temperance and justice, its trees are useful studies and their fruits the conduct of the righteous; the Tree of Life is wisdom and the Tree of Knowledge the experience which comes with the transgression of a commandment. Alternatively, Paradise can be understood as the Church; its rivers the four gospels, the trees and their fruit the saints and their works; the Tree of Life is Christ himself and the Tree of Knowledge man's personal control of his will. Both interpretations of Paradise, briefly expressed in *The City of God*, were to prove long-lived and fundamental to medieval attitudes to landscape. In time they were developed and enriched in the diverse works of theologians, artists and poets.

Through the example of Augustine, the concept of the Philosophers' Garden became the Christian cloister – a place of peace and contemplation, separate from the distractions of the world outside. Gathering together a religious community in his town of Hippo, 'I assembled, in a garden that Valerius had given me, certain brethren of like intentions with my own, who possessed nothing, even as I possessed nothing, and who followed after me.' To this nucleus, a villa with a peristyle garden, he added a church, so establishing the basic elements of the monastic houses which would be built throughout the Western world in the ensuing centuries.

As the Empire crumbled, the movement for a communal life of contemplation and prayer grew in strength. Wealthy Romans endowed religious communities with their villas and estates, often joining them or leading them themselves. This trend was not a rejection of the world or an escape from its problems, indeed, it was seen as meeting the needs of an age when the foundations of civilised life were fast disappearing. The communities were founded as centres of ordered spiritual life which could lead men through temporal anxieties and the breakdown of the state, and prepare mankind for the imminent second coming of Christ. The combination of spiritual and practical ideals were fundamental to what became the monastic movement and so, also, the preservation of the learning and texts of the ancient as well as the early Christian world.

Some of the churches of this time survive today, relatively intact with their mosaics, but their cloisters and ancillary buildings have been replaced in later ages. But there is little reason to suppose that the cloister gardens of the Middle Ages differed from those of earlier centuries, for their function had not changed. They provided a setting for relaxation and quiet study, the covered walks giving shade from the Mediterranean sun, or shelter from the wind and rain in northern climates; useful herbs and fruits were grown and flowers for the church; in the centre stood a well or fountain. Today, almost all are neglected, for fruit, herbs and flowers have long been freely obtainable outside and the community, if it still exists, has no need to grow its

1. See (i) P. A. Feurier: 'Les Quatre Fleurs du Paradis', *Rivista di Arceologia Cristiana* (1956). Vatican. (ii) A. N. Didron: *Christian Iconography*. George Bell and Sons (1896). It would seem likely that the mounts which occur in the Gospels relate to the ancient tradition of the sacred mountain. They are the scenes for the Transfiguration, Calvary and the Ascension. In the Old Testament, Moses receives the Law on Mount Sinai.
2. This great work of learning, interpretation and synthesis was written following the capture of the city of Rome by a Gothic army, a shattering event to civilised men which seemed at the time to herald the Apocalypse itself. Augustine sought to show a divine purpose through the history of man, combining both the holy scriptures and the Roman histories, in order that men could view the collapse of their ordered world in a wider perspective of challenge and hope. His interpretation of Virgil's *Fourth Eclogue* as foretelling the birth of Christ has already been noted.

own. In Rome three cloister gardens survive; two are on sites of great age although reconstructed in the early Middle Ages – St Paul's outside the Walls and the Quattro Coronati; the third, S. Giovanni dei Genovesi, dates from the fifteenth century. All three well repay a visit, but perhaps the small cloister of the Quattro Coronati is the most perfect, a direct link with the gardens of the early religious communities and with the peristyles of Roman town houses under the Empire. The court is a deep rectangle cut off by the surrounding building complex from the noise and bustle of the surrounding streets. At ground level it is surrounded by an arcaded cloister, above which rise the loggias of domestic rooms from which the viewer can appreciate the ordered plan of the garden. In the centre stands a fountain, fashioned to represent the source of four rivers and leaving no doubt of its intended symbolism or that of the garden. Tall trees rise to shade the court from the glare of the noonday sun, the luxuriance and variety of their leaves contrasting with the formal geometry of the walls and floor permitting a dappled light to penetrate the cool recesses of the cloister. Once seen, this garden seems to compel one to revisit and the visitor must wonder what peculiar qualities it possesses; they are not easy to analyse. In terms of function, the light and heat of the Mediterranean summer are controlled, herbs may grow unparched and daily tasks continue in shade and coolness. The hum and dust of the surrounding city are shut out: the hum replaced by the murmur of the fountain, the dust filtered by the leaves of the trees. The senses, isolated from the macrocosm outside, are delighted by contrasts: the geometry of architecture and the abundance of natural foliage, hard surfaces and the dynamic sparkle of water, shade and shafts of brilliant light, the bright colour of flowers offset by the green of trees and shrubs. An added dimension, that of time, is given by fragments of antique carving and inscriptions built into the fabric of the cloister.

The plan of the garden itself is one of the oldest religious symbols: the mandala, a form to which Jung devoted much research and found associated in his patients with strong feelings of harmony and peace [3]. Thus an unconscious need for underlying harmony is answered in the form of the garden in addition to the requirements of function and conscious delight of the senses. This seems the explanation for the quality of greatness that lies in the small garden of the Quattro Coronati, once one of thousands and now, in the twentieth century, a rarity.

In cloisters such as this, medieval man could contemplate the divine order of God as reflected in the order of the garden, or consider allegorical interpretations on the lines begun by St Augustine: the garden as man's soul tended and nurtured by Christ, the divine gardener. While the garden looked back to man's origin and fall in Eden, it also beckoned to his ultimate quest: the last great paradise garden at the end of Heaven and Earth and of time itself, to which Eden was but an earthly prefiguration. Here the blessed souls would dwell in the company of the saints in eternal bliss, perfection for medieval man had thus begun and would end in a paradise garden.

In England, grass and graves, occasionally dignified by cedar trees (planted at a much later date), fill the spaces where monks and canons had their miniature paradises; the cloister courts of the cathedrals and abbeys, once centres of communal life, are now melancholy backwaters of remembrance. Perhaps this is best so; restoration would be

Fig. 3.2 Divine lamb and source of four rivers (A. N. Didron).

Fig. 3.3 Christ and Apostles in form of sheep (A. N. Didron).

3. F. Fordham: *An Introduction to Jung's Psychology.* Penguin (1968).

Fig. 3.4 Cloister garden of the church of the Quattro Coronati, Rome.

an anachronism, flowers are no longer symbols for saints and virtues, herbs are rarely grown for their healing properties and fruit is available from shops at all seasons; Eden itself is now regarded as a myth and the symbolism of the cloister paradise forgotten, although perhaps the fountain and the mandala would arouse some atavistic response. In England the Little Cloister at Westminster Abbey, maintained with taste around its fountain, alone preserves an echo of one purpose of the cloister: a garden of delight.

The Christian cloister evolved from the Roman peristyle as early it seems as the fifth century. In the East the concept of Paradise was given a new and complex imagery in the Quaran as the celestial garden, but based still on the *char-bagh*, the quadripartite oasis garden

Fig. 3.5 Fountain in the cloister garden of the Quattro Coronati.

that had inspired the description in Genesis and existed perhaps for millennia. The fusion of sacred and secular, the ideal and the functional in the gardens of Islam was similar to that of the cloister, but richer and technically more sophisticated, as befitted the heirs of the Paradise inheritance.

Islamic gardens

Arab armies swept out from the Arabian peninsula in the seventh century to conquer Persia, Mesopotamia and Egypt and continued on to subdue North Africa, Sicily and most of Spain [4]. With the Abbasid revolution, in AD 750, Persians assumed the dominant role in the artistic and political life of the Empire and from this point it becomes difficult to assess how far Islamic culture was a revival of Persian traditions under Arab stimulus and how much it owed to other subject peoples. The Persians accepted conversion to Islam, but did not accept the taboos on representations of people and animals in secular buildings and the applied arts. There was the influence of the Byzantine Empire, whose aniconic phase was short-lived and whose lost provinces provided the architects and craftsmen who built and decorated the early Arab palaces. While the Arabs provided the vigour, organisation and new creed, they were no doubt initially bewildered by the rapidity with which they found themselves possessors of an empire. In adapting to a settled life with huge resources and skills at their disposal, it seems that the Arabs learned most from the Persians, a people with whom they had long contacts, and shared the tradition of the oasis.

Unfortunately, little remains to be seen of this early period in Persia and Mesopotamia, mainly as a result of the devastation caused by the Mongol invasions of the thirteenth century. Samarra, the Abbasid

4. *Though the expansion was by military force, this was under very strict discipline and Abu Bakr the first Caliph (632–634), in setting the war machine in motion, gave the order that no palm trees were to be destroyed, no cornfields burnt, no orchards cut down. Unlike the Greeks who ravaged the fields of their fellow Greeks with whom they were at war, cutting down their olive groves, the Muslims were at pains to avoid destruction and, as soon as possible, restored peaceful government and prosperity to the countries they overran.*
John Harvey: *Medieval Gardens.* Batsford (1981).

Once secure in their conquests the Arabs proved tolerant rulers, absorbing what they found to be of use in the cultures of their diverse subject peoples and bringing a fresh vigour to the arts and, in particular, to the useful sciences. Philosophy, botany, medicine and mathematics flourished; algebra and our numerals remain a legacy from the Arab civilisation of this time. From the Persians they inherited the technology of irrigation and horticulture, and a love of plants and trees which they adopted and developed with the zeal of a people accustomed to the sandy wastes of arid lands. Above all they brought a veneration and love of water, the source of life itself which had sustained the oases of their country of origin, and throughout their new realms the Arabs planted gardens and permanently set their mark on the functional landscape by the introduction of the citrus fruits and the date-palm.

capital on the Tigris, survives only as a ruin in which remains of pavilions, canals and fountains can be discerned: the relics of a garden
and palace complex which covered 70 hectares. Surviving, but later
gardens in Persia are in poor shape. V. Sackville West, writing during
her visit in 1926, described the disparity between ancient poetry and
art, and the modern reality; Persian gardens had become very unimaginative with straight canals and avenues, blue tiles and pavilions,
but few flowers. For surviving examples, which are still gardens of
delight, we must turn to Spain, and although these have been much
altered, archaeological discoveries give a picture of their original appearance and could enable reconstruction [5].

Two other paths of approach shed light on the gardens and parks
of Islam's great period, which influenced development in the West.
First, the written record in both the works of poets and the accounts
of actual landscapes given by travellers. Secondly, the features of gardens depicted by Persian painters, and although these are relatively
late (14th–16th centuries), the Persian tradition of conservatism suggests that these could be a reliable guide to earlier centuries. Thirdly,
there is the record of archaeological evidence from Spain.

In essence, the Persian/Islamic garden is a grove around a fountain,
formalised into a mandala. The trees give shade and protection
against the relentless heat and light, the water is the source and sustainer of life. It reflects the ultimate Paradise described in the Quaran
and is an anticipation of the reward of the faithful, while embodying
earthly delight for the senses: flower-studded swards to delight the eye,
fruit to taste, sweet-scented herbs and flowers, the sound of water and
bird song:

> It gives a setting and a pattern for the quality of life that touches
> the infinite. Rest in a garden is contemplative; there a man
> composes his soul and is at one with his world; it is the place of
> unification within and without. Nor is this realisation of the self
> and of its coherence with the universe achieved only in isolation.
> The garden is the place of friendly intercourse, where mind
> meets mind in conversation touched with poetry and spirits
> intermingle, while the amber Shiraz wine passes in fragile
> turquoise pottery bowls. Life was lived largely in the garden and
> lived there at its best [6].

The spiritual and contemplative aspects of the Islamic garden accorded with Persian traditions before conversion. The Zoroastrians
addressed their God under the sky and sacred places under the Achaemenians were open with stepped fire altars. Under Islam this pref-
erence produced the wide vaulted liwans, niches facing an unroofed
central court.

The garden is an anticipation of Paradise and also a reflection of
the world in microcosm, with the canals or paths aligned to the cardinal points, intersecting at the source of life. It reflects the changing
seasons, the fecundity of the earth and the renewal of life. A complex
poetic imagery attaches to the trees and flowers to describe human
emotions and physical beauty. 'She was like ivory from head to toe,
with a face like Paradise and a figure as graceful as a tree. Her cheeks
were as red as pomegranate blossoms and her lips like its seeds, while
two pomegranates grew from her silver breast. Her eyes were like the
narcissus in the garden, and her eyebrows stole the blackness from the

Fig. 3.6 Palace of Mirrors, Isfahan, from P. Coste: *Monuments Modernes de la Perse* (1867). The palace, built
in the seventeenth century and destroyed early in this,
is of a type that recurs in Persian and earlier history
(compare Fig. 2.1), the lofty pavilion resembling a
grove of palms.

5. See James Dickie's account: 'The Islamic garden in
Spain',*The Islamic Garden*, E. B. Macdougall and R.
Ettinghausen (eds). Dumbarton Oaks (1976).
6. Arthur Upham Pope: *An Introduction to Persian Art.*
Davies (1930).

crow's feathers. She is a Paradise to look upon' [7]. The garden de-lights the senses as it does the mind and spirit, and is the setting for love as well as contemplation.

Often an owner would build his tomb in his garden, to rest in the scene he had enjoyed in life, itself a terrestrial reflection of divine order and promised reward. The most famous is the Taj Mahal, but an eleventh-century Cordoban text describes an enchanting garden where a famous poet lies buried beside his friend the Vizier who owned it. In youth they were companions and shared the pleasures of alternat-ing sobriety and inebriation. 'The foliage of the garden prevents the sun seeing the ground; and the breeze, blowing day and night over the garden, is loaded with scents.'

Possibly the earliest eye-witness account of Islamic garden design is given by two Byzantine ambassadors to the Caliphal palace in Baghdad, dating from 917. A large central pool feeds a surrounding stream, all lined with tin, more lustrous than polished silver. Four pavilions are set around the pool, covered with gold work and adorned with gilt and embroidered seats. Lawns extend beyond with lofty palm trees, bearing full grown dates, and their stems enclosed for their full height in carved teak wood, encircled with gilt copper rings. Around the sides of the garden were fruit trees and melon plants. Elsewhere, in another palace, a large artificial tree rises from an artificial circular pond with branches of gold and silver on which roost mechanical sing-ing birds [8]. The ambassadors were impressed and wrote accord-ingly, for these were clearly landscapes designed for this purpose; however, they have some truly Persian characteristics: the central pools and the ambiguity between natural elements and artifices.

Persian painting developed under the Abbasid Caliphate and prob-ably had its roots in the Sassanian period. It flowered, paradoxically, under the brutal and bloodthirsty Mongol conquerors who had an eye for quality in the arts. Miniature painting flourished from the late fourteenth century through to the revival of a true native dynasty, the Safavids, in 1501 and finally withered after 1600; there was to be no Persian equivalent of the High Renaissance or baroque. The parallel development with the West in miniature painting, with the obser-vation and depiction of natural forms, suggests an affinity too close to be coincidental and it seems likely that the Persian tradition influ-enced the West in this respect.

These relatively late Persian paintings abound with garden scenes and natural landscapes that appear directly observed from nature before reduction to the formality of the miniature. The gardens and palaces accord with the written and poetic record, with their formal pools and the lofty, airy pavilions that give shade and comfort. Persian ambiguity is present in the designs of rugs, screens and the woven clothes of the courtiers, reflecting flowers and trees in perpetual blos-som. Springtime is eternal in these paintings. Long-established sym-bolism is evident in the trees: the plane (chenar), symbol of shade and protection, and the evergreen cypress, representing immortality. Monu-mentality is wholly absent, nature is never dragooned and the scale is always human, set by figures, trees, shrubs and flowers.

The trees may be formally planted, but the floor is never so, except where paved. The designers seem to delight in informal combinations of herbs and shrubs, contrasting the architectural framework of pool, canal and pavilion with the profusion of nature and in particular

7. Firdausi: *Shahnamih*. Quoted by William L. Hana-way in 'Paradise on earth', *The Islamic Garden*. The essay gives many examples of poetic imagery.
8. M. L. Gothein: *A History of Garden Art*.

Fig. 3.7 Babur inspecting the planting of a garden, c. 1590 (Crown copyright Victoria and Albert Museum, IM 276-1913, IM 276A-1913).

flower-rich turf. The contrast, being softened by the patterns on the rugs and screens, is subtle and never harsh.

Always the painters seem to be casting their eyes beyond the garden pale to the wild landscape beyond: the rock formations and self-sown trees, growing in wind-blown shapes and foaming with blossoms. The court is seen enjoying picnics in these wild landscapes much as the Achaemenians and Sassanians must have done on their hunting excursions. Techniques and skills in painting could now describe an element of Persian life that must always have been present.

An exquisite miniature survives from the memoirs of Babur (1483–1530), a Mogul ruler who loved gardens and created them in his conquered territories in Afghanistan and India. The garden is a formal *char-bagh* with crossed water channels, and surrounded by a wall. Peripheral placing of fruit and bay trees is irregular, and the planting of the beds is clearly intended to create an irregular and in-formal effect of flowers and leaves. Beyond the pale there are wild trees among the rocks, a gazelle and birds, all clearly identifiable as are the trees and flowers of the garden. Babur himself directs the planting with the workmen shown in postures of hurried activity, while anxious messengers are left outside the gate.

The period following the Mongol cataclysm saw rapid development in the applied arts as well as painting. The new freedom of expression and skill in depicting natural forms appears in the silks, brocades, velvets and rugs of this time. In Abbasid and Seljuk ceramics we find a delight in the forms of animals and birds, directly derived from Sassanian art, with the curiously arched and rounded forms of animals, running, leaping or standing at bay. Contemporary textile designs are more formal and stylised as were Sassanian. Now all design seemed to loosen with a new fluency and competence, and the Persians, ruled by the Safavid dynasty without outside constraints, attained many of their finest achievements in the arts. The threads come together and are woven into a rich fabric that embraces wilderness. Paradise on earth is unconfined and exists wherever beauty is evident in the forms of rocks, trees and flowers, and the presence of animals and birds. The enclosing wall of the *paradeisos* has been broken and the Persian love of nature has found its full expression, in which a verdant and abundant earth reflects the divine, unplanned and uncoerced. Eventually this vision faded; by 1750 it was virtually dead and has remained so. But given the past resilience of the Persians one hopes that their native genius to work with nature may one day surprise us again.

The third approach to early Islamic landscapes is through Moorish Spain and the recent work of archaeologists there. This has shown that planting that has always been vaguely thought of as Moorish, and illustrated as such, is nothing of the kind and derives from later European traditions. Even the famous and delightful jets of Patio de la Acequia in the Generalife are a post-Moorish introduction. As so often elsewhere, architectural features are respected by those entrusted with their care, whereas the garden features are considered unimportant, even in the light of specific and accurate evidence.

In Spain today, the garden courts of the Alhambra and Generalife at Granada survive in working order and can give some impression of the garden architecture of Al-Andalus (Muslim Spain) to the visitor, provided that he is forewarned that they have been much altered. They were built relatively late, in the thirteenth century, when the former castle was reconstructed as a citadel and palace; water brought up from the River Darro supplied the fountains and pools, and transformed the surrounding hills into wooded slopes where summer villas and retreats stood among gardens and orchards. The views from the Alhambra would have won the approval of the Younger Pliny himself, for its prospects are magnificent: miles of rolling hills are visible, culminating in the snow-capped peaks of the Sierra Nevada. Clearly the emirs loved them, for views are framed by arched openings in the external walls of the perimeter rooms and halls; the surrounding landscape is an element carefully included in the design to give a dimension of space and distance. Internally, the lightness of columns, arches and vaults, and the subtle use of textured surfaces and honeycomb vaults to modulate sunlight and its reflections, give a sense of ambiguity between open and covered spaces. The use of water confirms this sense; in the celebrated Court of the Lions, water flows from the central fountain into four 'rivers' which extend across the court into the arcades where they meet formalised springs bubbling from the floor. This extension of the floor and water channels into the building, the resemblance of the slender columns and filigree arches of the arcades to a grove of palms, and the weightless quality of the vaulted rooms

9. R. Pinder-Wilson: 'The Persian garden'. *The Islamic Garden*. Dumbarton Oaks (1976).

behind, give an impression of an encampment set among the trees and springs of an oasis, the stalactite form of the vaults suggests hanging fruit as the capitals in the palace of Persepolis; after 600 years the images and structures of the oasis still lay beneath the sophisticated forms of Arab architecture, translated here to a hilltop amid productive countryside. The inclusion of water sources within the building recalls an account of the tenth-century Abbasid capital at Shiraz, where streams were seen flowing through the rooms and arcaded courts [9].

The floor of the court is at one level today. Originally the open area was 80 centimetres below and planted, the water channels crossing the fountain on raised causeways [5]. This would prevent the planting obscuring the architecture and the sunken beds would have the appearance of a flowered carpet.

Across the valley from the Alhambra lies the Generalife, the sole survivor of the villas and pavilions which once surrounded the Alhambra. In essence it is a peristyle – a long rectangle with a central canal watered by a series of jets amid luxuriant planting of fruit trees, roses and flowering shrubs. Small fountains in the form of lotus cups stand at the ends and centre of the canal. Gardens cover the small terraces that rise in steps from the court, cut into the hillside. The architectural elements are original including the obliquely aligned water-stair, but the planting is anachronistic and the level of the beds false. Excavations in 1959 revealed their original level to be half a metre lower than today. Fragments of glazed tiles were found bordering the raised paths and evidence of basins used to confine the

Fig. 3.8 The Court of the Lions in the Alhambra. The shaded areas of the floor are shown at their original lower level and they would have been planted.

growth of trees and their consequent height. It seems extraordinary that the garden was not then restored as far as possible to its original appearance or, alternatively, in such a way that would reveal in part the original levels, while retaining attractive later features such as the jets.

At Seville a twelfth-century quadripartite garden has been excavated where the beds are sunken 2 metres and surrounded by blind arcading in brick on the sides, walls and causeways which carry the canals to a circular central pool. Orange trees were planted in the corners of the beds, confined in basins, and the survival of seed will enable a complete and accurate restoration to be made of both the architectural and living elements of this remarkable garden [5].

Part of another garden in Seville, dating from the eleventh century, has been discovered with the beds sunken about fifteen feet ($4\frac{1}{2}$ metres) and it can be identified with a description from the seventeenth century which refers to it as 'a subterranean garden of orange trees, divided into four quarters; and it is so deep, in relation to the courtyard that the tops of the trees almost reach the level of the paths'.

These remarkable discoveries show the potential for increasing our knowledge through archaeology. Clearly Spain has been fortunate in having skilled archaeologists on hand and one wonders what future knowledge will be gained elsewhere, particularly in countries spared the Mongol invasions. But even in Persia and Mesopotamia much evidence must lie below the surface that could be interpreted by techniques such as pollen and seed analysis.

Western landscapes

A version of the paradise garden occurs in the literature of romance which flourished from the eleventh century onwards. Highly idealised, the epics and songs extol chivalry, knight errantry and courtly love, with material adapted from a variety of sources: the Christian legend of the Grail, the classical traditions of Troy, Aeneas and Alexander, Celtic legends and the erotic imagery of the *Song of Songs*. The garden is the embodiment of sensual delight, a refuge of love and happiness, sheltered by wall, hedge or pale from the unpredictable, disordered and potentially dangerous world outside. Natural reality is distrusted and the functional landscape of husbandry apparently does not exist. The garden is, in essence, an oasis, the wilderness of desert and waste replaced by the mountain, forest and fen of a northern climate. In the centre gushes a spring or fountain, probably a scion of the waters of paradise itself, for the belief persisted that Eden itself survived, hidden and inaccessible to man, but still the source of water flowing through the earthly regions and feeding the selected gardens of romance. Alexander himself, according to medieval mythology, had sought the garden and had failed.

The gardens of castles and manors were the preserves of ladies, and the gardens of romance soon became gardens of love. In the celebrated *Roman de la Rose* (13th century) paradise is essentially erotic, albeit with a bad conscience, for various disclaimers and sequels are added to the narrative. The landscape is designed for the delight of all senses: taste, touch, hearing and sight; tall trees, regularly spaced, filter sunlight on to a luxuriance of flowers and fruit, and lawns which remain evergreen and soft, and suitable for dalliance. Overall, the garden

Fig. 3.9 Lavabo in the cloister, Monreale from F. H. Jackson: *Sicily* (1904).

appears square and formal, planned around a fountain, the well of love itself, from which clear water flows over magic crystals and silver gravel. Much of the erotic content of the poem is expressed symbolically, culminating in the taking of the rose. A century later, in the poems of Chaucer, it is explicit, the garden is a secluded and private place more suited for love than the bower of the manor house.

The imagery derives from the East or from gardens designed under Eastern influence, particularly in Norman Sicily where they were built by Saracenic designers. Other principal contacts with the Islamic world were through the Kingdom of Outremar (following the capture of Jerusalem in 1099) and Spain. Despite sporadic warfare between Christian and Infidel, peaceful intervals, embassies and captivities in time nurtured a mutual respect somewhat similar to that between Greek and Persian. For the West, emerging from the renewed Dark Age following the invasions of the Northmen and safely passing the dreaded millennium when it was feared that the world would end, the cultural benefits were incalculable in the sciences, applied arts and architecture, the rich pollen of the East alighted on a fertile tilth.

Al-Andalus flourished brilliantly in the tenth century when civilised life in Western Christendom was at its nadir. The capital Cordoba must have appeared a miracle of urbanity: the streets were paved and fountains sparkled in arcaded courts; 900 public baths provided refreshment for the body and 400 mosques elevation of the soul, and in the countryside around peasants tilled fields of rice and sugar-cane irrigated by the skills of Arab engineers. Near Cordoba rose the terraced gardens of Al-Zahra which were said to rival those of Baghdad, with orchards, gardens, aviaries and cages on the lower levels, rising to the palace of the Caliph above, which he had decorated by artists brought from Constantinople. Later, crusaders travelling by ship to the Holy Land were to encounter the brief and brilliant civilisation, half Oriental and half Western, that flourished under Norman kings in Sicily; for after the capture of Jerusalem the island became an assembly point and supply base for the main route to the Levant [10].

10. Under these enlightened monarchs Sicily became a meeting place of cultures. The kings themselves adopted the customs and way of the emirs they had supplanted, installed harems in their palaces and appeared in public with the state of Byzantine emperors. Their ministers were Greeks, Saracens and Englishmen, and their subjects, Latins, Greeks, Moors and Jews, were allowed to practise their religions and encouraged to live in amity. In Arab fashion they encouraged the sciences and arts, geography, Aristotelian philosophy, astronomy and medicine flourished and the Norman passion for building produced the unique architecture that is the surviving memorial of their rule in which Greek cupolas crown structures articulated with the Saracenic pointed arches and interiors encrusted with Byzantine marbles and mosaics.

Outside the capital Palermo, a vast park encircled the town containing palaces and gardens 'like a necklace which ornaments the throat of a young girl', as an Arab poet described them in the twelfth century. It is a sad area today, covered with urban sprawl and containing only a few architectural fragments, left like flotsam as the green tide retreated. But contemporary accounts exist that record their magnificence: the enclosed hills and woodlands where exotic beasts and birds roamed wild, the artificial canals and lakes [11], the pavilions and palaces with their water chutes, fountains and porticoes – in one a central fountain adorned with lions, similar to that in the Alhambra. The palace of William I, called the Zisa, survives and has been restored. Outside it is somewhat forbidding, but the interior is in pure Saracenic style with lofty honeycombed ceilings, tumbling in stalacite vaults – a shady, cool haven for the King to relax, sheltered from the summer heat and the turbulent happenings of his reign. A water source, set in the wall, flows down an inclined marble chute into a channel leading to the gardens outside, originally planted with fruit trees and planned with canals and fish-ponds of which nothing remains to be seen, although one wonders what archaeologists might make of what may lie beneath the surface of the ground. Some indication of the garden architecture is perhaps given by the amazing lavabo, or wash-room, of the monks of Monreale which consists of a monumental Arab fountain enclosed by an elegant arcade of Saracenic arches with zigzag ornament – an extraordinary fusion of Eastern luxury and the Rule of St Benedict. Of the birds, beasts and trees, we have only the written records and the mosaics that encrust the upper walls and vaults of a joyful little room in the royal palace: the Sala di Ruggero. Peacocks fly up to seize dates from the palms, lions and leopards confront each other, swans preen themselves, and archers stalk stags among fruit-laden trees. Luxuriant flowering climbers cover the vaults and frame mythical beasts and smiling lions.

The importance of Norman Sicily to Western culture lay in the strong links its kings maintained with Norman courts elsewhere, particularly England, and its focal position as staging post to the Levant. Oriental influence disseminated northwards through royal and courtly contacts, and returning crusaders such as Robert of Artois who visited Palermo in 1270 and returned to Hesdin to create a garden with fountains and automata that was still renowned in the fifteenth century when the influence of Italian gardens reached France. Henry I of England enclosed the royal park at Woodstock with a wall of stone and introduced exotic beasts: lions, lynxes, leopards, camels and a porcupine, and about three centuries later, Henry V had a moat built around a summer pavilion at Kenilworth which suggests the distant influence of the Favara even at this late date (c. 1414). But interest in gardens, parks and the natural scene was not limited to magnates and kings. Enclosed parks had been established in Saxon England [12] and in France may have had links with the vast emparked areas referred to by Columella [13]. The concept was not new, but from the Norman period onwards emparking had fresh impetus, and in England licences to enclose waste and woodland on manorial demesne rapidly increased in number, and although functional and sporting considerations were primary, it seems likely that they were not exclusive. Geoffrey de Montbray, Bishop of Coutances in Normandy, created a park surrounded by a double ditch and palisade – 'Within he sowed

11. *In order that none of the joys of land or water should be lacking to him, he [King Roger] caused a great sanctuary for birds and beasts to be built at a place called Favara, which was full of caves and dells; its waters he stocked with every kind of fish from divers regions; nearby he built a beautiful palace. And certain hills and forests around Palermo he likewise enclosed with walls, and there he made the Parco – a pleasant and delightful spot, shaded with various trees and abounding with deer and goats and wild boar. And here also he raised a palace, to which the water was led in underground pipes from springs whence it flowed ever sweet and clear. And thus the King, being a wise and prudent man, took his pleasure from these places according to the season. In the winter and in Lent he would reside at the Favara, by reason of the great quantity of fish that were to be had there; while in the heat of the summer he would find solace at the Parco where, with a little hunting, he would relieve his mind from the cares and worries of state.*
Romauld of Salerno from J. J. Norwich: *The Kingdom of the Sun*. Faber and Faber (1976).
12. The earliest documentary evidence in England is for Ongar Great Park, 1045.
13. Columella: Book IX.

acorns and took pains to grow oaks and beeches and other forest trees, filling the park with deer from England.' [14]

While the poetry of romance preserved the concept of the garden as an oasis in a hostile wilderness – a walled enclave of tranquillity within the wildwood, records survive that many Normans took a practical and realistic view of their own estates and the landscapes through which they travelled. An observation of the natural scene worthy of the Younger Pliny is contained in the description of Fecamp in Normandy by Baudry, Archbishop of Dol (1107–30). He begins by extolling the beauty and size of the abbey and describing a church organ that seemed a wonder of the age. Passing to the site, he says:

Fig. 3.10 Southwell Minster, capital in chapter house.

> It is like a garden of Paradise, set in a lovely enclosed valley, between two hills, surrounded by farmland on one side and a charming little wood on the other. This seems to be of such even growth that it might be thought to have grown on a single day or to have been cropped back in height. The summits of its boughs and leaves and twigs are so thick that by their shade and strength they favour both the earth and the view; they keep off the heat of the sun and repel the onset of the rains. The trees stand up somewhat from their stocks, not very tall, but pleasant to stroll under [14].

Baudry goes on to describe the functional landscape; a harbour where the quayside is lapped with clean water, land where there are springs of fresh water suitable for orchards growing good apple trees, and the winding bends of the river beside the strong walls of the castle. The abbey itself stands on a cliff, 'surrounded with very fine high walls', its church is called the gate of heaven and the palace of God himself, and is likened to the heavenly Jerusalem. The description recalls the scenes depicted in the *Tres Riches Heures* of the Limbourg brothers in which castles and towns are set in working landscapes shown as ordered and beautiful. Yet Baudry was writing 300 years earlier, when the tradition of romance reserved order to gardens and meadows, separated by great tracts of wild and disordered forest and the landscape of farming was beneath consideration in the songs and poems of chivalry.

If Baudry had written a century later, his description would perhaps have seemed tuned to a new appreciation in the West of the beauties of the natural world. A vigour and sense of springtime prevades the thinking and art of the thirteenth century – the age of St Francis who saw a oneness in the universe as God's creation and of St Vincent of Beauvais who wrote: 'I am moved with spiritual sweetness towards the creator and ruler of this world when I behold the magnitude and beauty and performance of his creation.' A spirit of scientific inquiry and direct observation was evident in the works of Roger Bacon and in Albertus Magnus who sought a balance between experience and inherited revelation, a characteristic of the age reflected in remarkable leaf and flower carvings, such as those of Southwell Minster whose freshness and accuracy was something quite new in Western Europe [15]. The sculptors appear suddenly awakened to beauties previously hidden or deemed commonplace and in the spirit of Christ's dictum on the lilies of the field, they observed and carved the forms of woodland and hedgerow trees and flowers: maple, oak, hawthorn, hop, buttercup and briony.

Fig. 3.11 Southwell Minster, capitals at entrance to chapter house.

14. John Harvey: *The Medieval Architect.* Wayland (1972).

15. In the course of the thirteenth century the leaves of Gothic carving began to follow the characteristics of specific plants. It is as though the sculptors gathered specimens from woodlands and hedgerows and looked at them with wonder, translating their forms and patterns into stone. The masterpieces at Southwell came late in the century and have been described and illustrated by Sir Nikolaus Pevsner in *The Leaves of Southwell*; elsewhere he refers to them 'throbbing with life, yet kept under the strict discipline of architecture, economic in treatment, nowhere fussy or ostentatious, and of a precision of surface to be compared only with the classic Greek art of the Parthenon'.

Fig. 3.12 Wells Cathedral, retrochoir high roof. Early fourteenth century.

Above all achievements, the thirteenth century saw the full development of a new architecture whose forms reflected the organic structure of broad-leaved trees. Lethaby wrote: 'Gothic was an art of the northern forest lands [16]. Although branching trees and long vistas were not consciously imitated, yet the forests were in the minds of the people who built and they could do no other than express their love.' Spengler wrote similarly:

> ... the character of the cathedral is that of the forest, the transformation of columns into clustered piers grow up out of the earth and spread on high into an infinite sub-division and interlacing of lines and branches; the giant windows by which the wall is dissolved and the interior filled with mysterious light – these are the architectural actualising of a world feeling that had found first of all its symbols in the high forest of the Northern plains.

Thus a Gothic cathedral can be seen as a metamorphosis of the broad-leaved forest into stone just, as we have seen, Arab buildings appear to reflect the forms of the desert oasis. The organic quality of mature Gothic, so apparent in its structure, is consistent in its details. At St Denis, the first building in which the elements of pointed arch, flying buttress and rib vault fused to produce the new style, the capitals were still derived from the form of the Corinthian order used by the architects of the Romanesque. So too at Canterbury (c. 1175), the first Gothic building begun in England, but soon after at Wells the Corinthian convention was abandoned and the capitals break into flowing leaf forms similar to axillary shoots on trees where lateral branches leave the main stem. There is an exuberance in these Wells carvings which seem to express a joy in living and the excitement and freshness of new discovery and invention. The mood follows at Lincoln Cathedral where the whole structure seems alive, breaking into leaf at the junctions of its members, meeting in clusters at the apex of the vaults or dropping in leafy pendants from the corbels. Angels sing or

Fig. 3.13 Crown post dating from the third quarter of the thirteenth century *photograph by Mr P. M. Richards).*

16. This view of Gothic is not by any means generally accepted and there is no contemporary documentary evidence to support it. Therefore the view remains essentially subjective and a matter for the individual to come to his or her own conclusions. Technical advance played a large part in the development of Gothic and a delight in showmanship and virtuosity as new techniques evolved and were perfected.

play instruments and dragons frolic harmlessly among the leaves of the capitals. It is an ideal landscape in stone [17].

Parallel with the achievements of the masons and stone-carvers was the work of carpenters who developed structures similar to branching forest forms, most notably at the Cistercian barn at Great Coxwell and the remarkable roofs of the retrochoir and chapter house at Wells [18]. In the domestic architecture of this time, one of the oldest and most revered symbols of mankind makes its reappearance: the sky pillar as the World Tree supporting the heavens. This is the essence of the crown post, the central feature of the manorial hall with its four branches reaching out to the cardinal points and often appropriately carved and moulded befitting its importance [19].

Not only dragons and angels occur in the work of wood-carvers and stonemasons; the Green Man is often present, leaves springing from his mouth, hair and beard, his face sometimes fine and dignified, sometimes half-animal. He lurks among the foliage of Southwell and as late as the sixteenth century in the roof bosses of Segovia Cathedral. The Church seems to have tolerated this survival of animist beliefs, the Silvanus of the northern races, vegetation sprite and guardian spirit of the woodlands that produced the imagery and much of the raw material for the Gothic achievement. His presence is significant; his woodlands were by now intensively managed, not by techniques resembling modern forestry but as a self-renewing resource; his oaks were selected, felled and worked 'green' to become the manor houses and farms of East Anglia and other regions without stone, the high roofs of cathedrals and priories, the barns that held the fruits of the land, and the visible achievements of the wood-carver. His co-operation was needed as in the time of Cato, and his image, ever watchful, appears in the final fruits of stone and timber.

Fig. 3.14 Southwell Minster, Green Man carving in chapter house.

The later Middle Ages

The spirit of optimism and confidence so characteristic of the thirteenth century did not survive the repression of restrictive doctrine and the miseries of the Black Death and Hundred Years War. *Pietas* obsessed the fifteenth century as surely as the smiling and youthful madonnas of the thirteenth, and men's thoughts dwelt on death, purgatory and the sufferings of the damned rather than the felicities of the blessed. Yet the influence of the natural world persisted despite the pessimism; accurate paintings of flowers and insects filled the margins of manuscripts and around 1400 landscapes began to form the backgrounds and settings in paintings of the Flemish school.

These paintings record the hunting parks of the age, of which there were many, for it was the ambition of every lord to obtain a licence from the Crown to enclose land for this purpose. In the ordered and funtional landscape of the later Middle Ages, parks must often have appeared relatively 'natural' and even wild. In *St John the Baptist in the Wilderness* (late 15th century) Geertgen tot Sint Jans places the saint in a scene clearly recognisable as a hunting park; the land is undulating and boggy, with rock lying close beneath the surface, providing a convenient seat for St John; the turf is cropped by deer and rabbits which are seen in the distance and grassland flowers bloom around the saint's feet. Trees stand singly and in clumps, forming glades and vistas, their lower limbs browsed by animals and the bare

17. There is a certain dichotomy in Gothic architecture deriving from its origins; if the spirit is the memory of a forest people, as Lethaby and Spengler suggest, the geometrical discipline derives from the works of Euclid which had been preserved by the Arabs and introduced to the West with the pointed arch either through Sicily or Spain, or from the Crusader states. This dichotomy leads to what might be termed 'creative tension' and a changing emphasis according to the spirit of the time. The contrasts are evident, for example, in the 'organic' forms of the chapter house and retrochoir at Wells compared with the rectilinear discipline of the choir at Gloucester. In the choir of Lincoln both elements are emphatically present.
18. Wells is fortunate in still possessing most of its original high roofs, for their destruction in many other cathedrals in recent years is a crime that will be as surely condemned by future generations as certain acts of 'restoration' by the cruder nineteenth-century restorers; respect has been shown only for the visible works of the carpenter such as at Westminster Hall, and the hidden achievements considered unimportant.
19. This interpretation of the four-branched crown post is a personal opinion.

Fig. 3.15 *Conversion of St Hubert* by the Master of the Life of the Virgin, active *c*. 1463–80 (National Gallery, London).

trunks, perhaps deliberately 'shrouded' to produce good timber stems. The scene is reminiscent of landscapes usually associated with eighteenth-century planned designs; if the saint is removed, the bog tidied up to form a lake, and a temple or two artfully positioned, the transformation is complete.

This it seems is much what happened in England from the 1750s onwards and the example was followed on the continent, for what is generally still regarded as a specific invention of that time was, in fact, an adaptation of far older landscapes. Other examples confirm this view; the *Conversion of St Hubert* by the Master of the Life of the Virgin (active *c.* 1463–80) shows hilly country, useless for agriculture, in which groves of clear-stemmed forest trees rise from swards of close-cropped grass, as composed and balanced as a view from the windows of an English country house. Clearly these parkland scenes were landscapes of beauty to artists of the time, although their form derived from the needs of the chase and the bonus of land to grow stands of structural timber. Historically they must be placed in the category of the informal hunting park, a landscape type that must have changed little since the second century when Columella described parks covering kilometres of hill country in Gaul [13].

Numerous illustrations survive of late medieval gardens in manuscripts, books of hours, tapestries and paintings mainly of the Flemish and Italian schools. These are reproduced abundantly in Sir Frank Crisp's *Mediaeval Gardens* and show formal, often raised, flower beds, pergolas and arbours, turf seats and the surrounding pale, varying from a lattice fence to a stone wall. Water is almost always present in a cistern pool often serving as as outdoor bath, and its source an elaborate fountain designed in Gothic or Moorish style, sometimes achieving the size and complexity of an Eleanor Cross or the grandeur of the fount at Monreale, and sometimes the miniature delicacy of a toy, but always the focus and pride of the garden, sometimes erotic with scenes of Bathsheba bathing, but more often the centre of courtly scenes of social intercourse, conversation and the enjoyment of music. Flowery turf is evident, as in Eastern paintings, but above all the visual record confirms the essential informality of these gardens. Symmetry and grandeur at this stage of garden design are absent.

The mount, a feature of Assyrian gardens, makes its reappearance; the Louvre of Charles V (1350–64) had four, and in the fifteenth century the mount became usual in the larger English gardens. Its purpose was to provide a view across the garden pale into the park and occasionally its summit was crowned, as in Assur with a pavilion.

The conventions of medieval illustration shrink the gardens they depict into tiny plots. Some undoubtedly were very small when situated behind the walls of a castle or in the limited space available in a town. But it is clear from the literature of the time that the ideal garden was a much grander affair. In the *Decameron* the courtiers flee the plague-ridden city to a country estate where they are wonderstruck by the beauty of the walled garden. The account has been quoted countless times, but its relevance is such to any description of the ideal landscape of its time (14th century) that it must be described [20].

> It was bordered and traversed in many parts by alleys, each very
> wide and straight as an arrow and roofed in with trellis of vines,
> which gave good promise of bearing clusters that year, and,
> being all in flower, dispersed such fragrance throughout the
> garden as blended with that exhaled by many another plant that
> grew therein made the garden seem redolent of all the spices that
> ever grew in the East.

The sides of the alley were walled, as it were, with white and red roses and jasmine, and even at noon one could walk the alleys in shade and fragrance. The rarer species of plant allowed by the climate grow in abundance, and in the centre of the garden is a lawn of the finest turf.

20. G. Boccaccio: *Decameron*. Trans. J. M. Rigg. Dent (1930).

... pranked about with flowers of, perhaps, a thousand sorts and girt about with the richest living verdure of orange trees and cedars, which showed not only flowers but fruits both new and old, and were no less grateful to the smell by their fragrance than to the eye by their shade. In the middle of the lawn was a basin of whitest marble, graven with marvellous art. In the centre rose a column supporting a figure which sent forth a jet of water of such volume and to such a altitude that it fell, not without a delicious splash, into the basin in quantity ample sufficient to turn a mill-wheel.

The overflow was carried away by a hidden conduit to re-emerge in tiny channels flowing round the lawn and then on in similar channels to penetrate almost every part of the garden.

Re-uniting at a certain point, it issued thence, and, clear as crystal, slid down towards the plain, turning by the way two mill-wheels with extreme velocity to the no small profit of the lord. The aspect of the garden, its fair order, the plants and the fountain and the rivulets that flowed from it, so charmed the ladies and the three young men that with one accord they affirmed that they knew not how it could receive any accession of beauty, or what other form could be given to Paradise, if it were to be planted on earth.

Turning from the features of the garden, they notice that it is peopled with a host of living creatures, perhaps a hundred different sorts including the coney, hare, goat and fawn, harmless and all but domesticated. Clearly, the garden was both complex and large, even allowing for Boccaccio's tendency to add a nought when describing numbers. The *Decameron* was written in the mid fourteenth century and the garden with its fountain and irrigation channels stands at what might be termed a 'point of departure' in Western planned landscapes. While still deriving from the Arab tradition it points the way to the achievements in the management and use of water in Italian landscape gardens of the sixteenth century culminating in the Villa d'Este. The basic technology was there ready to develop in the image of the torrents and cascades of the Italian hills rather than the springs and pools of the oasis. The force of water was such to drive mill-wheels.

By the fifteenth century, the influence of Persia was again apparent in the applied art of tapestry design and in painting. Both depict Persian delight in the forms of animals, birds and plants. The great series of *La Dame à la Licorne*, woven probably between 1509 and 1513 in the Loire district, embodies the elements of the paradisal tradition with superlative artistry. The lady delicately experiences the five senses in a verdant paradise enclosed by a wall; rabbits, dogs, monkeys and foxes gambol in the rich turf, while a lion and unicorn hold painted poles with banners curling and floating in the breeze. Every plant is in flower and the trees are rich with fruit. Outside the pale, the wider landscape of the earthly paradise teems with wildlife and flowers. It is a landscape at once marvellous and crazy, embodying Eastern ambiguity in its depiction of both the heavenly and earthly nature of the garden, the blending of artefacts with the natural scene, the apparent ability of carnivores to forget their natural instincts and the seasonal

Fig. 3.16 'A mon seul désir' from *La Dame à la Licorne* set of tapestries (Cluny Museum, Paris).

anomaly of perpetual spring. But the Lady is unaware of these problems and her grave young face shows her concentration on the serious matters that concern her: her refined appreciation of the arts and senses and the apparent absence of love. Perhaps the garden is a preparation.

These and other tapestries of the time reflect the paradisal influence of the East and the skills of Persian designers of fabrics. Paintings in Germany and Italy in the fifteenth century reflect the art of Persian painters of miniatures and the eagerness of artists in the West to develop this vision in their own way. A favourite scene is that of the Madonna and Child, relaxing within a walled garden filled with flowers and roses while angels, in place of beasts and birds, frolic and amuse the holy pair. These paintings must rank among the most delightful in Western religious iconography; springtime is as eternal in the Madonna's garden as in those of the Islamic East. The same influence permeates Florentine painting of the time: the rocks and trees of Gozzoli's *Adoration of the Magi* and the landscape elements of Botticelli's *Birth of Venus* and the flowered turf and clothing of his *Primavera*. But the flowers are fleeting; the freedom of Botticelli and

Filippo Lippi reflected the cosmopolitan brilliance of the Medici court soon to be replaced by the heavy classicism of the High Renaissance and Mannerism in which the observation of landscape had little place. In the meantime there is the miracle of Flemish painting, included here under the heading of *The Middle Ages* since its origins seem to lie more with the Gothic tradition than that of the revival of classical forms which characterised the Renaissance.

Landscape painting

Since the end of the Roman Empire painters had been content to express landscapes symbolically and regarded accuracy as irrelevant to the immediate and spiritual content of their work. Strange terraced structures inherited and debased from Hellenistic painting had symbolised mountains and wilderness: the untamed world beyond the walls of the cloister, garden and orchard. With the rise in population from the eleventh century onwards this view became increasingly untenable, for more and more land was needed to grow food, and the woodlands and wastes which had separated settlements at the time of the Domesday Survey (1086) progressively diminished. Already in the thirteenth century, stone-carvers had sought inspiration in the natural world and in the fourteenth, illustrations of everyday life began to appear in the calendars and occupations of the months, expressing the ordered conduct of husbandry according to the seasons. By 1300 most available land in the fertile lowlands of north-west Europe had been brought into cultivation or grazing, the forest remnants enclosed as parks or managed as productive woodlands, and even on land subject to Forest Law, customary rights of lopping and pasturage would often remove any illusion of disordered and untamed wilderness. Only rocky outcrops, cliffs and mountains retained, as today, the appearance of nature uninfluenced by the activities of man. This land-

Fig. 3.17 *St John the Baptist going into the Wilderness* by Giovanni di Paolo, 1402–82 (National Gallery, London). Symbolic mountains derived from the Byzantine tradition which inherited and debased the Hellenistic and Roman. Direct observation is only evident in the small farmhouse and fields.

scape was recorded faithfully in paintings and miniatures of the Flemish school of the fifteenth century, finding its culmination in the
landscapes of Bruegel in the sixteenth.

The point of arrival of true landscape painting in the West can be
dated to around 1416 with the Limbourg brothers' remarkable series
of months for the *Très Riches Heures* of the Duc de Berry, in which
fields, vineyards and woodlands are rendered with confidence and
delight, it seems, in a new-found ability to observe and depict the
countryside as a unity. Above each scene the chariot of the sun crosses
the vault of the heavens, watched by the relevant signs of the zodiac
and expressing the divine order which governs the celestial bodies
which in turn govern the seasons, the fruitfulness of the earth and the
conduct of husbandry. The spirit of the *Très Riches Heures* is very close
to that of Varro and Virgil. The month of March shows a peasant
ploughing an open field for the spring sowing while a shepherd tends
his flock; others prune vines within walled vineyards and at a cross-
roads stands a Gothic structure which may be a shrine or a water
source, or possibly both, but so resembles the fountain conventionally
depicted in contemporary paintings of Paradise that the symbolism
is clear: here, in the wider garden of husbandry, God has placed the
descendants of Adam to 'dress it and keep it'. In the month of April
a betrothal takes place in a meadow framed by groves of trees; the
walled garden with its peripheral arbour and formal beds lies deserted

Fig. 3.18 *St Jerome* by Patenier, *c.* 1520 (National Gallery, London). However fantastic the landscape, all the
elements – rocks, clouds, fields and buildings – are
directly derived from observation of reality.

to one side, the company have chosen the countryside with its spring flowers for this important event in their lives.

Throughout the *Très Riches Heures* the observation is meticulous: pollard willows line watercourses, peasants mow their meads in strips, and trees in woodlands are promoted from stubs to form high forest for structural timber. In the background are the stately castles of the Duke which look out on to these pleasant scenes and recall the description of Fécamp by Archbishop Baudry three centuries earlier.

Fig. 3.19 'March' from the *Très Riches Heures du Duc de Berry* (Musée Condé, Chantilly, MS 65).

With the Limbourgs, the symbolism of medieval landscape painting had been replaced by the direct observation of nature; what Lord Clark calls the *landscape of fact* [21], and he describes the work of the Limbourgs as having an objectivity and truth of tone only to be surpassed by Bruegel. At around this time Flemish painting emerged into maturity with the work of the Van Eyck brothers who were both concerned with landscapes as an essential element in their paintings, and henceforward landscape assumed a dominant role in the work of many

Fig. 3.20 'April' from the *Très Riches Heures du Duc de Berry* (Musée Condé, Chantilly, MS 65).

21. K. Clark: *Landscape into Art*. Murray (1949).

painters of the Low Countries, in particular the Master of Flemalle (usually now identified with Roger Campin), Geertgen tot Sint Jans, Simon Benninck, Hieronymus Bosch and Pieter Bruegel. These artists sought their material in the real world around them which they rendered with obsessive care and accuracy, and with a quality of revelation that only appears when familiar scenes and objects are newly perceived. The new skills of perspective, the ability to depict objects in light and the technique of oil-painting all contributed to a spirit of exitement and growing confidence channelled into a new departure in the visual arts and freedom of expression. It has something in common with the spirit of contemporary mariners opening up new routes to India and the Far East and the discovery of America, but also recalls the freshness of vision which had produced the leaf and flower carvings of Southwell and Lincoln two centuries earlier.

These Flemish Landscapes of Fact have much to tell of the appearance of the functional landscape of their time and form a historic record that has been surprisingly neglected. The landscape of the hunting park in the painting by Geertgen tot Sint Jans has already been noted: eight surving miniature painting of the months by Simon Benninck of Bruges depict in detail the pursuit of husbandry. *December* shows a boar hunt in a 'coppice with standards' woodland, a form of management that was general in the Middle Ages when surviving woodland began to have scarity value. The scene is a glade where a coppice has been recently cut as 'underwood' and the 'standards' of oak and elm left to grow on to form a crop of structural timber. It is a scene that can be seen today in the few woodlands still managed in this excellent and economic manner, the only difference lying in the costumes and quarry of the hunt, and the use of axes rather than chain-saws. The bracken in the ground flora suggests that the wood covered the ground least suitable on the manor for arable cultivation; a situation familiar from observation of ancient woodlands.

Benninck's *March* shows the pale of the garden broken down to reveal the varied and interesting Landscape of Fact and Function beyond – the garden now embraces the total landscape of husbandry. Small irregular fields are surrounded by vigorous hedges or woven wattles; elms are carefully grown up as standards and are 'shrouded': the practice of stripping the woody 'trousers' growing from the stem in order to produce timber with small knots and to provide winter kindling for the farm worker.

May and *June* show the conduct of husbandry on small farmsteads independent of nucleated settlements or common-field agriculture. They are clearly accurate and describe the appearance of the land while the occupations of mowing and shearing are carried on. Again, shrouded elms form part of the tree cover while others grown for shelter or shade surround the farmstead. The landscape depicted must be very similar to that of much of south-east England at this time, the only divergent element being the distant rocky hills which by this time had become a convention of Flemish painting: a reminder of the unproductive wilderness beyond the fruitful landscape of ordered husbandry. Interest in the wilderness, expressed in the backgrounds of Benninck's paintings was a characteristic of the time. Patinir (1485–1524) painted wild, remote landscapes, both romantic and menacing, in which human activity and habitation is an incident; his detail is superbly observed and drawn. But it is in the landscapes of

the Germans, Altdorfer and Grünewald, that this vein achieves a quality of horror and it is not the 'pleasing horror' of the eighteenth century. In this *Isenheim Altar* Grünewald depicts scenes that used to be described as lunar (before men landed and looked on the moon); they are malevolent, inhuman and redolent of decay, and could be described as an assault on the senses.

Bosch and Bruegel

Many reasons have been put forward for this trend: men could now regard the remnants of wilderness with interest, for the landscape was largely tamed and farmed, and natural areas no longer seemed menacing; dragons and monsters were myths and even predators were becoming scarce. At the same time there were deep fears that the world would end in 1500 and the world order itself seemed to be called into doubt, particularly in the sixteenth century when the horrors of the religious wars became a reality in the Low Countries, France and Germany. The logical end of this development is the landscape of hell itself, and in the works of Hieronymus Bosch it was realised. Bosch's work ranges into the wildest fantasies, but the detail is always meticulously observed; farmsteads, trees and implements give a bedrock of credibility and reference, but the underlying symbolism is medieval, fam-

Fig. 3.21 *March* by Simon Benninck, early sixteenth century (British Library Add. MS 18855, f. 108).
Fig. 3.22 *December* by Simon Benninck (British Library Add. MS 18855, f. 108v).

Fig. 3.23 *Garden of Earthly Delights* by Hieronymus Bosch (Museo Nacional del Prado, Madrid).

iliar from the 'dooms' on chancel arches, a source of deep unease to all classes in the uncertain world of 1500. Bosch exploits the effects of fire in these landscapes, familiar in his troubled age from the destruction of villages and farms, and the punishment the heretic or necromancer.

In the complex imagery of his tryptich *Earthly Delights* in the Prado, Bosch shows the path of man to perdition from the Garden of Eden in the left-hand panel to hell on the right. Swarms of nudes frolic in the sunshine in the company of huge birds, and feast on enormous fruits while in the centre, a crowd of women bathe in the Fountain of Youth; impossible structures of rock rise in the background and appear semi-animate. It appears to be Bosch's interpretation of the erotic paradise garden of sensual delight. The Garden of Eden by comparison seems relatively straightforward, apart from its details: the Tree of Life is a strange cactus-like growth, perhaps derived from a description of a Dragon Tree, and the Fountain of Life a bizarre red structure composed of organic forms rising above a hollow disc in which an owl, a symbol of evil, lurks, for the garden is already threatened and the animals have begun to prey upon each other. The innocent figures of Adam and Eve gaze gravely out from the picture, unaware of the evils which will tempt their progeny into mortal sin, while God himself beside them appears intent and sad, sensing that Satan has begun his work and devils will dominate His creation and pervert its perfection into a landscape of venality and ultimate doom.

Earthly Delights is the last great paradise of the Middle Ages, and in its pessimism the antithesis of the flowery gardens where the Madonna and Child sit among angels enjoying the fruits of the earth remote from the threat of evil. All Bosch's landscapes are menacing; his is a paranoid world in which legions of demons ensnare mankind and the Apocalypse is ever imminent.

Pieter Bruegel, born in the 1520s a few years after the death of Bosch, was his equal in imaginative power as well as accurate observation, but his landscape is that of the Limbourgs where divine grace is achieved by good husbandry in the cycle of the seasons under a benevolent God. Virgil's vision of the fusion of the functional and ideal in the practical countryside was expressed again in the paintings of the last 11 years of Bruegel's life [22].

Initially, Bruegel achieved fame through his engravings of moral themes such as the *Seven Virtues* and *Seven Deadly Sins*, expressed as complex allegories and crammed with imagery derived from Bosch and traditional Flemish proverbs but adding a strong sense of humour and a distinct vein of ribaldry. In *Allegory of Lust* (1557) the garden of earthly delights has become the antithesis of the medieval Paradise while using many of its forms. The fountain which feeds the River of Sin, and a ragged bower are the scenes of various erotic goings-on and in the foreground the tree has become a grotesque hollow structure within which Lady Lechery (or Venus?) herself entertains. Its branches grow into a stag's head (a symbol of lust) and bear golden apples and at its crown is a love-bower in the form of an oyster, a traditional aphrodisiac. Humans, animals and monsters disport themselves, often obscenely, and in the distance the fires of hell glimmer. The whole is a travesty, indeed a rejection and bizarre valediction to the medieval Garden of Love.

The legacy of travels to Italy were studies of sweeping Alpine landscapes with mountains dominating cultivated plains and river valleys, which were transcribed into engravings on his return; but their true significance lay in providing the material for the backgrounds of his later landscapes, conveying a knowledge of distance and mountain structure only to be grasped by direct observation. Probably no one before or since has painted mountain scenery with such magnificent breadth of vision. Forms of rock formations are accepted on their own terms and recorded without elaboration. Scale is given by the fields and farmsteads in the valleys.

22. Not very much is known of his life, but the long-held belief that Bruegel was a simple peasant turned painter now seems far from the truth. The epithet 'Peasant Bruegel' stems from the bucolic subjects of some of his paintings. He seems to have moved in a distinguished circle, for which education and culture would have been prerequisites and he was a close friend of the geographer and cartographer Ortelius. Virgil's *Georgics* were widely read and admired at this time and it is inconceivable that Bruegel would not be familiar with the work.

Despite his humanity, Bruegel had his dark side [23]. He challenged the achievement of Bosch in depicting the landscape of hell and won at least equal laurels. But his masterpiece in this morbid theme is the *Triumph of Death* (1562), a scene of total horror and pessimism. The dead arise from their graves, not as in the Christian Apocalypse at the command of the Archangel's trumpet to be judged for reward or punishment, but as a malignant and vengeful force to overwhelm and destroy the living. Triumphant cohorts of grinning skeletons wield their coffin lids as shields and scythe and crush the disordered rabble that remains alive. The landscape is of parched and arid soil bearing a crop of gibbets and tall poles surmounted by sinister wheels with broken bodies; a bell hung from a stunted tree tolls the knell of mankind and in the distance, smoke and fires obscure the sky. It is the landscape of evil and the total destruction of life, more terrible and hopeless than Bosch's visions of hell which at least allowed men a prior choice before a terrible and eternal retribution [24].

Bruegel seems to have overcome his pessimism and in 1565 painted his masterpieces, a series of the *Months* of which five now survive, the culmination of an epoch that began with the seasonal tasks in the calendars of the Middle Ages and expressed in the first 'true' landscape of the Limbourgs. Now, with the mastery of landscape and light achieved by the Flemish school, Bruegel painted the countryside as an aspect of the divine. All are boldly and marvellously constructed with sure draftsmanship and sense of colour and tone. In the foregrounds rustic figures pursue their tasks: pruning, tilling, harvesting and hunting: or relaxing from their toil: picnicking, slumbering in the summer sun, or warming themselves by a fire in the snow. Noble and lofty trees contrast with the rounded and muscular forms of the peasants and at the same time are permanent and rooted structures in the landscape which gave stability and vertical divisions to the composition. In the middle distance the countryside with its vernacular buildings, ordered fields, trees and groves stretches to distant mountains and wilderness. The sky with its cloud formations sets the mood of each picture through the quality of light and tone, always dominating but never melodramatic. Every detail, distant or near, is minutely and truthfully observed, but is never allowed to detract from the overall unity of the whole.

In *Winter* (*Hunters in the Snow*), the huntsmen trudge in deep snow carrying spears for stalking wild pigs and followed by a motley collection of hounds. The air has the stillness of frost and the light, the clarity of reflection from snow. Birds perch in the traceried branches of elms, black against the sky which is a leaden grey-green, portending a further fall.

Brick houses of sturdy shape have high-pitched roofs, now the same white as their surroundings, and in front of the doors of an inn, the landlord's family tend a warming fire perhaps in preparation for roasting the pig. Beyond, the land slopes into a vale with a great series of fish-ponds on which the peasants frolic and skate. The water is diverted from a distant river and passes from the ponds beneath a bridge to a water-mill, with its wheel now hidden beneath a cascade of icicles. Pollard willows line the fields beneath villages and hamlets and afar foothills rise rapidly to bare crags rising sheer out of snow-covered mountains.

Hunters in the Snow is a painting that can be regarded and analysed

23. Beggars and cripples fascinated him and he painted the blind, epileptics and other unfortunates with observation but not it seems with any underlying compassion for their condition. These paintings are strangely clinical with the grotesque forms of the subjects set in landscapes of quiet and natural beauty. The Renaissance ideal of human physical beauty seems to have held no interest for him.

24. The context may have been the political and religious climate of his time. The Spanish Inquisition had been introduced into the Netherlands (a dominion of the King of Spain) in 1522 and as religious doubt and schism grew, repression became increasingly draconian. Five years after the *Triumph of Death* the regime of the Duke of Alva set out to extirpate heresy and unrest, a development that civilised and sensitive men must have dreaded, and it must have seemed that Bruegel's vision of horror was coming to pass.

in many ways. Judged as an abstract composition of line, tone and colour it is totally balanced and satisfying and in some ways recalls the work of Bruegel's later countrymen Mondrian and Van Doesburg. As a landscape it conveys the stillness following a snowfall, the transformation of a familiar scene and the crisp coldness and the sense of exhilaration that fresh snow evokes in many people. It is also a record of a historic landscape, accurately depicted with minute observation of detail, frozen in time as surely as the fish-ponds and the mill-wheel. But these are but aspects of a unity and control evident in every detail of the canvas and reflecting the vision of the wider unity of man through husbandry with the creation, the triumph of life itself.

The other *Months* are equally optimistic. In *February (The Gloomy Day)* peasants prune their pollards and thin their groves for firewood in the mysterious fleeting sunlight of a storm-clouded winter day. *In July (Corn Harvest)*, the weary harvesters relax in the noonday sun and eat their picnic lunches in a landscape of fruitfulness and golden corn, gathered around a pear tree which dominates the picture, uniting sky and ground like the World Tree of ancient belief, and for a moment it seems as though the landscape is revolving around it. In *October (The Return of the Herd)* the cattle are driven home in the russet landscape of autumn from their summer grazing in the uplands. The rocky

Fig. 3.24 *Winter* or *Hunters in the Snow* by Pieter Bruegel (Kunsthistorisches Museum, Vienna).

hills in the distance which have provided pasture for fattening now seem verdant and less menacing; even the wilderness contributes to the fruitfulness of the earth.

The awareness and appreciation of wilderness balances the immediate and productive landscape of husbandry. There is both ease and confidence in the *Months*, in the breadth of vision from stormy skies and mountain peaks to the depiction of the minute details of farming and peasant clothing. Similarly Virgil moves from considering the 'tiny republic of the hive' to celestial constellations. In both the *months* and the *Georgics*, farming is set in the wider context of the cosmos, and in the fulfilment of its seasonal tasks, good husbandry achieves a unity with divine order.

Chapter 4

The Renaissance and its aftermath

Florence and Venice

For the student of ideal landscapes from the sixteenth century onwards there is an extensive literature to consult, with copious illustrations and descriptions; moreover, many of these landscapes still
survive to be visited, studied and enjoyed. Since it is a field well tilled,
this section is concerned with the later expression and development
of the concepts described and followed through Antiquity and the
Middle Ages in the form of ideas, the achievement of painters and in
the actual landscapes of parks and gardens.

The survival of the written heritage of the Ancient World in the
Latin language was the legacy of those last vital years of the Empire,
when the Church assimilated the traditions and learning of Rome.
Throughout the Middle Ages the texts were preserved and transcribed
in the libraries of cathedrals and religious houses; the works of writers
and poets such as Chaucer were full of references to Antiquity and
often used antique legends as themes for their work; Dante took Virgil
himself as his guide in the *Divine Comedy*. Thus the culture of the Ancient World was never dead or even dormant in the Middle Ages, yet
the vigour of the Gothic style in architecture and the visual arts was
such in northern Europe that there was little interest in the forms of
Antiquity until the sixteenth century, when the secular character of
the age welcomed and adopted the new style that had evolved in Italy.

The Renaissance was born in Florence, cradled and brought to
maturity by three generations of the Medici family. From the return
from exile of Cosimo in 1434 until the death of his grandson, Lorenzo
il Magnifico, in 1492, the family effectively governed the city, wisely
and by consent of their fellow citizens. In Florence they themselves
were private citizens; in Europe they were merchant princes whose
banking and trading empire brought wealth for patronage of art and
architecture. Their circle included the brilliant and creative minds of
the age, and at our distance Florence of the fifteenth century appears
a ferment of creativity, each building, painting, sculpture, poem and
fine artefact seems now as then a new achievement and discovery.

The landscape of Tuscany formed the setting to this achievement;
today, it is still extraordinarily verdant and rich, giving an impression
that every metre is cultivated and productive, however hilly and

daunting it might seem to farmers from other regions. The Medici, as other wealthy urban families, held estates which supplied their wine, fruit, cheese and oil and provided a surplus for the city markets. In summer the family would leave the heat of the city to live in the villa, the centre of the estate as in the days of Cato and Varro, but fortified still against the perils and marauders of the Middle Ages.

Paintings show the family villas of the Medici as they appeared in the sixteenth century, two of which, at Fiesole and Cafaggiola, retain their gardens today – the latter little altered from the time of Cosimo. They are homely and functional, essentially still manor houses without aggrandisement or imposition of architectural ideas other than pergolas and fountains embellishing the immediate environs of the house. The views of the landscape beyond is the important element in the design, accepted on its own terms as it had been in Pliny's day. As in Antiquity, the Medici regarded the villa and its gardens as the natural setting for discourse on philosophy and the arts.

A member of their circle was Leon Battista Alberti, author of a treatise *De Re Aedificatoria* (1452) in which he gives a detailed description of the design of an ideal villa. It must be sited on rising ground, the house above the garden in order to see over the walls (still necessary for defence) to embrace the prospects of the countryside: woods, plains, hills and distant mountains – the view is all important. The layout of the gardens must reflect in plan the geometry of the house, extending it into what are effectively outdoor rooms, the scale still intimate and domestic. Alberti deals with vine pergolas, recalling the one at Cafaggiola which he must certainly have known, porticoes and a mass of architectural detail for the garden mostly lifted from Pliny's description of the layout of beds and features around his Tuscan villa. Grottoes and artificial caves fascinated him, probably taken from examples from Roman times still surviving to be seen and emulated. Notably absent from Alberti and from the Medici villas is the concept of axial planning, overriding symmetry and grandiose architectural adornment. The garden is still an adjunct of the house and combines functional considerations – the growing of herbs, vegetables, flowers for picking and vines within its planned architectural framework. The links with the garden described by Boccaccio a century earlier are still strong; the scale that of the garden of a man content to remain a citizen of Florence.

An early winter destroyed the Tuscan spring. The Medici heirs returned from exile to rule Florence, not as citizens but as grand dukes, and by imposition rather than consent. Predictably, bombast replaced the earlier family reticence expressed in public statuary and the design of the Boboli gardens behind Pitti Palace, laid out as a setting for court functions and pageantry, and above all imposing display. Today the gardens are a sad sight; the quality that impressed visitors to Florence in their heyday are difficult to envisage and there is no compensating patina of 'pleasing decay'. Historically they look towards the landscape of Versailles, designed for prestige, and mark a stage in the trend to exclude functional elements from the planned ideal landscape. Florentine painters, unlike the Flemings, seem to have taken their familiar landscape for granted, concentrating on composition, figure drawing and the subjects of mythology. Giotto had painted a series of frescos depicting the life of St Francis which lack any sympathy with the saint's love of the natural world and sense of brotherhood with all living things; Giotto's trees are purely symbols and their forms would have aroused Francis' pity. Later, the paradise garden found echoes in Florentine art, notably in the work of Fra Angelico (1387–1455) and expressed in the flowery mead and formal trees of his *Noli me Tangere*, and the wider paradise forms the setting of Benozzo Gozzoli's *Journey of the Magi* (1439). But in neither painting is the landscape more than a setting. Gozzoli's interest lies in the human figures, their faces and clothing, the horses with their rich caparisons and trappings, and the hounds; these appear observed at first hand whereas flowers, trees and rocks seem to derive from a formula.

Flemish developments in the techniques of landscape painting reached Florence through banking and trading connections in the Low Countries [1]. Development of the pictorial arts in Italy and Flanders was separate but not isolated; landscape was a matter for the individual artist's sense of priorities. Sandro Botticelli (1447–1515) only tentatively tried his hand at it. In the *Adoration of the Magi* (1481), ruins of classical buildings form the structure of the picture, but in the distance a delightful landscape is briefly glimpsed – but it is a scene from northern Europe rather than Italy, and like most Italian artists, Botticelli observed this scene at second hand, reserving direct observation for flowers, leaves and trees that would form an immediate and enclosing background to his compositions. An inner struggle between the pagan beauty of *Primavera* and the *Birth of Venus*, and the intensity of his religious paintings became ultimately resolved when, according to Vasari, he became a follower of Savonarola. Tormented by visions of apocalypse brought by the papacy of the Borgias he was an early victim of the Florentine winter. Other younger artists of talent left the city for new centres of patronage at Rome and Fontainebleau.

A few Italians painted landscapes with the same interest and observation as the Flemish masters of 'fact'. True landscapes appear in the backgrounds of Piero and the Pollaiuolo brothers, but most of their contemporaries were content to follow in the manner of Roger Van der Weyden, producing decorative and romantic scenes with little reference to reality or observation of nature at first hand; nevertheless, in the work of masters such as Pinturicchio and Perugino these romantic landscapes have a haunting beauty, depicting an unreal world where the mundane problems of growing and harvesting crops are an irrelevance. They are a townsman's view of the landscape.

Perhaps the finest romantic landscapes of this time occur in the backgrounds of works by Leonardo, notably the *Virgin and Child with St Anne* and the *Mona Lisa*. These are composed of mountain ranges with rocky foothills and outcrops, sweeping plains and lakes bathed in a mysterious blue-green light, man is absent, and only the outline of a bridge in the middle distance of the *Mona Lisa* indicates that the land was once inhabited. Even stranger is the *Madonna of the Rocks* where the Virgin, seated in a grotto, has become the attendant goddess of a landscape of rocks and wild flowers from which man has been utterly purged, or perhaps has never reached. However remote these landscapes may seem, a sense of truth is carried by the quality of the observation; the elements, whether flowers or distant mountains, derive from the studies from life which appear in Leonardo's sketchbooks and he was clearly fascinated by their structures and intricacies. Sketches of functional landscape in the valley of the Arno survive, but

1. Flemish paintings had reached Italy through diplomatic missions, trade and the connections of the Aragonese rulers of Naples. A direct link was the painter Antonello da Messina (1430–79) whom Vasari believed to have studied under Jan Van Eyck himself at Bruges and brought the new technique of oil-painting to Italy. Since Van Eyck died in 1441 the story is apocryphal, although Antonello may have studied under Jan's pupil Petrus Christus, possibly in Milan. He settled in Venice in 1475 where he was highly esteemed and widely commissioned, and it is sometimes suggested that Bellini learnt the technique of landscape painting from him. By this time, however, Giovanni's style was accomplished and mature and there was little that Antonello, fine painter though he was, could teach him; it was more likely to be the reverse.

In Florence, a painting of *St Jerome in his Study* by Jan Van Eyck was owned by Lorenzo de Medici and influenced the murals in the Ognissanti by Botticelli and Ghirlandaio. The splendid painting by Hugo van der Goes *Adoration of the Magi*, which now hangs in the Uffizi, was commissioned by the Medici's agent in Bruges (1476–78).

they did not appear to have interested him sufficiently to transfer them
to his paintings. It is the forms of nature which seem to have held his
attention: mountain ranges, storm clouds, waves and wild flowers, but
the landscape of husbandry seems to have eluded his concern.

In the Roman High Renaissance the ferocious personality of
Michelangelo gave support to the use of the human body, derived from
the study of antique sculpture, as the true concern of the artist in expressing the heroic and ideal. He detested the Flemish landscape
painters, dismissing their works as for 'young women, monks and
nuns, and certain noble persons who have no ear for true harmony'.
The awe in which he was held by his contemporaries ensured that his
view prevailed among Italian painters of the sixteenth century, except
in Venice, for the Venetians were an independent people who followed
their own rules and went their own way, and it was here, paradoxically in a city surrounded by the sea, that a new concept of an ancient
idea evolved: the landscape of the Golden Age.

This change in interest from the Flemish Landscapes of Fact to the
Age of Gold can be traced in the works of Giovanni Bellini through
his long life (1430–1516). From his youth he was a true observer of
the natural scene and in his middle years he painted landscapes that
can be compared with, but are earlier than, those of Bruegel. The
sublime vision of husbandry as an aspect of divine order is expressed
in two paintings by this great Venetian: his *Madonna of the Meadows*
and *St Francis*. In both landscapes the scenery and buildings of the
Low Countries are replaced by those of northern Italy, each observed
in the clear sunlight of an Italian morning. In the *St Francis*, hills with
ordered fields are crowned by a castle in the manner of the Limbourgs,
but built in the Italian vernacular and no longer dominating the landscape. A walled town beside the river crossing is peaceful and settled,
with houses and gardens outside the walls and, in the middle distance,
a fenced field and a shepherd driving his flock reminds us of the seasons. A rocky outcrop in the foreground has a cave which is the saint's
home, with a vine climbing over a trellis at the entrance and a raised
bed of herbs, while wild flowers and climbers grow in the crevices of
the rock. Every detail is observed and depicted with humility and extraordinary patience: sky, hills, rocks and the construction of the
saint's desk and stool; every animate thing, plant, tree, beast and bird,
seems to exist in its own right as a creation of God and a part of the
community of living things. St Francis greets the sun in the attitude
of the stigmata, welcoming the light and warmth which sustains all,
the symbol of a good and caring Creator who has not abandoned his
world to demons. Brother Ass basks happily in the sunlight to which
the saint expresses his wonder and welcome, his equal, perhaps, as
a sentient being that experiences pleasures as well as pain. It is a superbly optimistic painting, a vindication of the concept of the world
as the garden which Adam was enjoined to 'dress and keep'. The careful tending of the vines bears witness that Francis himself is a
husbandman.

Arcadia revived

It seems strange that this master of the Landscape of Fact who expressed the unity of God, nature and humanity, should have turned
in his later years to the creation of a different landscape, pagan and

Fig. 4.1 *St Francis in the Wilderness* by Giovanni Bellini (copyright the Frick Collection, New York).

remote in time and place. But the change was in keeping with the spirit of the age and accorded with the interest in classical literature and mythology, and with the figures and forms of Roman sculpture and sarcophagi which formed the inspiration of Michelangelo and his followers. Increasingly the belief prevailed that the Classical Age had achieved the highest human culture from which a later age could benefit through adaptation of its forms and imitation. Raphael coined the term *Gothic* for the architecture of the Middle Ages, a scornful epithet which has survived for lack of an alternative, and we have seen the dislike of Michelangelo for the Flemish Landscape of Fact. Permanent schism in the universal church was imminent, to be followed by the horrors of the religious wars, and a man as sensitive as Bellini may have felt a prescience leading to pessimism and a need for escape. Be that how it may, his youthful pupils Titian and Giorgione had little use for the countryside of husbandry and maybe influenced the old

Fig. 4.2 *The Feast of the Gods* by Giovanni Bellini (National Gallery of Art, Washington; Widener Collection).

man, and after achieving landscapes of the quality of *St Francis*, one may ask to what such an artist can turn if he is not to repeat and imitate himself. But, whatever the origin, the fact is that the new concept in landscape painting appears fully developed in Bellini's *Feast of the Gods* dated to 1514

This remarkable painting has the essential elements of a genre that was to continue through the Venetian tradition to the landscapes of Claude and Poussin in the following century. The scene is one of perpetual summer, a pastoral landscape of clumped trees, full and free-growing and all bathed in a golden light. A rocky eminence looms mysteriously in the distance and in the foreground gods, goddesses and satyrs feast rather self-indulgently on nectar and the fruits of the earth. Escape is total, to a world described by Ovid in his *Metamor-*

phosis or to the Golden Age as described by Evander in Virgil's epic. The concept of Arcadia, the age of simple rusticity when gods, heroes and natural spirits walked an earth where the plough was unknown, has returned.

The ingredients of this new Arcadia and its subsequent development are derived from several sources and fused together most successfully. The mood and inspiration derive from the eighth book of the *Aeneid* and from the pastoral *Eclogues*, and the subject-matter often comes from Ovid. The landscape setting, however, originates in the pastoral semi-natural landscape of Flemish painting where husbandry in the form of fields, hedges and crops is excluded; in essence it is the medieval hunting park, with its deceptively 'natural' appearance, which, in fact, derived from a variety of functions for which it was managed. Trees stand singly or in clumps or groves to provide structural timber or successive crops of 'underwood' through lopping or coppicing; open grass swards provide grazing for cattle or sheep as well as deer and the small beasts of the warren and plains into which the deer were driven for hunting. Areas of scrub and bracken provide coverts and browsing for the deer, and springs, streams and boggy areas the water to slake the thirst of grazing animals in summer months. It is a controlled landscape, not a wilderness, and hence its appearance of mysterious order and repose.

The debt of the new Arcadia to the traditional hunting park is borne out by an essay on 'the situation of the parkes, and the manner of ordering the wild beasts therein' from Liebault's *Maison Rustique*, translated into English and printed in 1616 as *The Country Farm*. This was written before the fashion for imposing straight avenues or vistas on the parks, and well over a century before the English rediscovered the virtues of the 'natural scene'. The following passages are relevant as describing the landscape desired:

> The parke would be seated (if it be possible) within a wood of high tall timber trees, in a place compassed about and well fenced. . . . You must foresee that there bee some little brooke of spring-water running along by the place, or, for want of springwater and naturall streames, you must prepare ditches and pooles, walled and daubed in such sort, as that they may receive and keepe the reine water. Nor ought the parke to consist of one kind of ground only, as all of wood, all grasse, or all coppice, but of divers, as part high wood, part grasse or champion, and part coppice or under-wood, or thicke spring. . . . Neither must the parke be situated upon any one entire hill, plaine or else valley, but it must consist of divers hills, divers plaines, and divers valleys; the hills which are commonly called the viewes or discoveries of parkes would bee all goodly of tall timber, as well as for the beauty and gracefulnesse of the parke, as also for the echoe and sound which will rebound from the same, when in the times of hunting, either the crys of the hounds, the winding of hornes, or the gibetting of the huntsmen passeth through the same, doubling the musicke, and making it tenne times more delightful: the plains which are called in parkes, the lawnds, would be very champion and fruitful. . . . The valleys which are called the coverts or places of leave for wild beasts, would be all very thicke sprung or underwood, as well for the concealing of

them from potchers and purloyners, as for giving them rest and
shadow in the day time. . . . Thus you see the parke must consist
of view, lawnd, and covert, and the situation of hill, valley and
plaine. Now for the water, of which formerly we spoake. You
shall know it is very right necessarie in parkes, as well for the
reliefs and sustenance of wild beasts, as for the watering,
washing and moistening of the grounds to make them fruitfull.
Besides, whensoever your game is extremely hunted, and brought
to the pitch of extremitie, then he will flie to the water, which is
called the soile, and there find releife and rescue: for, according
to the profit David, As the Hart desireth the water brooks, so a
deere in his greatest extremitie findeth reliefs and is refreshed by
drinking and bathing in the water [2].

The description recalls the setting for Actaeon surprising Diana bathing with her nymphs, and subsequently being transformed into a stag
and pursued by his own hounds; also the banquet of Evander, when
'the woods all rang with their singing, the hills echoed it back'. It
makes it clear that aesthetics were involved in the selection of the sites,
planting and maintenance of traditional parks and these provided a
fitting setting for Arcadia revived.

Although the landscapes of this new Arcadia derived from the
wood-pasture of the northern European countries, later painters living
in Rome introduced elements based on studies of the Campagna and
its hills, which added a different, more Mediterranean feeling [3].
Nicolas Poussin (1594–1665) studied this landscape and his sketches
suggest that in a previous age he would have been a master of the
Landscape of Fact. Some of these elements were transferred into his
paintings in the Arcadian tradition, others became the inspiration for
a tradition of lesser men who painted peasant landscapes, romantic
and delightful in their way, for the northern gentry who flocked to
Rome on the Grand Tour. Poussin reinterpreted the rocky outcrops
of Flemish tradition in the crags and ravines of the Apennine foothills,
and the seeming wildness of the hunting park is supplemented by the
scrub and natural growth on steep and rocky slopes and wetland
areas. The quality of light, golden and pervasive, in the paintings of
Poussin and his contemporary Claude recall both the mood of Virgil
and the vision of the Van Eycks who first revealed light as the medium
to express objects and distances.

Above all innovations, Poussin and his contemporary Claude introduced buildings into their paintings that directly evoked the imagery
of the Golden and Heroic Ages. Temple fronts, miniature Pantheons,
columns and funerary monuments; also ruined structures recalling the
crumbling monuments on the Saturnian and Janiculum as shown to
Aeneas by Evander on his tour of the future site of Rome. Fallen columns and ruins also recall the Rome of their own time; romantic reminders of the Imperial Age, neglected and plundered for building
materials by succeeding generations, but still evident and dominating
the baroque city. A century later, the ruins of the Roman Forum inspired Gibbon to embark on his *Decline and Fall*, and the romantic
scene of architectural elements overgrown by nature and worn by time
is preserved in the engravings of Piranesi.

The vision of Poussin and Claude was to appeal deeply to eighteenth-century Englishmen. A classical past, viewed romantically,

2. The full description in *The Country Farm* can be
read in E. P. Shirley: *English Deer Parks*, Murray
(1867).

3. A notable painter of rocky and romantic landscapes
of these foothills was Salvator Rosa (1615–73) who
was much admired by English collectors for the qualities of awe and wild nature and influenced the later
cult of the 'Sublime'.

suited the spirit of the age and they hastened to adapt their parks to give an appearance of Arcadia. In this they were aided by the formal structure of Claude's and Poussin's paintings which provided scenes which could be adapted into the English 'picturesque'.

The inhabitants of Arcadia were provided by classical mythology as interpreted by Giorgione and Titian, and developed by Poussin. Heroic nudity had been a theme of Florentine painting, deriving from antique sculpture and sarcophagi and surviving Roman domestic paintings. In Venice, this theme followed its own distinctive course, with figures rounded and observed in light, in contrast to the linear tradition of Florence. Beautiful and superbly sensuous nudes were painted by Giorgione in his *Fête Champêtre* derived from classical precedent, but observed from models drawn from the renowned Venetian courtesans of his own day. They are frankly erotic and seductive, plump and used to a life of opulence, and fitting subjects for the attention of Jupiter and the gods, heroes and satyrs who pursued the nymphs in their endless leisure hours. Titian, in his *Bacchus and Ariadne*, added the Bacchanale in which a host of satyrs, nymphs, goats and tigers join the young god and his companion, the fat and usually stupefied Silenus, on a drunken jaunt. The Bacchanale was a favourite theme in Antiquity and had already been revived in painting and sculpture in Florence and Rome, but Titian introduced it into the new Arcadia, and subsequently Poussin painted many variations of the subject. One suspects that the owners of parks gained a vicarious thrill from observing these uninhibited scenes of nymphs and their hairy lovers in familiar surroundings, but safe from the censure of the Church or prying eyes of the peasantry.

The development of Arcadia revived can be followed in a series of paintings. First the traditional park posing as wilderness in the *St John* of Geertgen tot Sint Jans (late 15th century). 'Mature' Arcadia appears in Bellini's *Feast of the Gods*, but the figures do not seem wholly at ease and the nymphs of Giorgione's *Fête Champêtre* and the bacchantes of

Fig. 4.3 Pastoral scene by Claude Lorraine. Northern wood-pasture modified by distant views of the Apennine foothills and ruins. See also Fig. 1.1.

Titian's *Bacchus and Ariadne* seem more suited to their surroundings. Finally, a formal structure adorned with the buildings of Antiquity and with landscape elements, derived from the Campagna, appear in Claude's *Ascanius and the Stag* and *Temple of Apollo*, and Poussin's *Gathering of the Ashes of Phocion*.

Parallel with the development of scenes from the Golden and Heroic Ages, this landscape provided a new vision for painters of Paradise itself. Thus the formal parks of the Babylonian kings reappeared in the guise of the informal parks of northern Europe, enriched by the imagery of Virgil. Soon, with Milton's *Paradise Lost*, a poet of similar calibre would describe the new Paradise in the English language.

Italian and French gardens

The enthusiasm of Italian humanists for the classical world did not lead to a revival in Italy of the understanding of landscape as a totality as expressed by Virgil and Pliny and, more recently, by artists in the Low Countries. Landscape painting, estate management and the designs of landscape architects developed in strictly separate compartments. Landscape painting, as we have seen, reconstructed the remote landscape of the Golden Age and although it used certain contemporary material, essentially excluded the landscape of husbandry. Humanist landowners managed their estates on the precepts of Virgil, Cato, Varro and Columella, spending most of the year in their town *palazzi*, but moving out to their manor houses in the heat of the summer months. Those of the Veneto employed Palladio to redesign their country houses as Roman villas, which would have delighted Varro, but would probably have offended Cato by their elegance. Palladio extended his designs from the house to the agricultural buildings that attended it, thus fitting it to its immediate setting; granaries, cowsheds and stores were designed as wings and pavilions and united into a composition by colonnades, screen walls, stairways and ramps. Gardens seem not to have interested him and it is in Rome and its surrounding countryside that the remarkable achievements of the Italian garden architects of the High Renaissance and Mannerism evolved.

Fortunately, many of the gardens survive today and can be visited; we are not dealing with fragments, as is the case with Arab gardens, or travellers' reports as with the gardens of the Ancient East. Moreover, an excellent manual can be consulted: Miss Masson's book *Italian Gardens* describes their evolution and regional development, is lavishly illustrated and essential reading for the student of the subject and the fortunate visitor.

The garden described by Boccaccio illustrates the high level of development of the art in the fourteenth century. It is a formal, enclosed garden in the Arab tradition, with the skilful handling of water in fountains and channels characteristic of Arab gardens. These elements were retained in the developments of the next three centuries, although the sense of enclosure was modified by planned views of the countryside and distant hills or mountains, very much in the manner of the Alhambra, thus providing a link with the greater world outside, but in no sense seeking to include it in the garden. Sometimes these are glimpsed framed in an opening, or accented by a standing figure, or form the end to a vista. Formal planning appealed to Renaissance designers who loved order and symmetry, which they elaborated into a complex hierarchy of axes and cross-axes which divide the overall composition into areas of different character – often 'outdoor rooms' or semi-enclosed gardens, each with their individual character. It was similar to the design of a *palazzo* or villa in which rooms may vary considerably, but are subordinated to the geometry of the overall plan and, indeed, the garden was seen as an extension of the house plan itself, with all its variety of spaces and corridors. In their handling of water the Italians proved to be brilliant, and at Tivoli, the variety of its use in jets, cascades, fountains, channels and pools achieved a mastery that has been much imitated, but never surpassed.

To this vigorous tradition, Italian Renaissance designers added the forms, statuary and architectural detailing of ancient Rome and eagerly studied the descriptions of gardens by Roman authors. The full account given by Pliny of the formal surroundings of his Tuscan villa was of particular importance and so influential that it reads like a description of a Renaissance garden. It is clear that Pliny regarded it spatially as an extension of the plan of the house, providing outdoor rooms where plane trees could grow and fountains murmur and sparkle; he enjoyed an ambiguity between indoor and outdoor space, describing one room decorated with a ceiling fresco of birds perched in the branches of trees. Both rooms and courts enjoy views of vineyards, meadows and the distant mountains – the landscape which really interested Pliny, who seems to have looked on his outdoor rooms rather

Fig. 4.4 Villa d'Este, Tivoli, in the sixteenth century (engraving by Duperac).

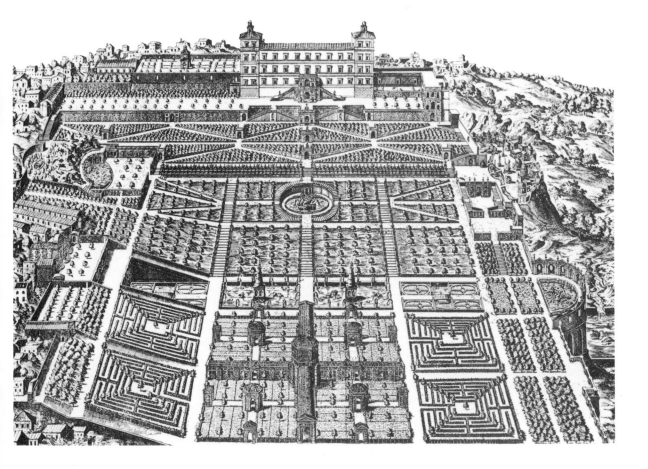

less seriously than his later admirers. The plant material includes plane trees overgrown with ivy, box clipped hedges, obelisks and innumerable shapes including the letters of his own and his gardener's names, laurel, roses, grass lawns and rippling seas of acanthus, all familiar in gardens of the Renaissance. The mechanics of the manipulation of water fascinated him and he describes an outdoor dining room [4]. Beside the 'room' is a marble pavilion with an alcove with windows in all its walls, but the light is dimmed by the dense leaves of a flourishing vine which climbs over the whole building. Here, as in Governor Mucianius' hollow plane trees, one can lie on a bed and imagine oneself inside a wood, but without the risk of rain; again, the division between the indoor and outdoor spaces is ambiguous.

Pliny's descriptions of his gardens and pavilions, designed to amuse and delight him, became a case-book for Italian designers in much the same way as Vitruvius books for architects. A major contribution of the Romans to landscape design was a revival of the formal terraced hillside, known from the ruins of the temple of Sulla at Praeneste (Palestrina) and the gardens of Lucullus on the Pincio. Both were measured and drawn by Pirro Ligorio, the architect for the Villa d'Este at Tivoli where this Roman concept is combined with the brilliant use of water. A sixteenth-century print survives, showing the garden formally planned and planted throughout, all subject to overriding geometry and man-made order. Today the rigidity of the concept is softened by the maturity of the trees, and the lichens and mosses that encrust the stonework. The patina of age and the stealthy conquest by nature have added to the quality of this man-dominated landscape, giving it the dimension of time.

Villa d'Este is incomparable, the supreme example of the Italian water garden grafted on to the Roman hillside landscape. Those who have not yet seen this masterpiece should choose a summer weekday (but not a saint's day), leaving the bustle of Rome early in the morning as Cardinal Ippolito d'Este would have done four centuries ago. The gardens can be explored before the sun reaches its zenith and the heat grows stifling, when a picnic lunch with wine can be followed by a siesta accompanied by the murmur and spray of the fountains in the shade of the trees, again, just as the Cardinal would have done. Then in the cool of the afternoon, the traveller can visit the ruins of Hadrian's Villa nearby [5].

A very different garden is that of the Villa Giulia (now the Etruscan Museum) at Rome. In the tradition of the Caesars it lies outside the walls of the antique city and formed the nucleus for the vast pleasure groves of Pope Julius III which stretched to the Tiber and included fountains, aviaries, grottoes, pavilions, monuments and statuary. All have now gone, except the distinguished building of the villa itself and the series of outdoor rooms that comprise its garden. Built from 1550 to 1555, the finest architects of the day had a hand in its design: Vasari and Vignola and, possibly, Michelangelo. It is a building for the summer, a casino, and the division between garden and indoor space is undefined, as with Pliny's villas, the two elements are intended to interpenetrate. Curving arcades embrace the main court in a hemicycle, the vaults, decorated with frescos of vines with fluttering birds and butterflies, open to the air. Originally, this court was filled with sculpture and a fountain taken from the Baths of Titus stood in the centre, but all were removed to the Vatican after Pope Julius' death.

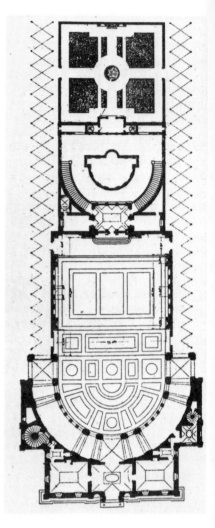

Fig. 4.5 Villa Giulia, ground plan of gardens (Letarouilly, Paris (1860)). See also Fig. 2.9.

4. *At the upper end of the course is a curved dining seat of white marble, shaded by vine trained over slender pillars of Carystian marble. Water gushes out through pipes from under the seat as if pressed out by the weight of people sitting there, is caught in a stone cistern and then held in a polished marble basin which is regulated by a hidden device so as to remain full without overflowing. The preliminaries and main dishes for dinner are placed on the edge of the basin, while the lighter ones float about in vessels shaped like birds or little boats. A fountain opposite plays and catches its water, throwing it high in the air so that it falls back into the basin where it is played again at once through a jet connected with the outlet.*
Pliny (the Younger): *Letters.* Trans. B. Radice. Penguin (1963).

The three courts are separated by loggias on a central axis, which allow a fleeting giimpse from the villa entrance through to the greenery of the third court with its formal planting. In the second court is a sunken nymphaeum, leading to underground rooms providing a cool retreat in the summer heat. Time has been kind, as to the Villa d'Este, giving a patina of pleasing decay; ferns grow in the cracks of the stonework of the nymphaeum and tall pines and cedars rise beyond but above the walls of the villa, recalling the vast gardens that once encompassed it.

The composition can be interpreted in two ways: as an exercise in Mannerist space and perception, subtle and glimpsed indirectly through screens, compared with Renaissance formality or baroque clarity. Alternatively, it can be seen as a substitute on level ground for the hillside garden, with the succession of glimpses, followed by concealment and then revelation as the terraces are ascended. Perhaps, both approaches played their roles in the design of this subtle and sophisticated villa. The Villa d'Este is undeniably the most impressive of surviving Renaissance gardens, but Villa Lante at Bagnaia, which is tiny by comparison, may be considered by some the most beautiful. Deliberately, it seems, its designer Vignola eschewed the temptation of monumentality, choosing delicacy and understatement. Water tinkles and sparkles, rather than roars as the garden descends from the water source in a wooded grotto to the water parterre, opening up by stages to reveal magnificent views over the old town of Bagnaia to the plain beyond. Although the garden is symmetrical and formal, it enjoys an easy relationship with the adjoining hunting park – the garden was created within the enclosed area, sited on the most steeply sloping ground with the finest prospects. A print of 1614 shows it united with the park by walks and rides through the woodland meeting points where interest is provided by an obelisk, pavilions and the surviving Pegasus fountain.

Villa Lante is a magical place to which time has added its patina. The plane trees now are huge and the resting river gods in the Fountain of the Giants are encrusted with mosses and ferns which give a timeless dimension to these figures of Antiquity and earlier ages when a belief in animism was accepted. Virgil's Father Tiber seems credible as one regards these grave figures – earth giants sprung from stone. So today, Villa Lante has the added quality of the historic dimension; Montaigne had awarded it the prize for use of water, while in this century that acute critic Sacheverell Sitwell described it as the most lovely place of the physical beauty of nature that he had seen with his own eyes.

Villa Lante was begun in 1564 and completed in the 1580s. Flowers and herbs may have formed the material for the planted beds when it was created. Miss Masson draws attention to trellises for climbing plants evident in the 1614 engraving. Similarly, at Tivoli she shows that flowers and herbs were still an essential part of garden design in the original layout until banished in the seventeenth century [6]. Links with the gardens of the Medici were strong in the sixteenth century and the functional elements of the garden still had a place in the ideal landscape.

A fine example of the Renaissance garden, which maintains the union of the functional and decorative, lies not in Italy but in the soft landscape of the Loire valley. Villandry, built in the 1530s, predates

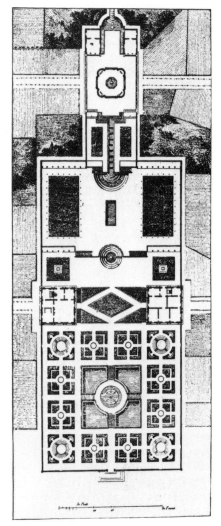

Fig. 4.6 Villa Lante, ground plan (Percier and Fontaine (1809)).

5. Features have disappeared that impressed the visitors of the seventeenth and eighteenth centuries, such as the water organ, the weird noises of the dragon fountain, but they would probably seem as unimpressive in the 1980s as the side-shows of Edwardian piers. It is the planned set pieces which still impress today: the terrace of a hundred fountains, the cascades and jets, and the stone stairways all now enriched with mosses and lichens, and softened by their union through time with nature.

Elaborate effects propelled by hydraulic power were admired in the sixteenth century, including water organs, joke fountains which soaked visitors and all manner of automata, notably at Pratolino designed by Buontalenti in 1569 (see J. Shearman: *Mannerism*. Pelican Books (1967), pp. 126–33. Automata had a long history dating back at least to the Hellenistic and had been reintroduced from the East at Hesdin in the thirteenth century.

6. G. Masson: *Italian Gardens*. Thames and Hudson (1966).

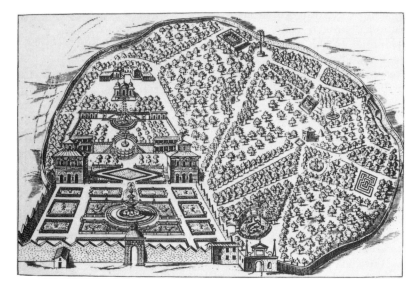

Fig. 4.7 Villa Lante, view of garden and adjacent park (Laurus: *Antiquae Urbis Splendor*).

Fig. 4.8 Villa Lante, view over the water garden towards the roofs of Bagnaia.

Fig. 4.9 Villa Lante, sculpture of river god.

the Villas d'Este and Lante; it was the work of Jean le Breton, financier and Minister to Francis I, who had served as an ambassador in Italy where he had the opportunity to study Renaissance gardens at first hand. The site is gently modelled into three broad terraces, the highest collecting the waters of a small stream into a large formal pool which then feeds jets and irrigating fountains at the lower levels and through a linking canal, the moat beside the château and around its formal approach. The middle level is planted with flower gardens and surrounds on three sides the lowest level, the *Jardin potager* or kitchen garden. Avenues of pleached limes define the upper level and give added height to its terrace. The gardens are organised within a structure which is reticent but retains a subtle control, conveying a sense of quiet breadth and leaving the eye to dwell on the intricacies of the planting, either close to or from the terraces, or from the belvedere created on an eminence beside the château whence the design as a whole can be seen and appreciated. There is no attempt to exclude the surrounding landscape: the village and its church remain in view and are linked into the gardens by a complex of stables and utilitarian buildings (rebuilt in the 18th century) which also serve to give protection from northerly winds.

The most remarkable and beautiful feature of Villandry is the kitchen garden which occupies the central area and pride of place. Its planning is as complex and decorative as the flower parterres, but is devoted to the growing of vegetables which provide the variety of colours and textures. The scale is fine due to the functional requirement of gathering the crop without treading on the borders and the discipline of planting and spacing dictates an orthogonal layout. Each of the nine great squares follows a different geometrical pattern, the constant element being small box hedges which define the edges of all the beds and low trellises which contain the squares, and the vertical forms of fountains and rose-clad arbours at the intersections of principal paths. Probably such grand but functional gardens adorned other châteaux of the time, but today Villandry is unique [7], a garden that stirs and satisfies the senses of sight, touch, smell and taste – the last reserved for the fortunate owner to whom the saying 'it is so beautiful I could eat it' is literally true.

In our distant perpective these surviving gardens of sixteenth-century Italy and France seem to mark both a climax in the art of garden design and a watershed. They look back to the landscapes of ancient Rome, the East and the European Middle Ages; they also contain the seeds of monumentality and the change from the gardens of the manorial villa, maintaining its essential links with a productive hinterland, into a theatre for courtly displays from which the embarrassing presence of the producers of wealth from the soil is removed. Artificiality and divorce from reality had set foot in the garden with attendant risks, but as yet a delicate balance had been held.

Symptomatic of this coming divorce was the banishment of the fruit trees, herbs and vegetables, and even flowers that had formed an integral part of the gardens of the Medici. Cosimo and Lorenzo kept their grip on the reality of a culture sustained by horticulture and agriculture, although their immediate enrichment came from trade and banking. Both the princely and bourgeois tastes of the seventeenth century preferred to ignore these roots, and an indication of the new role of garden art as the handmaid of prestige can be seen in

7. The extraordinary freshness of the planting at Villandry which may enable the visitor to feel transported back four and a half centuries, compared with d'Este and Lante where age is evident, derives in part from the fact that it is largely a reconstruction where the original appearance of le Breton's day has been deliberately sought. In the nineteenth century the gardens had been redesigned in the style unfortunately known as Jardin Anglais, and the restoration of both château and gardens is the work of Joachim Carvallo who purchased Villandry in 1906. Restorations, however good, inevitably reflect their restorers and the exquisite taste and fine colour sense of the flower gardens as well as the *jardin potager* must reflect the quality of Carvallo.

See Christopher Hussey's account of Villandry: 'Le Château de Villandry, Touraine', *Country Life*, 18 June 1948; 'Villandry – the ultimate kitchen garden' in *The Garden – Journal of the Royal Horticultural Society*, January 1976; K. Woodbridge: 'Doctor Carvallo and the absolute', *Garden History*, Vol. VI, No. 2.

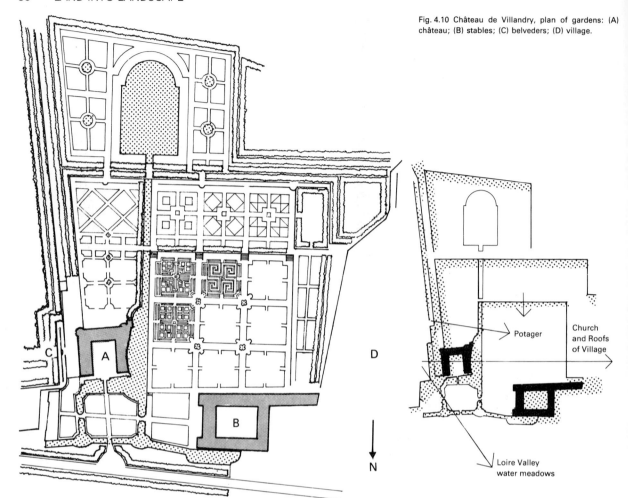

Fig. 4.10 Château de Villandry, plan of gardens: (A) château; (B) stables; (C) belveders; (D) village.

D

N

Potager

Church and Roofs of Village

Loire Valley water meadows

Fig. 4.11 Château de Villandry. Analysis.

numerous prints of the late sixteenth and seventeenth centuries which depict gardens designed in interminable and convoluted geometric patterns, useless for any purpose other than display of wealth of the owner. A similar trend seems to have occurred in the Islamic tradition of the Moguls in India at much the same time; their gardens display monumentality and a mastery in the use of water, but the earlier Eastern values in garden design – intimacy and human scale – appear rejected [8].

Giganticism and the divorce of the ideal from the functional and productive, the development of landscape as the setting for royal display, found their apogee in the gardens of Versailles, planned and constructed from 1661 onwards. It is said that much of the land was formerly swamp, which makes this achievement of Louis XIV and his landscape architect Le Nôtre the more remarkable in transforming a wilderness into a vast complex of water gardens, canals and formal promenades linked into surrounding woodlands by avenues and a network of rides. Enormous sums of money and human effort were expended on monumental fountains, statuary and stairways which adorned the basic earth-moving, excavation and planting.

8. This could be a harsh comment on the Mogul gardens. The problem today is the loss of the trees and flowers which were such essential elements in their design. The Taj Mahal stands now in a bleak landscape which enables us to concentrate on the beauty of its architecture originally only seen as a whole along the main axes.

It is the landscape of the centralised state, centre of the known universe, ruled by an absolute monarch, himself the essence of ordered government which radiates from his presence and is expressed on one side of the palace by the buildings housing government departments, civil service and guards, and on the other by the seemingly endless vistas of the gardens. Trees and plants are dragooned and coerced into formal shapes and parterres – every growing thing appears clipped and organised into a framework of geometrical preconception. The productive and fruitful landscape is banished from sight and links with images of Eden or Arcadia are severed.

It is virtually impossible to form a considered opinion, let alone judge, such a landscape from the distance of the late twentieth century. Centralised states and despotisms are repellent to most people who have observed recent regimes which by comparison make King Louis' France seem benevolent. Versailles removed the King from direct contact with his people and inefficiency and delay in government followed, just as had happened a century earlier when Philip II sought to govern his empire from the fortress palace of Escorial. With hindsight it is easy to regard Versailles as the visual embodiment of the causes of the French Revolution. The visitor today may find the endless acres of gravel and water tedious, and long for the human scale of earlier gardens.

On the other hand no effort of imagination can recreate the fêtes and royal displays for which the gardens were the setting and at which thousands of guests were entertained. Inevitably today they have an empty feeling, and fellow visitors one may encounter appear (as oneself) most unsuitably attired for the grandeur of the surroundings. In his later years the King himself escaped to the intimate little Trianon de Porcelaine, built in 1687 in the grounds of Versailles, with its flower and vegetable gardens where he delighted in the scents and colours of flowers, the pruning and training of fruit trees, and the culture of rare plants. But this was a tiny area relative to the whole of which Saint Simon said 'the King loved to tyrannise over nature to bring it into subjection with the aid of art and money'. Yet this 'tyrant' loved the cultivation of flowers and vegetables, second only to his greater passion for hunting [9].

Versailles and its immediate predecessor Vaux-le-Vicomte should not be judged by the boring copies that subsequently appeared as European kings and princelings followed the fashion for absolutism. Their imitations lacked the touch of Le Nôtre and illogically diffused the apparent centre of the universe to a multitude of different points. A rather feeble copy was begun at Hampton Court, but it seems that the English had little heart for expressions of royal power and prestige; interestingly, Wren's rebuilding falls far below his usual standard of design and compares very poorly with the buildings of Versailles which have an easy scale which never overawes and is always human, in spite of the vast area the palace covers. Perhaps the last word in this brief discussion of Versailles should lie with a contemporary Frenchman: Pierre Huet (1630–1721), bishop and tutor to the Dauphin, described the gardens of Versailles as a 'factitious parterre, composed of earth brought together to a plan of M. Le Nôtre, having for its whole decoration but a few rows of box, which never distinguish the season by change of colour; surrounded by vast sanded alleys, very compact and very bare; such a parterre forms the delight of polite

9. Lucy Norton: 'The Country King', *Country Life*, 11 July 1974.

society'. Huet's comments are caustic but not alone [10]. and such Frenchmen were already looking forward to a new philosophy of landscape design which subsequently developed and found expression in England.

10. Edward Malins: *English Landscaping and Literature (1660–1840)*. Oxford University Press (1966).

Chapter 5

The English contribution

English landscapes

Perhaps the most interesting development in landscape planning following the Renaissance occurred in eighteenth-century England where
the owners of parks sought to re-create the Arcadia of the painters,
in their grounds. To see this development in perspective it is necessary
to consider the English landscapes which preceded it, which, in any
case, are full of interest. The Tudors had brought stability to the land
after a period of dynastic civil wars in which most of the old noble
families had perished or had their lands expropriated. The destruction
of the monasteries followed and their estates passed to the new ruling
class, ruthless and grasping men it seems from their portraits and from
the record of their deeds, but united in loyalty to the Crown which
had chosen them as its instruments and made them wealthy. Below
them were the gentry and yeomen, prosperous and independent
classes who had also benefited from the changing social and economic
order. Only the poor and dispossessed suffered, for the monastic welfare service had gone and on good sheep pasture ruthless landowners
evicted villagers to seek a more profitable return from the land in wool
– a trend which, to be fair, the Crown sought to prevent. But England
was spared the religious wars that tormented Western Europe in the
sixteenth century and men were relatively rarely made to suffer for
their beliefs. In the next century, prosperity, independence of thought
and a civil war to curb the power of the King prevented the establishment of an absolute monarchy, as became usual abroad. In due
course, the architecture and landscapes associated with absolutism
were also rejected and England made her own peculiar contribution
in this field.

By 1600, the landscape of much of lowland England was a patch-
work of small fields with scattered hamlets, villages and farmsteads
which must have looked much like the farming landscapes depicted
by Benninck and Bruegel. The medieval open fields survived over
large parts of the kingdom, notably in the Midland zone and, elsewhere, on poorer soils there were extensive commons and heaths.
Scattered through this landscape were the old manorial parks, varying
greatly in size according to the wealth and resources of their owners,
and in Essex alone there are records or evidence for over 160 existing

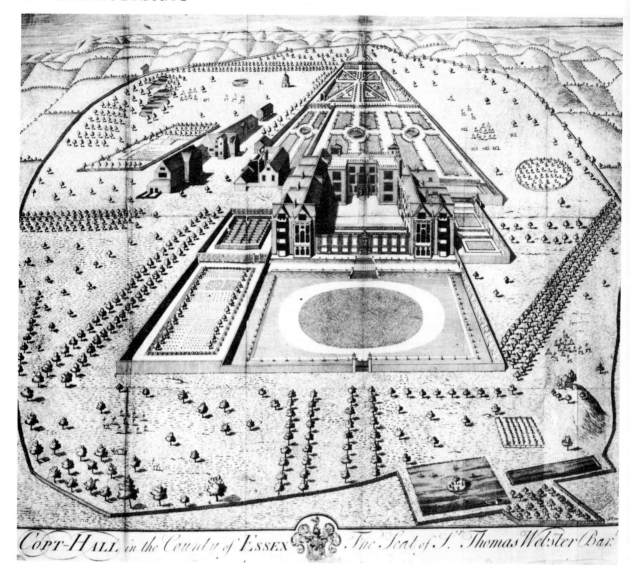

CÔPT-HALL in the County of ESSEX The Seat of S.ʳ Thomas Webster Bar.

in the course of the Middle Ages (not necessarily all at the same time). With the decline of the feudal nobility many were disparked to bring a return in rents as tenant farms and Speed's *Map of Essex* of 1610 shows forty-nine parks surviving. Those that remained were kept for prestige as much as for hunting, forming adjuncts to the great houses that were being erected by the new ruling class, enriched by changes in the social order, the spoils of the monasteries and by trade. Often the new owners built on sites within their parks, away from the sight and sounds of the village community, choosing for their mansions the position of the hunting lodge with its commanding prospects. Names such as Easton Lodge for a great house reflect this trend. At Henham the ancient manor survives as a moated farm near the village and church, but when Robert Ratclyffe, High Chamberlain of Henry VIII, acquired the manor, he built a new house in the middle of the park, described in a survey of 1530 as being on high and champion ground

Fig. 5.1 Copt Hall near Epping. Engraving from J. Farmer, *The History of the Ancient Town and once Famous Abbey of Waltham in the County of Essex, from the Foundation to the Present Time* (1735).
The engraving shows the Tudor house with formal gardens set on an eminence away from the site of an earlier house. The park, shown with a paling, is far older, a licence to enlarge having been granted in 1293. Eighteenth-century features, formal avenues and a roundel, overlie the earlier wood-pasture. A Palladian mansion, now a ruin, replaced the Tudor house in 1753. Many features including the line of the park pale are still visible today.

and well wooded. The house was a grand affair with hall, galleries around a court and a three-storey gatehouse, probably much like a Cambridge college of the time. It had vanished by the mid seventeenth century and its ground disparked, and today a farm named Henham Lodge stands on or near its site.

There are many examples of this desire for seclusion away from the old communities, perhaps arising from the unease of the newly rich. Their great houses were far fewer on the ground than the medieval manors and sub-manors which tended now to become the farms of the gentry and yeomen, with their parks converted to farmland. The surviving parks were retained for their amenity and sporting value and also, no doubt, as a token of respectability inherited from the older social order. And respectability was needed; the mansion of Robert Ratclyffe still belonged to the late Gothic tradition, which we know from surviving buildings of the time such as Compton Winyates was a harmonious fusion of function with the forms of prestige. But over the next 100 years the piecemeal introduction of second-hand foreign styles, the break in tradition and the excessive wealth available to spend on building led to the erection of enormous structures which one can admire for their qualities of ambition and vitality, while recognising that they were often of unparalleled vulgarity. The parks which attended these piles preserved the appearance and manners of an earlier age relatively unchanged.

From the 1660s onwards land was accumulated by the territorial aristocracy which became increasingly powerful at the expense of the gentry. Views of their 'country seats' published by Kip, Knyff and Badeslade early in the 1700s provide an accurate and invaluable record of the development of the gardens and landscapes of major country houses of this time. The houses themselves represent evolution from the manor house of the late Middle Ages, through the hybrids of the Tudor and Jacobean period, to the more disciplined and reticent buildings of the later seventeenth century. The gardens are equal to the houses in their variety; some are clearly on their old manorial sites, surrounded by stables, orchards, dovecotes, fish-ponds, and occasionally, the parish church or Tudor mount [1], while newly planted courts with parterres, dense plantations and formal sheets of water knit the different elements into a rectilinear composition. Others are either on new sites or have swept away the older buildings and features, allowing a greater freedom to plan the gardens which are always geometric and formal. Beyond or around the house, with its garden complex, there is often the older landscape of the park with its scattered trees set in grassland, sometimes forming dense wood-pasture, sometimes open and, frequently, with trees clustering inside the pale to make an enclosing belt. At Bradgate, Leicestershire, Knyff shows an Arcadian landscape of groves and glades rising on a hill above the house and its garden, a relic of the Middle Ages.

The grander houses show straight avenues of young trees stretching out from the gardens to impose an ordered pattern of vistas on the informal parkland. This reflects continental influence but also the passion for tree planting which gradually became a characteristic of English estates from the late seventeenth century onwards. Social and political upheavals had considerably reduced the carefully nurtured reserves of structural timber; the Crown had sold rights in the royal forests for felling without requirements to manage and restock and the

1. A description of an early Tudor garden complex survives in a survey of Thornbury Castle, Gloucestershire, which was drawn up following its confiscation by Henry VIII in 1521. The unfortunate owner had lived and built too well, arousing royal envy, a similar misfortune to that which later befell Fouquet, builder of Vaux-le-Vicomte. There was a small inner knot garden and a larger garden beside the castle with high embattled walls. Alongside, a large orchard was full of newly grafted fruit trees well laden, many roses and other pleasures, and many alleys with resting places (bowers) covered with whitethorn and hazel. A further orchard was enclosed with sawn palings, quickset hedges and ditches. Further beyond was the park, newly created and containing many hedgerows of thorn and great elms – clearly a landscape of small fields from which the tillers had been excluded. Except for the knots, the essential informality of garden, orchards and park conform with illustrations which survive of late medieval domestic landscaping.

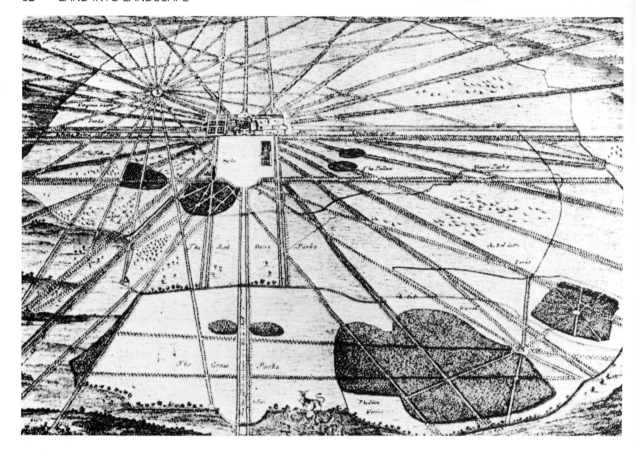

Fig. 5.2 Kip's view of Badminton, Gloucestershire.

Commonwealth, with similar improvidence, had sold off the forests and temporary encumbents of estates and livings under Commonwealth rule had felled the valuable timber of woodland, park and hedgerow for an immediate cash return. In the 1660s fears were roused that the supply of oak would soon be insufficient for maintaining the fleet and henceforward the growing of timber became a patriotic duty as well as a sound investment [2].

Two of the most interesting of Kip's engravings show the park at Badminton in Gloucestershire. It encompasses a great area and its boundary, sometimes sinuous and sometimes zigzag, suggests that it was demesne land originally abutting the small enclosures and strips of the manorial tenants. Within, there are irregular boundaries, probably reflecting stages in the park's expansion and providing divisions for the management of different kinds of deer. Blocks of woodland, also irregular in outline, are survivals of the manorial economy and contrast with new plantations which are circular and placed strategically on or beside avenues. Overall is imposed a network of newly planted avenues, radiating from the house or extending the lines of the formal gardens and orchards, the regimented lines of young trees contrasting with the informal scatter of ancient parkland trees. The whole landscape is a palimpsest of evolution in which the newest element, the avenues, would shortly be swept away by a change of taste.

Historically the gardens depicted in Kip's engravings have considerable interest, for virtually all would be altered out of recognition

2. In fact the fears proved groundless and difficulties lay in organisation and transport rather than supply. But the myth of ancient forests despoiled of oaks to maintain the fleet remains as persistent and erroneous as that of the reuse of ships' timbers in building (O. Rackham: *Trees and Woodlands in the British landscape*, 1976). The problems of the late seventeenth century derived from improvident management of resources, felling with little thought for replenishment. A similar situation occurred following the First World War when many woodlands changed hands and all trees of timber value were felled, followed by total neglect; natural regeneration under traditional management techniques would by now have made good the loss had this course been followed.

Much of the interest in woodlands and trees apparent in the last half of the seventeenth century was generated by John Evelyn's *Sylva, or a Discourse on Forest Trees*, a manual on the planting and management of woods and trees which achieved a wide readership and remained the standard work on the subject for 150 years. Evelyn loved nature and its irregularities and was never fully converted to the French fashion for rigid symmetry – his name deservedly remains preeminent in the history of British silviculture and arboriculture.

or wholly destroyed by subsequent changes of fashion. But judged as designs, the impression is one of total reliance on styles evolved abroad, principally France and, after the accession of William III, the Netherlands, when acres of topiary became the vogue. A dependent industry arose with a strong vested interest in promoting imported styles, notably the partnership of London and Wise, authors of an 'improved' version of *The Compleat Gardener*, John Evelyn's translation of the work of la Quintinye. Wise became royal gardener and together they dominated the scene during the years around 1700, securing influential patrons and huge commissions realised with plants supplied from their own nursery. When he died in 1738 it was said that Wise left £200,000. By this time the style he promoted was in disfavour, landscape and garden design followed very different aims.

A revolution had taken place in both the philosophy and applied design of landscape, apparently in a relatively short space of time but the underlying factors – a love of nature, an appreciation of the vision of the Latin poets and a desire to work with the Genius Loci rather than impose upon it – were not new. Direct observation of the forms of nature is evident in the carved decoration of Gothic buildings, notably the flower and leaf capitals at Southwell Minster. Appreciation of nature, husbandry and the seasons pervade Chaucer's work and in Shakespeare there are constant references to wild plants, notably the

Fig. 5.3 *Leyton Grange in the County of Essex, the Seat of David Gansel Esq. who Designed and Executed it himself.*

This engraving of *c.* 1720 shows another site where ornamental formal planting appears to overlie an older park. The home farm and fruit and vegetable gardens still have pride of place next to the house, and in the distance earlier fish-ponds adjoin a formal lake.

This attractive landscape is typical of those ruthlessly altered and partly erased by the change in fashion later in the century.

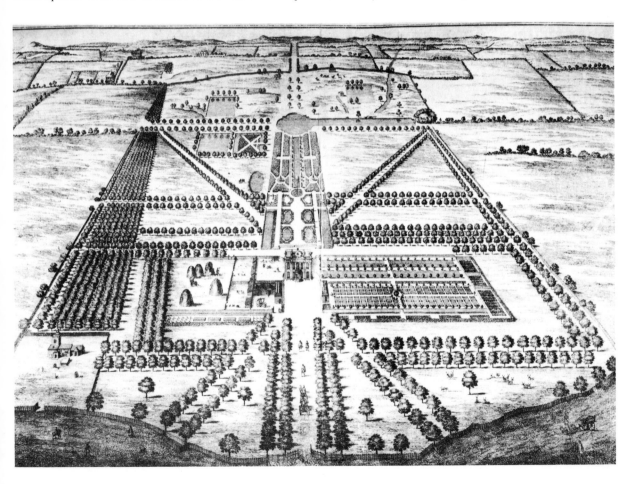

description of Titania's bower and Ophelia's fatal expedition to collect wild flowers. The artificialities of the formal garden did not appeal to the finer minds of the age who retained their regard for the natural. In Thomas More's garden, rosemary romped over the walks, feeding his bees and bringing thoughts of remembrance and friendship – qualities to which the herb was sacred. More had purchased the land beside the Thames at Chelsea, which allowed him swift access to London by water for his duties as Chancellor; with its flowers, fruit trees and views of the river, meadows and wooded hills, his garden was a place of marvellous beauty. Francis Bacon described his ideal garden a century later in *On Gardens* (1625), in which a heath or wilderness covered 2½ of the overall 12 hectares. His scheme included elaborate architectural features and a mount, but he eschewed 'knots, or figures with divers coloured earths' as toys, better seen as tarts – which recall the later censures of William Robinson on the pastry-work gardening of the Victorian parterre.

More and Bacon represent a strain of common sense as well as sensitivity, although the extremes of artificiality with the banishment of useful arts from the garden were to occur after their time in the late seventeenth century. But by then the days of such excesses were already numbered. A pastoral landscape, balanced and at peace, formed the setting for Bunyan's Delectable Mountains, the paradise on Earth where Immanuel's shepherds prepare pilgrims for their last ordeal – the crossing of the dark river to obtain entry to the Celestial City. In the 1660s a new imagery of Eden combining the scenery of traditional parkland with that of classical Arcadia found expression in Milton's *Paradise Lost*, a work destined to be a potent and lasting influence on attitudes to landscape and indeed, later described by Horace Walpole as the poetic inspiration of English landscape design. Leadership was passing to the poets and men of letters, Pope, Addison and Steel would follow, new patrons would appear to commission and direct new landscapes, and the architects and designers to implement them. In the 30 years between 1715 and 1745 England was to become a cauldron of philosphical, pictorial, literary and architectural ideas applied to landscape, and the resources and practical competence were there to implement them.

Milton and Pope

Milton's Paradise must be the most compelling description of a divine landscape in the English language. T. S. Eliot once commented, rather unkindly, that it is evident from its imagery that *Paradise Lost* was the work of a blind man, and this disadvantage certainly accounts for the lack of familiar detail that gives conviction, for example to the landscape paintings of the great Flemings. But, equally, it accounts for the idealised sweeping vision, unfettered by mundane considerations, its sense of wonder; the landscape of childhood and youth recalled in its essence by a blind poet in his later years. Hence, perhaps its sense of distance and remoteness, but also its familiarity, being based on remembered imagery of the English scene. Exotic trees, animals and birds grace the landscape of Eden, but underlying all are the lineaments of the traditional informal hunting park, the contribution of a northern temperate climate with its rich verdure and noble broad-leaved trees to the paradise tradition.

Milton describes Adam's awakening to a world unsullied by sin and the ill effects of the dominion of his progeny. It is a landscape vision similar to that of Virgil's primeval world and the comparison is relevant, for Milton was an accomplished classical scholar. The vision of the Roman poet was known well to this late humanist and the connection between Virgil's Golden Age and Milton's Earthly Paradise is a direct one and not coincidental. The description of Adam's first impression and arrival in Eden is as follows:

> A woodie Mountain; whose high top was plaine,
> A circuit wide, enclos'd, with goodliest trees
> Planted, with Walks, and Bowers, that what I saw
> Of Earth before scarce pleasant seem'd.

A fuller description of the approach to Paradise and the garden within accompanies Satan's arrival in the Fourth Book. He sees the slopes as a steep wilderness of overgrown thicket, grotesque and wild [3]. Towards the summit the dense wilderness gives way to woodlands to cedar, pine, fir and branching palm, but above them towers the 'verdurous wall' of Paradise, itself overtopped by trees laden with blossom and fruit. The air is so pure it inspires the heart with joy and delight, driving away all sadness and despair. Satan leaps over the thicket, woods and wail, and alights in the garden. In the guise of a cormorant he flies to the middle and rests in the branches of the Tree of Life, the highest tree of all, laden with ambrosial fruit. From here he surveys Nature's whole wealth contained within the confines of the garden. The noblest trees for sight, smell and taste, groves of odorous gums and balms, trees with golden fruit and, nearby, the source of man's Fall and expulsion: the fateful Tree of Knowledge. Water rises in a fountain, spreads in rills to water the garden and then descends to join the great river that passes through the Land of Eden, underneath the mountain [4].

Between the groves are lawns and level downs grazed by flocks, hillocks of palms, valleys verdant with flowers and thornless roses, dark grottoes and caves overhung with luxuriant vines, and murmuring waters and pools. Milton compares this landscape with that of Pan dancing with the Graces and the Hours and with the renowned scenes described by the Latin poets: the fields of Enna where Proserpine was seized by Dis, the sweet grove of Daphne and the renowned Castalian Spring, but these are not its equal. The beasts of the earth that have subsequently become wild and live in the wilderness or forest, here frisk and play [5].

Satan espies the first man and woman:

> Of living Creatures new to sight and strange:
> Two of far nobler shape erect and tall,
> Godlike erect, with native Honour clad
> In naked Majestie seemd Lords of all,
> and worthie seemd, for in thir looks Divine
> The image of thir glorious Maker shon. . . .
> So hand in hand they passd, the lovliest pair
> That ever since in loves imbraces met,
> Adam the goodliest man of men since born
> His Sons, the fairest of her daughters Eve.

3. ... so thick entwined, As one continu'd brake, the undergrowth
Of shrubs and tangling bushes has perplext
All path of Man and Beast that past that way:
One gate there only was, and that look'd East.
4. Which from his darksom passage now appears,
And now divided into four main streams,
Runs divers, wandring many a famous Realme
And Country whereof here needs no account,
But rather to tell how, if Art could tell,
How from that Saphire Fount the crisped Brooks,
Rowling on Orient Pearl and sands of Gold,
With mazie error under pendant shades
Ran Nectar, visiting each plant, and fed
Flours worthy of Paradise which not nice Art
In Beds and curious Knots, but Nature born
Powrd forth profuse on Hill and Dale and Plaine.
5. Sporting the Lion rampd, and in his paw
Dandl'd the Kid; Bears, Tygers, Ounces, Pards
Gambold before them, the unwieldy Elephant
To make them mirth us' all his might, and wreathd
His Lithe Proboscis.

So, true to the Judaic–Christian tradition, man and woman are created the superiors of the beasts, fashioned in the image of the divine being. But, with superiority, stewardship is expected and man has been placed in the garden with the duty to 'till and to keep it'. The world is anthropocentric, but not to be exploited.

Alexander Pope (1688–1744) was born 14 years after Milton's death. He loved landscapes and gardens and his keen imagination and capacity for clear analysis had a marked influence on the development of landscape design in Britain. His description survives (written in the early 1720s) of Sherborne in Dorset, which included a traditional hunting park, modified by gardens laid out before the Civil War and now mature.

> The house stands in a park crowned with very high woods on all the tops of the hills, which form a great amphitheatre sloping down to the house. On the garden sides the woods approach close, so that it appears there with a thick line and depth of groves on each hand, and so it shows from most parts of the park.

The gardens, although formal, are irregularly disposed, taking advantage of the sudden rises, falls and turns of the ground and of the views out, including the town of Sherborne in a valley, interspersed with trees. There are terraces, groves, a little wilderness filled with honeysuckle and cherry trees, a bowling green and a canal. Beyond is the natural river with green banks of turf above which rise terraces; a vineyard and then a wilderness with wild winding walks.

> When you are at the left corner of the canal and the chestnut groves in the bottom, you turn of a sudden under very old trees into the deepest shade. One walk winds you up by a hill of venerable wood over-arched by nature, and of a vast height, into a circular grove, on one side of which is a close high arbour, on the other a sudden open seat that overlooks the meadows and river with a large distant prospect. Another walk under this hill walks by the riverside quite covered with high trees on both banks, overhung with ivy, where falls a natural cascade with never-ceasing murmurs.

A bridge, built 'in ruinous state', crosses the stream and the ground rises past the Hermit's Seat to the highest terrace.

> On the left, full behind these old trees, which make this whole part inexpressibly awful and solemn, runs a little, old, low wall, beside a trench, covered with elder trees and ivies; which being crossed by another bridge, brings you to the ruins, to complete the solemnity of the scene.

These are the remains of a castle, with towers, pillars and arches 'through which the whole country appears in prospect'. Pope longs to landscape the ruins with evergreens, grass and parterres to create outdoor rooms and with seats placed to enjoy the views 'which are more romantic than imagination can form them'. He also envisages a little temple placed on a neighbouring round hill which is seen from all points of the garden and would make a fine termination to the river as seen from the deep scene by the cascade, appearing as in the clouds, framed by lofty trees forming an arch before it.

The account is interesting as a description of a mature garden and park of this time and it also gives an insight to the fertile imagination and perception of Alexander Pope, teeming with ideas while appreciating the best features and spirit of the place. So many elements in his description – the temple, cascade, ruined castle and bridges, and lofty trees framing the view – subsequently became commonplace and it requires an effort of imagination now to realise the originality and freshness of Pope's vision in the context of his time. But original it certainly was, and profoundly influenced his contemporaries when the private landscapes of the time were either the wood-pastures surviving from the past or the chopped and geometrical gardens reflecting contemporary fashions.

Pope's approach was empirical, analysing the particular qualities of a place and essentially different from both the 'bulldozer' attitude of Le Nôtre and that of Capability Brown 60 years later, in which an existing landscape would be dragooned to fit a preconceived concept. Pope valued the variety brought by enclosure, surprise and views outwards, and there is no distinct boundary between formal gardens and park. He reacted emotionally to different scenes, using words such as 'awful', 'solemn' and 'romantic'. Variety and contrast is also evident in his appreciation of formal gardens against parkland and a bowling green in the same overall landscape as a wilderness and area of elder and ivy. A historical dimension is noted and expanded; the crumbling ruins of the castle and bridges, the Hermit's Seat, ancient trees and Pope's wish to place an Arcadian temple on the hill contrasting, again, formal architecture with the informal shapes of 'nature'. There is no attempt to seclude this landscape from the outside world of which it remains a part; the view of Sherborne is valued and also the distant prospects from particular viewpoints.

Pope believed that 'the amiable simplicity of unadorned nature was the taste of the ancients in their gardens [6]. He wrote, summarising his philosophy, 'all the rules of gardening are reducible to three heads: the contrasts, the management of surprises, and the concealment of the bounds. I have expressed them in these verses:'

> He gains all who pleasingly confounds
> Surprises, varies, and conceals the bounds.

But there was far more to Pope's landscape philosophy than these succinct and elegant lines. His 2-hectare garden in Twickenham (begun in 1719) became a focus of interest for a new approach to landscape design and when he invited William Kent to advise on the design of fountains and pavilions Kent may have been the beneficiary in terms of originality and ideas.

The reign of the Whigs

Pope has been quoted because his influence was seminal in the early years of the English landscape school, but other personalities must be considered as thinkers who influenced events, patrons and practical men who implemented the ideas of the age. With the advantage of distance the school divides into two periods. The earlier period, ending with the deaths of its leading figures in the 1740s, gave way to the second in 1751 when Lancelot Brown, dominant figure of the later phase, set up his practice in London. The former is notable for the

6. *The Guardian*, 1713

variety and inventiveness of ideas and eagerness to experiment, the latter for the opposite: the age of the 'package deal' and preconceived solution. This section concerns the first phase, termed the 'reign of the Whigs', for Whig thinking, poets, artists and aristocratic patrons set the standards for the arts as Whig oligarchs dominated the polity of the realm [7]. Landscape design in this phase divides into four main lines of development: the first might be termed 'formal survival' in which Bridgeman and Vanbrugh sought to come to terms with a new and freer approach, secondly the picturesque of William Kent, thirdly the literary approach realised at Painshill and Stourhead, and lastly the *ferme ornée*. This division is one of convenience, and no line is exclusive.

Before considering specific landscapes, it is essential to explore the political scene that fostered an approach to landscape design radically different from that of the European mainstream. Dislike of France and its social order led the Whigs to re-examine their own cultural ideals and to evolve an alternative philosophy of art and architecture, and, as a result, landscape design [8]. Dislike of Catholicism and the Counter-Reformation predisposed the Whig establishment to an appreciation of the work of Milton. Republican and Puritan, he is none the less represented in the pantheon of British Worthies at Stowe.

The social and aesthetic philosophy was supplied by the writings of the third Earl of Shaftesbury. In *Characteristics* (1711) he wrote that harmony, balance and proportion are the ultimate foundations of morality and beauty. The same principles governed ethics and the arts, and the taste of the cultivated man expressed them both in his conduct and his appreciation of the arts. Judgement for the man of breeding and politeness must be based on the right models: in ethics, the writings of Antiquity and, in the arts, the remains of the Roman world. Shaftesbury hoped for the development of a new 'national taste' to improve the arts and industry, and this would be based on Roman and Italian models, not French. Travel in Italy became an essential part of the education of a young Whig, as a result of Shaftesbury's teaching.

Shaftesbury had strong views on landscape: wild nature has a 'magnificence beyond the mockery of princely gardens', he wrote in the *Moralists* (1709); the primitive state unspoilt by man expresses genuine and divine order. He cites 'rude rocks, the mossy caverns, the irregular unwrought grottoes and the broken falls of water, with all the horrid graces of the wilderness itself', all as first created, without fault. This 'passion for things of a natural kind' related to the scientific discoveries of the time, new telescopes revealing the ordered courses of the stars and planets, and microscopes showing the structure of organisms invisible to the naked eye. Newton's physics demonstrated the concept of the balanced and immutable 'clockwork' universe as one vast mechanism, reassuring Shaftesbury in his 'idea of Sense, Order, Proportion everywhere'. Thus, carefully selected examples of apparently unspoiled nature that appealed romantically to a temperament reacting from applied formalism could be justified as examples of divine order. The concept is almost as foreign in its way as that of Le Nôtre to the recognition of ordered husbandry as the union of man with the divine. Shaftesbury was by no means alone in his view of nature. A few years earlier Joseph Addison (1672–1719) had written reflections on his travels in Italy, where he admired the smoking plain

7. By the 1700s the Whigs had evolved far from the vicious faction of the 1670s. The new generation was cultured and aristocratic and dedicated to prevent the emergence of absolute monarchy in the British Isles. The political coup of 1714 established a constitutional monarchy and the failure of the revolts of 1715 and 1745 confirmed it. Voltaire lived in England from 1726 to 1729 and, smarting from his imprisonment in the Bastille without trial for challenging a nobleman, was confronted by the prospect of a 'free, animated and cultured people'. Astonished, he wrote that England had the lineaments of a free and happy society, where a man was free to say or publish what he liked and there was no torture or arbitrary imprisonment; 'an Englishman goes to heaven by the road he pleases'. Montesquieu, writing at the same time, declared England to be the freest country in the world, because 'the sovereign, whose person is controlled and limited, is unable to inflict any imaginable harm on anyone'. One might comment in the manner of *1066 and All That*: 'except for the common people', but England of the early eighteenth century was undoubtedly advanced by international standards in respect for the individual.

A remarkable product of Whig culture was the coterie known as the Kit-Cat club who met regularly to dine and exchange ideas. It included the oligarch politicians who ran the country, such as the Dukes of Newcastle and Grafton, Henry Pelham, Lord Cobham the creator of Stowe, the poet Alexander Pope, John Vanbrugh and the writers Steele and Addison. Such a gathering on terms of social equality would have been inconceivable in any other European country at that time.

8. An analysis of the historical and philosophical basis for English planned landscapes is contained in the late Christopher Hussey's introductions to *The Work of William Kent* (M. Jourdain, 1948) and *Capability Brown* (D. Stroud, 1950).

on the summit of Vesuvius. Most of all he was pleased by the Roman Campagna ...

> ... where the eye loses itself on a smooth, spacious plain. On the other side is a more broken and interrupted scene, made up of an infinite variety of inequalities and shadowings, that naturally arise from an agreeable mixture of hills, groves and valleys. But the most enlivening part of all is the river Teverone, which you see at about a quarter of a mile's distance, throwing itself down a precipice, and falling by several cascades from one rock to another, till it gains the bottom of the valley, when the sight of it would be quite lost, did it not discover itself through the breaks and openings of the woods that grow about it. The Roman painters often work upon this landscape.

Addison would have seen the works of Claude and Poussin and the painter Salvator Rosa, who more specifically depicted the landscape around Rome, all of whom were avidly sought by English *cognoscenti* and were to exercise a considerable influence on the English landscape scene.

The conceptual framework for a new approach to landscape deriving from his own observations, was developed by Addison in *The Spectator* (No. 414, 25 June 1712).

> Our trees rise in cones, globes and pyramids. We see the mark of the scissors upon every plant and bush. I do not know whether I am singular in my opinion, but for my own part, I would rather look upon a tree in all its luxuriancy and diffusion of boughs and branches, than when it is thus cut and trimmed into a mathematical figure: and cannot but fancy that an orchard in flower looks definitely more delightful than all the little labyrinths of the most finished parterre.

The Spectator was short-lived, ceasing publication in 1712, but in collaboration with Steele who shared his misgivings on the formality and extravagancies of contemporary gardening, he went on to found *The Guardian*, publishing in 1713 Pope's oft quoted *Catalogue of Greens* ridiculing topiary and the absurdities the craft had reached. At this stage antipathy to the French political system did not imply dislike of the gardens of Versailles or the approach of Le Nôtre; Addison admired the 'Grand and August' and Switzer writing in 1718 regarded Louis XIV as having brought gardening to the 'most magnificent Height and Splendour imaginable' although he eschewed political judgement on his motives. Essentially it was the Dutch style, with its neatness, artificiality and total reliance on the 'scissors', which Addison and Pope most disliked [9].

To Pope, the concealment of the bounds to unite the garden with the countryside was all important. Addison suggested the further step of extending the garden into the contiguous landscape: 'why may not a whole estate be thrown into a kind of garden by frequent plantations?' Stephen Switzer (1682-1745) was the first to put this concept into practice. At Grimsthorpe, the surrounding countryside with its cornfields, pastures, orchards and woodlands was the most important feature; there was still a formal area near the house (possibly an earlier feature) which Switzer enclosed, allowing the eye to concentrate on the wider scene. Unfortunately this important work, the first ex-

9. Both Addison and Pope developed their own gardens which reflected their personalities. Pope's garden at Twickenham applied the ideas latent in his inventive, fastidious and practical mind. 'Though containing but five acres, enclosed by three lanes, he had managed it with such art and deception, that it seemed a wood, and its boundaries were nowhere discoverable' – this is Horace Walpole's description before the garden was wrecked by 'improvement' in the manner of Lancelot Brown. Serpentine walks contrasted with formal plantings, although formal architecture was banished; a grotto formed the link to his house beneath the road from Hampton to London, and orangery, vineyard and kitchen garden were discreetly included in the layout. It is possible that this garden, since utterly lost, was the most important in terms of experiment and dissemination of ideas ever constructed in Britain. The regard in which Pope was held and its position near the capital would have ensured that everyone interested in landscape design and in a position to commission such works would have seen it.

Pope preferred his fame as a gardener to that as poet and man of letters; indeed, he neglected his writing for gardening. From 1718 until his death in 1744 he constantly experimented and altered his garden until finally, running out of space, he turned his attention underground, extending, elaborating and embellishing his grotto. For a description and history, see James Boutwood: 'Alexander Pope's garden at Twickenham', *Country Life*, Vol. CXLIII, No. 3705.

Addison's garden was a complete contrast and best described by himself: 'it is a confusion of kitchen and parterre, orchard and flower-garden, which lie so mixt and interwoven with one another, that if a foreigner should be conveyed into my garden at his first landing, he would look on it as a natural wilderness, and one of the uncultivated parts of our country'. He collected any flower that appealed to him and planted it, including those of hedgerows. His plantations emulated wilderness, and a small fountain in the highest part of the garden disappeared in a winding rivulet among the trees. Many later gardeners would have found in him a kindred spirit.

ample of the *ferme ornée*, has perished, but sketches by William Stu-
keley survive, recording its appearance in 1736 [10].

Switzer combined writing and theory with a thorough knowledge
of horticulture; he had worked under London and Wise at Blenheim,
had charge of the kitchen garden at St James's Palace, and ran his
own nursery garden. In *Ichnographia Rustica* he treats the immediate
surrounds of the house with formality, but flowers and topiary are to
be avoided and he would prefer a plantation of trees right up to the
walls of the house to borders worked in patterns. His views accord
closely with those of Pope and Addison; landscape schemes must submit to Nature rather than make Nature submit to them; ancient trees
should be respected and he regards with horror their felling 'to
humour the regular and delusive schemes of some Paper Engineers'.

'Formal survival' is characteristic of the landscape of Charles
Bridgeman, royal gardener from 1728 until his death in 1738. He
worked with Vanbrugh at Eastbury and Stowe, and his designs have
something of the breadth of vision and control that Vanbrugh
achieved in his buildings. Horace Walpole (the son of the Prime Minister Robert Walpole and our main source of information on landscape
designs of his time) describes Bridgeman as a designer of straight
walks with high-clipped hedges, although he banished topiary; 'the
rest he diversified by wilderness and loose groves of oak, though still
within surrounding hedges'. He is believed to have introduced the
sunken wall, or ha-ha, from France, which removed the visual barrier
between garden and landscape but prevented deer, cattle or sheep
from wandering up to the windows. A plan of 1739 survives of his
works at Stowe showing the balance he achieved between formal and
diffused spaces, the irregular and the ordered. The outer park consists
of great vistas cut through woodland and heath, straight but not forming a symmetrical pattern and, in counterpoint to this, a network of
serpentine paths linking open glades with scattered trees within. It
seems likely to be an adaptation of an earlier landscape; the outer park
is linked by an avenue to the separate home park which included the
gardens for the house, enclosed by a ha-ha. Peripheral avenues link
semicircular bastions (a Vanbrugh touch?) and a formal vista from
the house crosses an octagonal lake, linked to a larger irregular lake
on one side. Beside the vista, woodlands and groves contain winding
paths within a governing network of straight walks and avenues. It
is a tragedy that a Bridgeman landscape has not survived intact, there
is a splendour and consistency of vision in the few plans and remnants
surviving which suggest a rare imagination.

Stowe subsequently became renowned for its garden architecture,
structures with intense literary, romantic and sometimes political associations, expressed generally in classical forms: temples, obelisks,
bridges and urns in the manner and spirit of the paintings of Claude
and Poussin. Aesthetically the contrast of geometrical shapes with
their silvan setting is often breathtakingly beautiful (for example the
Temple of Ancient Virtue and the Palladian Bridge seen in the long
vista of the lake), less successful perhaps when a proliferation occurs
or Gothic structures attempted. Vanbrugh appears to have been the
pioneer of this new relationship between landscape and architecture.
He had designed isolated buildings at Castle Howard (begun in 1701):
a mausoleum, Tower of the Winds and a classical bridge [11]. At
Blenheim he sought unsuccessfully to persuade the Duchess of Marl-

10. W. A. Brogden: 'Stephen Switzer', *Furor Hortensis*,
P. Willis (ed.) (1974).
11. In 1732 Vanbrugh wrote of Castle Howard as 'the
Top Seat and Garden of England. Of the House I say
nothing; the other [the grounds] I may commend because Nature made them; I pretend to no more merit
than a Midwife, who helps bring a fine child into the
world, out of bushes, boggs and briars'.

borough to retain the remains of old Woodstock Manor as a picturesque ruin (1707) to enhance the park; the historical dimension had entered the planned landscape.

In spite of his Whig connections, Vanbrugh felt the force of a change in fashion in architecture. In 1712, Shaftesbury attacked the architectural establishment in his *Letter Concerning Design*, essentially against Wren, distrusting his command of mathematics and empirical use of baroque forms and against the imaginative genius of the younger Vanbrugh. His aims were realised in what is termed the Burlington House Group. The guiding hand seems to have been that of Lord Burlington himself, a man who enjoyed the company of artists (a trait Shaftesbury would have disapproved of), while having a grasp of the technicalities of architecture and a firm belief in the direction that architecture should take. He appears to have been converted early in his career to the architecture of Palladio, as expressed in his *Architettura* which gives examples of Palladio's own buildings and his reconstructions of Antiquity. He returned to Italy to study Palladio at first hand and met there William Kent, an eclectic but talented young artist, who became the instrument who put his patron's architectural ideas into effect. His success was astounding. For a generation the rule of Palladio, as interpreted in Burlington House, governed British architecture and for a further 70 years continued to exert a basic influence on the practice of the art; indeed, Palladianism had become almost synonymous with the term 'Georgian architecture'. Burlington's choice of a national mentor was a sure one. The baroque at its finest and most subtle, as in the work of Borromini, requires the bright light of Italy; moreover, baroque was associated in the Whig mind with Catholicism and with France. The grave manners of the north Italian appealed to the English temperament and the maritime city of Venice has always had a special attraction to a nation whose wealth and survival has depended on seafaring. The disciplined adaptation of Roman forms, applied by Palladio to traditional manor houses proved irresistible to the English and resulted in innumerable country houses that came to be seen as a specifically British contribution to the evolution of architecture [12]. But repetition and rules tend to unimaginative building and it must be recognised that many of the country houses that have been lost in recent years were neither great nor unexpendable by standards dispassionately arrived at. A disconcerting tendency of the Palladians was architectural inflation; the little manor house of Palladio, with its elegant portico and colonnades connecting granaries, stores, dairies and stables, became the huge country house with massive portico and base linked to wings housing chapel, library or guest suites. A visit to Palladio's houses after seeing the English mansions can come as a shock to one unprepared.

As often with a new movement, the early seminal works have a freshness that can still delight the later visitor, although aware, with hindsight, of the pedestrian mass to follow. So it is with Chiswick House, a villa begun in 1727 by Burlington and Kent, combining many elements of Palladio principally from the villas Capra and Malcontenta with delicacy and erudition. The gardens, and they are essentially gardens rather than a park, have suffered from age and a long period of neglect. In their original form they bore little relation to the traditional hunting park and derived from the Italian tradition, both

12. It was a reaction against the freedom of what can now be seen as a national school, paradoxically to further a 'national taste'. Shaftesbury wished for a more rigid canon in architecture, based on the rules of the Ancients laid down in Vitruvius and, more specifically, a return to the style of Inigo Jones as expressed in the many buildings he designed or was associated with before the Civil War. He deplored as false and counterfeit Wren's St Paul's and Hampton Court, and regarded the spires of the rebuilt city as a product of hasty and sudden growth, 'retaining too much of what artists call the Gothic kind'. Shaftesbury's reaction was successful, for the tide was in his favour and, subsequently, Wren lost his post with the Board of Works to a nonentity and both his buildings and friends became widely discredited.

of painting and gardens. What was new in the design was the network of serpentine woodland walks linking set scenes, conceived as paintings of temples, grottoes, fountains, cascades and obelisks, and it is this planned informality that must have seemed a striking innovation to his contemporaries, used to the symmetry of formal gardens [13]. The straight walks and canal which give an overriding discipline to Chiswick are probably the earlier work of Bridgeman, leaving the local scenes around the buildings and features to Kent, at this stage probably still feeling his way as a landscape designer.

Kent was aware of the value of contrasts of light and shade; evergreens, particularly yews, were planted to give a dark background to sculptures and buildings, or to finish a vista, and yew and myrtle were clipped to make semicircular alcoves with niches cut for statues or urns. It is all very Italian, as is the approach to the house, a scene of considerable magnificence, where noble and mature cedars now line the avenue framing the Roman cupola of the house. Below them are the stone statues and sphinxes placed there by Kent. It is a unique scene where one can recapture something of the vision and excitement of the early Palladian school [14].

In this early and adventurous phase of the English landscape school there was considerable variety of approach and scope for the individual to explore new concepts. The formal garden was not yet banished, nor was the landscape of husbandry excluded. In 1728 Batty Langley, the author of many treatises on building and architectural detail, published a manual on gardening which is probably a fair summary of the ideas current in his time. He included parterres, but condemned the strict formality that could involve the destruction of a noble oak and the expensive levelling that had hitherto destroyed the hills and valleys which are 'Beauties of Nature'. In the 'several parts of a beautiful Rural Garden' he includes walks, slopes, avenues, groves, wildernesses, labyrinths, winding valleys, dales, purling streams, cascades, grottoes, serpentine meanders, precipices and amphitheatres. In addition, he lists rude coppices, haystacks, small enclosures of corn, woodpiles and rabbit and hare warrens. Langley approved of mounts to give a view, raised from earth removed for foundations. The impression given is one of great variety of choice and of vitality – perhaps too much so.

The increasingly literary nature of landscape layout and architecture may seem alien to our own age and one needs constant reminders when considering eighteenth-century landscapes, that the Classical Age was regarded as the pinnacle of human achievement and that the works of the Latin poets and writers were familiar to all educated men. Following the examples of Chiswick and Stowe, temples and monuments evocative of classical scenes as interpreted in the paintings of Claude and Poussin became fashionable and their nuances were well understood and appreciated by contemporaries. Today most of us can only judge them as landscape features, for their literary and pictorial associations are largely obscure and in any case have little meaning in our own time.

The most famous of these Elysian designs are the gardens of Stourhead, created from 1740 to 1760 by the banker Henry Hoare, with temples designed by Henry Flitcroft. The site is that of an ancient hunting park in which Hoare dammed the stream and flooded the valley to create a lake, planting the steep surrounding slopes with

13. Serpentine paths had already appeared in Bridgeman's work at Stowe, and as early as 1698 in the plan for the Petit Parc at Versailles.

14. Chiswick House has been restored by the Department of the Environment to its appearance in Burlington's day, with later accretions removed, and work continues on the buildings and monuments which survive in the grounds, now a local park. Particularly successful has been the restoration of the Ionic Temple and its original setting, an amphitheatre around a pool and obelisk, with its slopes adorned with orange trees (now bays) in tubs.

A mass of contemporary paintings and prints, as well as the early drawings of Kent, are on view in the house, showing the original appearance of the gardens and their growth to semi-maturity. The cedars, which are now such a striking feature, were little more than small, formal evergreens during the eighteenth century, but the gardens had from the outset a wealth of mature and semi-mature trees, inherited from the grounds of the earlier Jacobean house and good use was made of them. Burlington and Kent did not begin with an open field, and this aspect of their 'received' landscape is typically ignored by writers on the subject.

Fig. 5.4 The ruins of the Classical Age, regarded as the pinnacle of human achievement. Piranesi's view of the Roman Forum from the Capitoline Hill where Edward Gibbon was inspired to write his *Decline and Fall of the Roman Empire.*

beech and conifers. A sequence including temples, pantheon, grotto and rock arch are placed around the lake, forming an allegory of man's passage through the world. But the subtleties of Stowe are not evident and the scene gives an uneasy sense of fancy dress bordering on the banal. It is not helped by the eclecticism of other features, a medieval cross (genuine), a Gothick cottage and, now lost, a Turkish tent. The garish horror of later planting follows – exotic conifers, rhododendrons and azalias – utterly alien to the imagery of Claude from which the design derives. Today it is one of the National Trust's most popular gardens, and it may be that the exotic planting is the main attraction; which puts the Trust in a dilemma: whether to pay regard to the intentions of Stourhead's creator and the integrity of his landscape, or to accept the judgement of the public expressed in the numbers of visitors. Stourhead today has little value for the landscape planner except as an example of the disasters that can befall an historic landscape. He would better view it through early paintings and drawings which depict a pastoral landscape of bewitching beauty [15].

The landscape farm

Stourhead is a descendant of Romance although its imagery (as first designed and intended) is classical; it is a huge enclosed garden, shel-

15. After a visit to Stourhead, I noted that giant gnomes should be erected to fish in the lake and that these would not be unworthy of the scene. Having seen early depictions of this landscape, this seems an unworthy statement, brought on by a surfeit of trees and plants alien to both Wiltshire and to Hoare's landscape. Yet these aliens are beautiful at Westonbirt Arboretum, not many miles distant from Stourhead, where they have been planted with taste and discernment as well as horticultural skill. But there is a fundamental difference between the paradisal aim of a fine arboretum and a Golden Age re-creation in the manner of Claude – the former can garner the riches of world flora, the latter must be selective. The National Trust have published an analysis with proposals. *The Conservation of the Gardens at Stourhead* (1978), which envisages partial restoration.

tered and protected from the world outside by wooded slopes and sky-lines. Its precise opposite is the landscaped farm, or *ferme ornée*, in which the functional and ideal landscapes form a unity, a concept conceived and expressed by Joseph Addison.

Addison's inspiration was Virgil, specifically the vision of husbandry in harmony with nature described in the *Georgics*: 'a Collection of the most delightful Landskips that can be made out of Fields and Woods, Herds of Cattle, and Swarms of Bees'. In his early years at Oxford he regularly walked among the fields, orchards and woods, and water meadows of the Thames and Cherwell which bounded the medieval town and university. His rooms at Magdalen overlooked the Water Walks to his constant delight [16]. In later years, writing in *The Spectator*, he recalled those days: the sequence of views along woodland rides opening on to the water, the profusion of birds on the banks and thickets of the river filling the woods with their song at sunrise, slumbering under the trees and listening to the lowing of the cattle. Addison, it seems, loved the sounds of the countryside as well as its pictorial qualities, the humming of the bees and bleating of sheep as well as the embroidery of wild flowers and glistening of dew. It is a dynamic, working landscape, not one re-created from pictures.

Later he created his own garden at Bilton, the antithesis of the Dutch style with its artificiality and reliance on 'scissors'. One suspects that Gertrude Jekyll would have felt at home there. In his own mind there were paradisal undertones: pleasure taken in gardens was one of the most innocent delights in life, for a 'Garden was the Habitation of our first Parents before the Fall'. At the same time he remained firmly practical; Virgil's landscape was productive as well as beautiful and respectful of the natural order, it was well managed and fruitful; similarly Addison saw the whole estate 'thrown into a kind of Garden' combining profit as well as pleasure – it was wrong to alienate land from pasturage and plough when all that was needed was carefully designed walks improved by 'some small Additions of Art' and such trees and flowers for which the soil was suitable to set off the hedges. The prospects were what mattered: fields of corn and the natural embroidery of the meadows.

Addison's ideas were followed by Switzer who freely acknowledged his debt to him 'one of the greatest Geniuses of this Age', and advocated the *ferme ornée* in *Ichnographia Rustica* as the truest and best way of gardening. This seemed to have the sanction of Antiquity, according with the plans of Pliny's villas at Laurentum and Tuscalum as reconstructed in Robert Castell's *The Villas of the Ancients Illustrated* (1728), as well as following the spirit of the *Georgics*.

Several gardens were designed on these lines, notably those of Philip Southcote and William Shenstone. In 1735 Southcote purchased Woburn Farm in the Thames valley and began improvements over its 60 hectares 'joined to the more simple delights of the country'; 14 hectares were set aside as a garden and adorned with trees, shrubs and flower borders, while the rest remained as a farm with dairy, haystack ('an agreeable circumstance in any position'), pasture and tillage, with clumps of trees added. The whole area surrounded by an ornamental walk with native hedgerows and odiferous herbs, embellished with Gothic ruins, seats, alcoves and ruins. There was a small menagerie and a serpentine lake for water-fowl, and the descriptions suggest that there was far too much attempted within its modest area to leave

16. Mavis Batey: *Oxford Gardens*. Avebury (1982) and 'The Magdalen meadows and the pleasures of imagination' *Garden History*, Vol. 9, No. 2 (1981).

much impression of a genuine working farm. The buildings alone constituted a collection and the trees an arboretum. Today's 'farm park' seems a more appropriate description than *ferme ornée*.

William Shenstone (1714–63), a poet in the pastoral manner, embarked on a scheme in 1743 at the Leasowes, a small farm near Birmingham. Without interfering with the practical conduct of the farm, he skilfully created a winding path across and around his hilly estate, with no less than thirty-nine seats carefully sited at points to enjoy a particular scene or prospect: a temple of Pan, a cataract, ruined priory and a distant glasshouse resembling a pyramid. Along the route were urns, obelisks and trophies, all engraved with appropriate verses for contemplation. The background of surrounding country was of hills diversified with woods, scenes of cultivation, and enclosures. Shenstone's farm was much admired in its time and it is tragic that it has not survived; indeed it was destroyed soon after his death. Certainly it appears to have been far more self-assured and skilful than Woburn. How far it succeeded in realising the ideals of Addison and Switzer we shall never know; but the description and a plan of 1764 suggest great sensibility and care in the design.

The Leasowes was the last serious attempt to unite husbandry and landscaping. Already the spirit of the age had moved away from the *Georgics* to the *Aeneid*, the source it seems for the imagery of Stourhead, a legendary never-never land from which husbandry was banished if ever known. The divorce of the functional and ideal had returned.

Rousham and Stowe

There are many parts of Britain, particularly outside the Midland zone, where the basic lineaments of the landscape – field boundaries and patterns, lanes and trackways, woodlands and the sites of farmsteads – are those of the Middle Ages or even earlier times. Much modified landscapes elsewhere, including arable East Anglia, often retain functional features of great antiquity. Even in the planned landscapes of the Midlands, fields established by late enclosure may follow the lines of earlier furlongs. There is a great persistence of early features for those who look for them, which is perhaps not surprising; property boundaries have changed little until recent years, field divisions often reflect major changes in soil type and woodlands occupy the least productive soil. Compared with the relative stability of the functional landscape, the ideal landscapes of planned gardens and parks have proved highly vulnerable; the solid, architectural features may survive, as at Montacute, Chiswick and Stourhead, but the planting is frequently subject to every vicissitude – age and death, neglect, ignorance, changes in fashion, and the introduction of plants anachronistic to the site. Even on sites where the built structures are responsibly cared for, the decisions on planting may be delegated to a gardener untrained in an awareness of history or, worse, a local committee 'doing the right thing'. Too often planting does not matter and is regarded as a matter for individual taste.

Most seminal and important works have been lost or altered out of recognition: Pope's garden and Shenstone's Leasowes were wrecked soon after the deaths of their creators: Shenstone's through vandalism and neglect, Pope's through a change of fashion. Fortunately two planned landscapes of great importance and quality have survived and

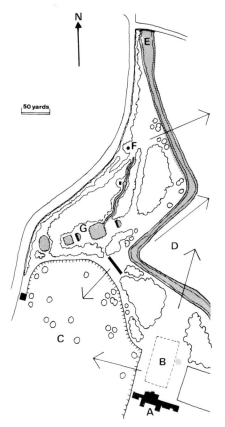

Fig. 5.5 Plan of Rousham House, Oxfordshire: (A) Rousham House; (B) bowling green; (C) Rousham Park; (D) water meadows; (E) Heyford Bridge (late 13th century); (F) Townesend's Temple of Echo; (G) Venus' Vale; (H) Praeneste.

the intentions of their designers respected and maintained. These are Rousham and Stowe.

Rousham is an Elysium, hidden on a steeply contoured terrace of the Cherwell from the miles of uneventful late enclosure farmland which stretches northwards from Oxford. Age has dealt kindly and Rousham is maintained with sensitivity by the descendants of its creator, General Dormer. It was first landscaped by Bridgeman, who planted extensively around 1721. In the late 1730s, when Bridgeman's landscape was maturing, Kent remodelled the gardens into a series of picturesque scenes, adorned by architecture and statuary, and intended to be seen as a sequence of surprises. Fortunately a letter survives from John McClary, the head gardener who carried out the works, describing the sequence and route intended with detailed descriptions of the planting [17]. There are the specific scenes: Venus' Vale, Praeneste and the watery walk with its rill – perhaps an echo of the spring in Addison's garden. A drawing of Kent's shows Venus' Vale as he intended, the rustic masonry of the cascades far larger than built and Bridgeman's trees thinned to give an informal effect reminiscent of Claude. In the background conifers give added distance with their dark foliage.

The circuit walk which leads to and through enclosed and planned scenes opens to include views which visually unite the garden with the countryside. First it includes the park with its cattle and deer, separated discreetly by Bridgeman's ha-ha. Enclosure follows, with a high wall bounding the peripheral road, densely screened by planting, then opening to reveal views over the valley and meadows of the Cherwell, the river itself a watery ha-ha, and the prospects focused on a distant eye-catcher erected by General Dormer by agreement with his neighbour to Kent's design. Thus Rousham combines the picturesque developed by Kent with Addison's walks overlooking the productive countryside, both approaches carefully controlled within Pope's theory of concealment and surprise – all within the small area of some 10 hectares, made seemingly much greater by inclusion of views over the surrounding landscape. Here in a nutshell, as it were, survives the essence of what was best and most inventive in the ideal landscapes of the first half of the eighteenth century. One senses a guiding hand and, although no record survives, Pope's imagination and breadth of vision seem to lie behind the overall design of Rousham, leaving his friend Kent to compose the set scenes. This would accord with Walpole's opinion that Pope had done much to influence Kent's taste, and Pope had practical gardening experience which Kent lacked.

Today Rousham has a magical beauty; wild flowers, huge carp and swarms of dragonflies inhabit the pools and lawns of Venus' Vale, suggesting that the goddess herself has once again become a rustic deity protecting the herbs and wildlife of her chosen locus. Elegant longhorns graze and browse the park. It is a place which Julian, the philosopher emperor, might have chosen for its pleasing solitude, as Walpole aptly suggested over 200 years ago.

We do not know the extent to which General Dormer may have influenced the design of Rousham and how far he was content to leave it to those he employed or consulted. At Stowe it is clear that the owners were more than interested patrons and played a guiding role throughout the evolution of the gardens over some 60 years. This timespan gave scope for second and even third thoughts: buildings were

17. Mavis Batey: 'The way to view Rousham by Kent's gardener', *Garden History*, Vol. 11, No. 2 (1983).

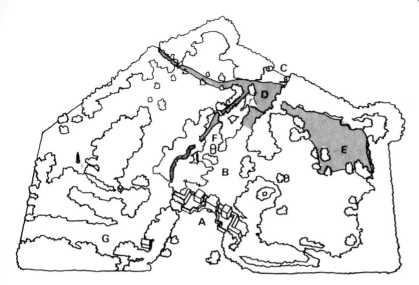

Fig. 5.6 The gardens at Stowe, adapted from Desmadryl's bird's-eye view of 1777: (A) Stowe House; (B) site of Bridgeman's parterres. Converted to lawns by Temple to be in scale with the new South Front. In the longer term the lawns provided the foreground in the long view from the portico over the Octagon Lake to the Corinthian Arch (Fig. 5.7); (C) Vanbrugh's two lakeside pavilions, originally built in 1717 and rebuilt further apart in 1764 (Fig. 5.8); (D) Bridgeman's octagonal lake altered to give an irregular outline; (E) Eleven Acre Lake; (F) the Elysian Fields; (G) the Grecian Valley.

moved or reconstructed, woodlands planted, thinned, reorganised or replanted, lakes extended and altered in shape. Cobham and Temple, the owners over this long period, had the means to employ the finest artists of the time, but it was their pursuit of excellence, of knowing their land constantly and intimately, that gave Stowe the particular quality of a masterpiece that has been slowly and carefully wrought.

When Lord Cobham, a distinguished soldier, inherited Stowe from his father it was a late seventeenth-century house with formal gardens stretching southwards towards the watercourse which would later be turned into lakes. With the conclusion of the wars against Louis XIV he turned his mind to politics and improving his estate, engaging Bridgeman to redesign the gardens and enclose them together with the Home Park and further land to the east within a peripheral belt

Fig. 5.7 View from the South Front.

Fig. 5.8 The Octagon Lake with the lakeside pavilions and Corinthian Arch.

of formal avenues and ha-ha, linking the semicircular bastions already referred to. Walking the perimeter beside the ha-ha, views of the surrounding countryside would be uninterrupted, but from within the gardens the effect of the avenues would be of almost total visual enclosure, only the view over the countryside northwards from the house remaining open. Work proceeded on landscaping the central area south of the house to the Octagon Lake and around the Home Park to the west, designed in the semi-formal manner characteristic of Bridgeman.

In the 1730s Kent was engaged to design buildings for the gardens, two of which, the Temples of Ancient Virtue and British Worthies, lie beside the winding lake in the gently contoured valley known as the Elysian Fields. This area could not be landscaped until soon after 1730 when the old approach road was diverted outside the grounds [18]. The subtlety of the ground modelling and planting, and the elimination of lines were a new departure at Stowe, and the contrast with the former planning of the adjacent areas must have been striking at the time, although now much softened by age and later modifications. The Grecian Valley, extending the grounds to the north-east, followed this approach.

This marked development has usually been ascribed to Kent, but it may owe much to Cobham himself, applying the ideas of his circle

18. L. Whistler, M. Gibbon and G. Clarke: *Stowe: a Guide to The Gardens*. Stowe School (1974).

to landscape design. The late Christopher Hussey described Stowe, under Cobham, as the capital seat of Grand Whiggery, the geographical and artistic centre of the cult of humane and political liberty subscribed to by the supporters of the Elder Pitt. Hussey saw this spirit as undoubtedly influencing Cobham's 'progressive loosening, with Kent's help, of Bridgeman's landscape design into harmony with the age's humanism, its faith in disciplined freedom, its respect for natural qualities, its belief in the individual whether man or tree, and its hatred of tyranny whether in politics or plantations'. The process of loosening was continued after Cobham's death in 1749 by his nephew, Lord Temple. A plan of 1753 [19] shows the $4\frac{1}{2}$ hectare lake with irregular outline and informal thinning and planting of the trees around the Home Park. While the intimacy of the Elysian Fields was retained, the landscape as a whole was simplified and broadened in scale; the gardens immediately to the south of the house had been transformed into a wide lawn. Temple's masterstroke followed, creating a vista from the south portico to the Corinthian Arch (1765) on the crest of the facing hill 1 kilometre away. Flanking woodlands doubled the apparent size of the grounds and Vanbrugh's two lake pavilions were moved apart to accord with the greater scale [20].

Happily, from Temple's death in 1779 until its acquisition in 1923 as the setting for a new public school, Stowe slumbered intact through an age when its qualities were little regarded. Its renaissance as the

Fig. 5.9 The Temple of Ancient Virtue, designed by Kent *c.* 1734, in the Elysian Fields.

Fig. 5.10 The Palladian Bridge, Stowe.

19. G. Bickham the Elder: *Views of Stowe* (1753).
20. As noted later, this phase of Stowe coincided with the achievement of wider horizons in British rule. The reality of empire was achieved by the Elder Pitt, but it had long been discussed by him and other leading Whigs at Stowe. There is perhaps a parallel between the fields of Stowe and British victories overseas, with Wellington's dictum on the fields of Eton and Waterloo. There is certainly a paradox when one considers Whig hatred of tyranny.

grandest ever Philosophers' Garden coincided with a new appreciation of eighteenth-century values; buildings, necessary for the school, have been sited with care and works of restoration – a fearsome burden – steadily pursued.

Stowe is 'Grand and August' in a manner that would gain the admiration of Addison and Switzer. It represents humanist ideals reflected in a re-creation of the landscape of Arcadia before tyranny, 'mad aggression and lust for gain' debased both man and nature. It also reflects the paradise tradition, seeking once more to raise Nature to her primal state of perfection as intended before man's Fall; indeed, it can be seen as Milton's Paradise, with its verdant grass and noble trees fused with the primeval, ideal landscapes of the Latin poets.

Chapter 6

Later British landscapes

The productive countryside

The mid eighteenth century was the threshold of what is termed the Agricultural Revolution, when the techniques of farming developed over the previous 200 years by progressive landowners interested in agricultural improvement, came to be accepted by most farmers and owners. New rotations, crops, implements, machinery and selective livestock breeding demanded a new pattern of husbandry and landholding over those wide tracts of central England where open-field farming still thrived. In areas of 'ancient countryside' where holdings had been consolidated earlier into compact farms or where open-field farming had never been the rule, the changes were accommodated relatively easily into the existing pattern of hedged fields (the greens and commons were another matter), but in central England the transformation wrought by parliamentary enclosure was drastic in its alteration of the face of the countryside and in the prospects and fortunes of its inhabitants – between 1750 and 1850 nearly 1 million hectares of farmland were enclosed and over 800,000 hectares of common pasture and heathland [1]. In their place a new landscape emerged of square fields, straight roads and occasional spinneys planted as game coverts; compared with the landscape of early enclosure which evolved over centuries, it appears hurried, often insensitive to topography, and smacks of the surveyor's tee-square. Today, these landscapes have acquired the irregularities of age and one regrets their loss to new 'open-field' landscapes.

Opinions may differ as to the social effects of the enclosure movement. Most will agree that the yeoman farmer benefited with the consolidation of his holdings, and the elimination of balks between the strips and headlands brought more land into cultivation; productivity rose. But the cottagers undoubtedly suffered; meagrely compensated for their rights to graze cows and geese on the commons, and customary rights such as gathering furze on the heaths, they became a class of landless labourers if they stayed, workers in the 'dark Satanic mills' of the Industrial Revolution if they left, as many did.

Thus the complex human ecology of the countryside was simplified; basically to landlord, tenant farmer, and labourer, a storehouse of social conflict to come when the native farming economy declined. Gone

1. W. G. Hoskins: *English Landscapes* (1973), pp. 77–86; E. C. K. Gonner: *Common Land and Inclosure* (1912).

was the largely self-sufficient peasant democracy of the English Midlands where village assembly or manorial court planned the crops, sowing and harvesting on behalf of the community [2].

Enclosure landscapes of this time demonstrate the relentless trend towards the exclusive and private ownership of land, unencumbered by customary rights, and towards single rather than multiple use of the countryside and its features. For example, the botanically rich hedgerow of ancient enclosure was a fence and often a boundary; it provided shelter, fruits and nuts such as elderberry, hazel, blackberry and hips, and protein in the form of small birds to add to the meagre diet of the countryman. It was a source of fuel – until recent times a farm worker would be given a length of hedge to 'face up' or coppice and the firewood cut warmed him through the winter. The hedgerow trees gave shade to cattle and, on roadsides, to the traveller; they also produced timber and firewood. The trees – usually oak, elm or ash – were managed either as pollards or standards. The surveyor's hedgerows of parliamentary enclosure are botanically poor, consisting solely of hawthorn with occasional ash or elm introduced to grow up as timber. They are essentially fences and little more. The social economy reflected in the management of woodlands illustrates a similar trend [3].

Poets traditionally attend the Ascendancy for their livelihood and there were none to record and lament the open fields. However, John Clare (1793–1864) saw the destruction of the commons in his native Helpstone and this must have been a factor contributing to his later derangement. Looking back to his boyhood, he saw this landscape as Paradise destroyed:

> I sat beside the pasture stream
> When Beautys self was sitting by
> The fields did more than Eden seem
> Nor could I tell the reason why.

Enclosure came and Clare recorded it in *Remembrances*; like Virgil he understood the countryside and its creatures as only a true countryman can, deploring the destruction of freedom to roam and the annihilation of wildlife.

> By Langley bush I roam but the bush has left its hill
> On Cowper green I stray tis a desert strange and chill.
> And spreading lea close oak ere decay had penned its will
> To the axe of the spoiler and self interest fell a prey
> And Crossberry way and old round oaks narrow lane
> With its hollow trees like pulpits I shall never see again
> Inclosure like a buonaparte let not a thing remain
> It levelled every bush and tree and levelled every hill
> And hung the moles for traitors – though the brook is running
>   still
> It runs a naked stream cold and chill.

Faced with the consciousness of dispossessing virtually a whole class from their livelihood, knowing of the Highland clearances and the exploitation of the Irish peasants by absentee landlords, it is not surprising that the landholding oligarchy turned its back on the functional landscape, preferring the land of an imagined Arcadia. In this context the unity sought earlier by Addison, Switzer and Shenstone

2. W. G. Hoskins: *Midland England* (1949), pp. 68–9.
3. O. Rackham: *Hayley Wood: its History and Ecology.* Cambridgeshire and Isle of Ely Naturalists' Trust Ltd (1975), pp. 24–41.

between functional and ideal had become contrary to the spirit of the age. Landowners interested in agricultural improvement tended to separate the ideal landscape of the garden and home park from the productive land where scientific experiments in stock breeding, drainage, rotations and developments in farm buildings were pursued. Those less interested in the functional management of their estates saw the wider landscape in terms of game cover and what might be described as foxscape. Merchants enriched by trade with the East and 'nabobs' by the plunder of India sought respectability, as many before and since, by the acquisition of land. Landscaped grounds surrounded the roads to London and clustered round prosperous market towns, some the seats of nobility and gentry, others the imitations by the newly rich, consuming useful land formerly tilled and the commons and greens of dispossessed villagers. The landscape style of Pope, Kent, Cobham and Temple had degenerated into a status symbol displaying wealth and influence.

A sinister development of the second half of the eighteenth century was the destruction of villages which lay in the way of new parks [4], a trend denounced by Oliver Goldsmith as breaking ancient traditions of peasant cultivation achieved by centuries of work by men and beasts. While the villagers might sometimes be rehoused adequately elsewhere, the traditions and continuity of a site expressed in its green, inn, mill, meadows and fields had gone for ever. Such a scene had no place in a landscape where function was banished.

While the lot of the yeoman farmer improved (until corn prices fell at the ending of the Napoleonic Wars), the lives of the labourers and remaining small cultivators reflected growing rural poverty. Cottage industry gradually declined, faced with competition from the towns. Protection of game involved barbarous methods that recall the forest laws of the Norman kings: mantraps and spring guns hidden in the brushwood, as likely to kill or maim the inadvertent wanderer as the poacher for whom they were intended. By a law of 1816 the cottager could be transported for 7 years if caught with nets to trap hare or rabbit for his starving family. Steadily the rural poor became a class apart and their latent resentment appears in Morland's paintings, the only artist who understood and was prepared to depict the lot of those occupying the lowest rungs of a society [5] where the old relationships, customary rights, loyalties and self-sufficiency had been destroyed.

The deprivation of the cottagers would sow a bitter harvest for the nineteenth century; in the mid-eighteenth century this was probably impossible to foresee except by such an acute critic as Goldsmith who actually observed on foot. The high ideals of Whig philosophy expressed at Stowe were not hypocritical, although we may think them ignorant with hindsight. The Seven Years War (1756–1763) added India and Canada to the British Empire under the guidance of the Elder Pitt (brother-in-law of Temple) at the same time as Temple was planning the wider horizons seen from his portico. In the southern American states slavery was the accepted social system which sustained Palladian buildings, notably those of Thomas Jefferson. Athenian and Roman history confirmed that liberty for the few might have disadvantages for the many, precedents not lost on a society which regarded the achievements and culture of the classical world as superior to those of later ages. Admiration for Antiquity and a guilty conscience for the lot of the labouring poor required a landscape

4. Mavis Batey in 'Oliver Goldsmith – an indictment of landscape gardening', *Furor Hortensis*, P. Willis (ed.) (1974) gives evidence for the destruction of dozens of ancient villages and hamlets to make way for Georgian pleasure grounds. In one rare case where householders fought for their rights for 10 years (Milton Abbas, Dorset), Lord Milton lost patience and released the dam holding Brown's lake, apparently with legal impunity.

5. J. Barrell: *The Dark Side of the Landscape* (1980).

of escape for the late eighteenth century rich. In the person of Lancelot Brown there was the man to effect it for them.

Capability Brown

From 1751 the invention and variety of the English school was submerged beneath the dominating personality and vast practice of Lancelot Brown. Miss Stroud in her work on Brown [6], describes 150 estates for which he was responsible and there were many more on which he gave advice. Moreover, his style was widely imitated. Such was the impact of this extraordinary man that today the mere rumour of a connection provokes a response in hushed tones that such and such is a 'Capability Brown landscape' [7]. Yet his style, in essence, was based on the traditional wood-pasture of trees set in grassland of the hunting park (many of which he adapted), whose forms are often consequently thought of as being of eighteenth century origin. The survival of some ancient parks may indeed be a debt to Brown.

He arrived, with some experience, at Stowe in 1741 where he was appointed to the post of head gardener and absorbed at first hand the landscape principles of Bridgeman and Kent, and of their active patron Lord Cobham [8] who recognised his ability and soon gave him responsibility for building projects as well as for the grounds. He studied the building manuals and textbooks which were now available and became a competent self-taught architect. It seems likely that he implemented Kent's later schemes at Stowe, for Kent was averse to travelling and Miss Stroud considers that Brown had executive responsibility for the Grecian Valley, formed by the removal of some 18,000 cubic metres of earth and planted with semi-mature trees in the hollow and with thick plantations on the slopes. Brown may have invented here the machine he used on later schemes to prise out large trees for transplanting. Cobham permitted him to undertake commissions elsewhere, including Warwick Castle of which Horace Walpole reported in 1751: 'The Castle is enchanting; the view pleased me more than I can express . . . it is well laid out by Brown, who has set up on a few ideas of Kent and Mr Southcote. One sees what the prevalence of taste does; little Brooke, who would have chuckled to have been born in an age of clipt-hedges and cockle shell avenues, has submitted to let his garden and park be natural'.

Following Cobham's death in 1749 Brown felt that the time had arrived for him to establish an independent practice. In 1751 he moved to Hammersmith to become the fashionable landscape designer of his time, sought by all, the inheritor of the mantles of Kent and Bridgeman. The elements of his approach remained based on his experience at Stowe, and Hussey has remarked on their similarity to the concept of beauty defined in Burke's *Inquiry into the Origin of Our Ideas of the Sublime and Beautiful* (1756). Burke saw the experience of physical phenomena as divisible into the Sublime, which aroused feelings of danger, and into Beauty characterised by delicacy of form, and waving and serpentine forms. Hogarth's 'line of beauty', Kent's reputed dictum that 'Nature abhors a straight line', the shapes of Chippendale's earlier furniture and Brown's serpentine paths and lakes all accord with Burke's definition. Brown avoided the Sublime, aiming to create a general and gentle serenity without sharp contrasts of topography or texture. The scenes at Sherborne which Pope has found 'inexpress-

6. D. Stroud: *Capability Brown* (1950).
7. The contemporary esteem in which Brown is held is in marked contrast to the scorn with which he was regarded in Victorian and Edwardian days, when he was seen essentially as a destroyer of earlier landscapes.
8. There was formerly a myth that Brown began as a sort of gardener's boy: this is far from the truth. He was born in 1716 of yeoman farming stock in Kirkharle, Northumberland, where he had a reasonable education and took employment with the principal local landowner, Sir William Loraine, who had already undertaken extensive landscape works on his estate. Loraine entrusted him with the reclamation and conversion to parkland of a tract of rough bog, which Brown carried out with great success, gaining basic knowledge and experience in earth modelling and the shaping of contours, and the planting and transplanting of trees. From Kirkharle he undertook other local commissions and, with his industry, proven ability and charming personality, rapidly achieved a reputation in the north of England.

One can speculate whether Brown's style would have evolved differently if the landscape of Stowe had been as rugged and varied as in Pope's description of Sherborne. It is not known whether he read the books of Burke and Hogarth, but perhaps the view of all three men was an expression of the *Zeitgeist*, rather as Hussey has suggested.

Fig. 6.1 Audley End House, Essex, where Brown initially advised on improvements to the grounds.

ibly solemn and awful' and the precipices of cascades which had thrilled Addison in the Campagna, had no part in his vision and it is, perhaps, not surprising that later critics found his landscapes lacking in excitement.

Brown practised architecture as well as landscape, designing competent country houses and buildings and monuments for his parks in the approved Palladian and occasionally, Gothic manner. Later he took into partnership the fashionable architect Henry Holland, who became his son-in-law; the two providing what we now term a 'package deal' for the Whig circles who favoured them. The epithet is not inappropriate, for Brown worked very much to a pattern, indeed a formula. First he would sweep away all vestiges of the formal garden; parterres and alleys were grubbed up, terraces obliterated and the grassland of the parks brought right up to the walls of the house itself, although the ha-ha still kept grazing animals at a respectful distance. Next, he attacked any formal elements that had been established in the park, felling within avenues to produce clumps and adding supplementary planting for irregularity, and altering the outlines of ponds and canals to give them a natural appearance. Brown's use of water was brilliant and by its means he would alter a landscape 'at a stroke', damming up streams to make limpid, meandering rivers and lakes, often levelling the beds and digging away banks and slopes beforehand to achieve a greater breadth. His masterpiece is at Blenheim, where by excavation and damming he turned the little River Glyme into a serpentine lake, winding through the valley below the palace and making the perfect foil for Vanbrugh's triumphal bridge, the water-level set to lap its bastions and the springing of arches.

A somewhat crude plan survives of Blenheim park showing the avenues, plantations and parterres originally planted by Wise and Vanbrugh early in the century. The park was the ancient setting for a former royal palace and one suspects that scattered trees were ignored in the plan and, almost certainly, the denser irregular tree cover shown south-west in the park, towards and around the High Lodge, was old wood-pasture. Brown's accurate plan of 1764 confirms this view and also suggests that the formal criss-cross alleys north-east of the house were impositions on a similar ancient pattern which Brown partly restored [9]. Around the perimeter of the park, extensive planting is shown to create a wooded pale; the earlier plan shows a bare boundary and, although one cannot be sure that a scatter of trees had not accumulated, as shown in engravings of traditional parks elsewhere, the device of the boundary belt was a favourite with Brown, separating the landscape within from the functional countryside beyond and providing a shady and pleasant route for viewing the park. With the removal of the formal gardens and the landscape enclosed and controlled within its verdant pale, the scene is set and the architectural elements, Roman bridge, column and temples, complete the metamorphosis of the informal hunting park into an English Arcadia.

Blenheim is a great landscape and the sensitivity with which Brown adapted and enhanced the existing features, modelled the contours and made use of the 'natural' pattern of tree cover traditional to ancient parks, mark him as a master and explains the willingness of his contemporaries to accept his dictates and annihilate their formal gardens and avenues, then approaching their full maturity and splendour. Unfortunately, his swollen practice often precluded the respect shown to the Genius Loci at Blenheim and tended to a hurried assessment and recommendations following a preconceived pattern. We can imagine the great man, invited to an estate to give advice, riding the grounds and expanding on the 'capabilities', judging where to dam the lake, thicken or thin the tree cover, excavate to soften contours and where to place the focal temples and eye-catchers – all elements

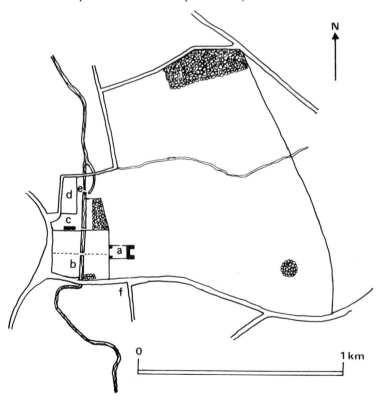

Fig. 6.2 Audley End. Plan of house and park from estate map of 1758: (a) house; (b) River Cam straightened into appearance of a canal; (c) late sixteenth-century stables; (d) walled garden; (e) corn mill; (f) Audley End village.

N

0   1 km

9. Both maps are illustrated in G. and S. Jellicoe: *The Landscape of Man* (1975).

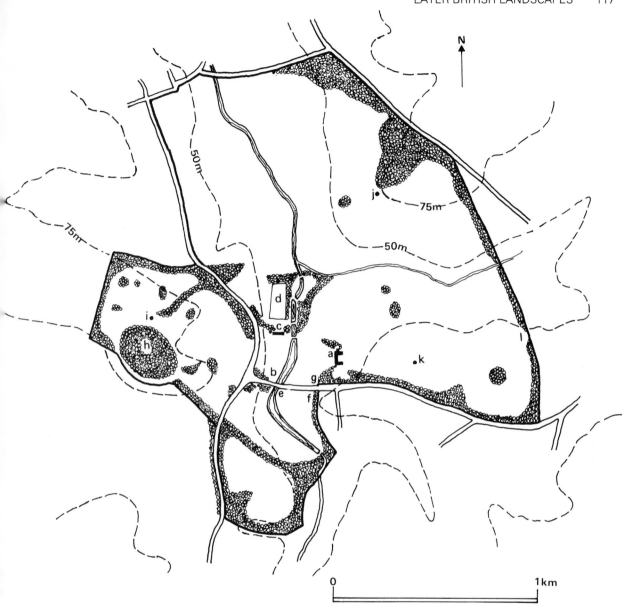

Fig. 6.3 Audley End. Plan of extended park from estate map of 1783. The woodland is much simplified and the extensive areas of wood-pasture and single trees not shown. (a) House; (b) reshaped River Cam; (c) stables; (d) walled garden; (e) bridge designed by Robert Adam; (f) area of village razed and included in park; (g) Lion Gate; (h) Ring Hill, Iron Age fortress; (i) Grecian Temple by Robert Adam, 1763; (j) column, 1774; (k) Temple of Concord (erected after Map in 1791); (l) park gate and lodge. Entrance from Saffron Walden.

of the Brown package, often as oblivious of locality as the architecture of the houses for which they formed the setting.

A fine example of an estate where Brown was initially involved with 'improvements' and which subsequently developed without his supervision but on the probable lines he had envisaged, is Audley End in Essex. The house is a Jacobean pile, standing above the flood plain of the River Cam on the site of Walden Abbey, just over 1 kilometre from the market town of Saffron Walden. Although no plan of Brown's survives, two fine estate maps of 1758 and 1783 [10] are preserved, which show the site before and after the works undertaken. The final landscaped park stretched across the Cam valley, rising on each side to boundaries on, or beyond, the hilltops; the topography is rolling and gentle, very much to Brown's liking. The patron was Sir John

10. Essex Record Office, D/DQ8 and T/M 123.

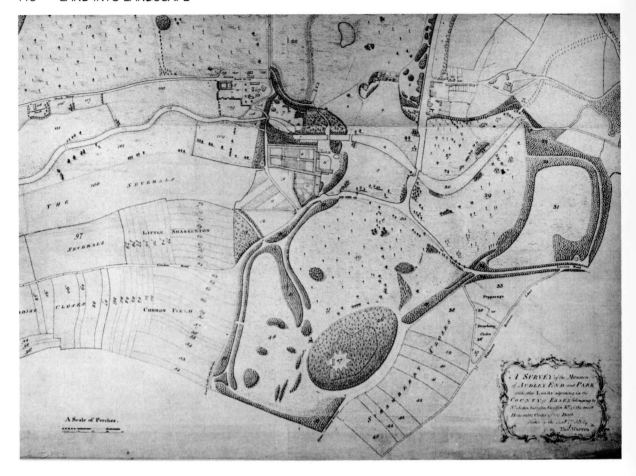

Fig. 6.4 Audley End. Part of the estate map of 1783.

Griffin Griffin, who was determined to restore his family seat to the renown in which it had once been held. The map of 1758 shows the estate he inherited in 1762, bounded by open parkland between the house and the town and ending in the west on the lines of a turnpike. Griffin lost no time in acquiring the land beyond the road on the western slopes of the valley and further land, extending the park to the north. He arranged the closure of two roads that crossed the estate and in 1764 secured, by private Act of Parliament, the removal of Audley End village which was visible from the house and encroached into the unity of the park he was seeking to create.

In 1763, Brown contracted to undertake to landscape the grounds, but 4 years later he fell out with Griffin over the payment of fees and interest and, as the work was far behind schedule, they parted company and the scheme was completed without his involvement. But one can fairly assume that it remained Brown's scheme in its essentials, for its elements have his characteristic stamp. All vestiges of the formal gardens were removed from around the house and a kitchen and flower garden, adjacent stables, estate buildings and workshops were discreetly planted to obscure them. Tree belts were planted and a brick wall built along the boundaries of the park and the tops of the valley slopes clothed with woods so that, except to the north-east where the topography made this impossible, all the boundaries are contained by woodlands and densely planted standing trees. Within the park, trees were scattered and clumped. How far existing trees were incorporated is difficult to judge, but the 1758 map shows a scatter of trees and a woodland, as today, on the northern boundary; probably these trees were retained and felled in due course as new planting grew up to take their place, for there are few trees standing now that seem likely to be older than 200 years. On the western side of the Cam it is impossible to judge what was there, as it was not shown on the early map, but it did contain an Iron Age fortress, which would probably have been wooded, and a hunting lodge nearby suggests that it may have formed part of an earlier park.

Major works were carried out to the River Cam and a new course was excavated to make it broad and limpid, on a scale with the house. Finally, Robert Adam was commissioned to design appropriate architectural features: a classical bridge to carry the road from Walden over the Cam, a Palladian bridge near the dam of the former abbey mill (which was converted into a cascade), a Grecian temple, column and splendid entrance gateway. Well before Griffin's death in 1797, the transformation was complete and he would have enjoyed in his old age the semimaturity of his earlier plantings, now adorned by the work of the finest architect of his time [11].

Audley End park survives in its essence and its elements can still be comprehended. Its natural topography was suited to Brown's vision and was spared the treatment he applied to more rugged landscapes elsewhere that he found uncongenial. It shows his approach to a medium-sized landscape at its best, enhancing the scene he found without undue destruction, other than the homes of the villagers.

Brown had his critics who conducted a vituperative campaign against his work, not on the grounds of earlier planned landscapes he destroyed, but on the claim that it was neither picturesque nor 'natural'; but they were of little account in terms of works as opposed to

Fig. 6.5 Audley End. View from Adam Bridge to the stables, showing the River Cam reshaped to give the appearance of a narrow lake.

11. Today, the main lines of this landscape are still apparent, in spite of depredations and division. The house is now owned by the Department of the Environment and its curtilage stretches westwards to the former turnpike, now the A11. Eastwards, it rises to an eminence crowned with a temple, built to commemorate George III's first recovery from insanity, a site earlier graced by a mount and temple, according to a crude map of 1750. From here the former lineaments of the park can be seen: to the south it is contained by its perimeter tree belt; to the west one looks over the house, with its cedars and later wellingtonias, to a wooded skyline, with Adam's Grecian temple on the site of the hunting lodge. Eastwards the view is contained by a belt of limes, separating the park from the town, above which the spire of Walden church rises, indicating the presence of the invisible town. Northwards the wooded ridge is enhanced by a Roman column, rising above former deer park, now a golf course. North-west the view extends for kilometres along the Cam valley to the distant village of Littlebury, with the skyline now, unfortunately, swathed in a cat's cradle of power lines.

words. Humphry Repton (1752–1818), who succeeded to his mantle
as the central figure of the English school, modelled his approach very
much on Brown and as late as the 1840s we find Hylands Park,
Writtle (earlier a Repton landscape) being extended on lines that both
he and Brown would have approved. So, Brown's dominance, living
and posthumous, lasted for the greater part of 100 years and, at this
point, it is relevant to consider both the achievements and limitations
of Capability Brown and his school.

First, it must be stated again that his patrons were an oligarchy,
well educated and versed in the classics. Many of them would have
been fluent, at least in their schooldays, in Latin and Greek. Though
they must have doubted the actual existence of the Golden Age, the
poetry of Ovid and Virgil as well as the paintings of Claude, were
basic elements in the culture of their time and, until the Gothic
Revival, the Roman world remained the reference point and source
of excellence which later ages could only seek to emulate. The sim-
ulation of Arcadia in the English countryside did not appear to them
as either anachronistic or out of place.

Brown's destruction of earlier, planned, landscapes is regrettable;
too much has been lost and today we look to Victorian reconstructions
to give an impression of these vanished scenes and to Kip's views
of the traditional parkland of wood-pasture, which ensured the survival of many ancient landscapes which had originally been emparked
from the woodlands and manorial wastes and retained direct biological links with the primeval landscape. Once destroyed, the complex
and long-established communities of plants and animals cannot be
replaced and the links are lost. Thus, the rehabilitation of the oak
savannah of the traditional hunting park, in popular esteem, surviving
as we have seen in Kip's and Knyff's engravings, is a considerable
debt to Brown; probably he appreciated the romantic qualities of ancient parkland trees and the grassland in which they had survived
and, with his practical eye, sought to retain and continue this scene
which accorded well with the landscapes painted by 'Arcadian' artists.
In sympathy with this approach, Brown planted the native hardwood
trees: oak, ash, beech, elm and, occasionally, the exotic Lebanon
cedar.

Although he incorporated earlier landscapes in his schemes,
Brown's technique tended to superimpose a preconceived 'package'.
The Genius Loci, extolled by Pope, was coerced by Brown where
necessary to fit his pattern and was not 'consulted' as Pope advised.
Pope's dictum 'all must be adapted to the Genius and Use of the
Place, and the Beauties not forced into it, but resulting from it' was
forgotten. Consequently, the average English landscape park often has
an 'anywhere' character reflecting the country house it surrounds,
copied from a Burlingtonian textbook and only reflecting locality in
the stone (if in the stone country) from which its materials were necessarily quarried.

A characteristic of Brown's landscape is the total exclusion of the
working countryside. Husbandry had no part in his vision, the rich
man's Arcadia was by now totally separated from the rest of his estate
and the wooded pale and high wall marked the bounds. Separation
of park and farmland allowed the landlord to pursue a purely utilitarian policy towards his productive acres, parliamentary bills legal-
ised the enclosure of the remaining commons and heaths to the benefit

Fig. 6.6 Audley End. The Lion Gate, a Jacobean structure adorned with sculpture and urns in the Adam style.

of food production but to the deprivation of the cottager, helpless before the alliance of 'squire, parson and lawyer'. This basic division of private amenity and efficient farming is reflected in Brown's landscapes and is a fundamental rejection of the total Virgilian vision and the *ferme ornée*.

But Brown's approach stood in the tradition of the informal hunting park, which had been a feature of medieval landscapes. Through him and Repton the tradition was transmitted to later generations of landscape designers and has influenced planned landscapes in Europe and America to this day. Olmsted's Central Park, New York (1857) and South Park, Chicago (1871) owe something to Brown, as does Bos Park, Amsterdam (1934). The image of a building rising out of Parkland turf appealed to 'modern' architects, particularly Le Corbusier, but unfortunately the need for car parks, play areas and other concomitants of high-density living have made the reality very different from the intention.

Enthusiasm for the English achievement of the eighteenth century has tended to obscure Brown's debt to the past and to ignore the landscape he inherited. It is often written, or implied, that he had little material to start with and that an act of faith was required of his clients. In fact, Brown usually 'improved' and often extended (as at Audley End) an existing park where ancient trees, woodlands and groves were likely to have formed part of the older scene and could well have been managed for amenity, as well as for hunting and functional considerations in the past. Where the land was not already parkland it may not, by any means, have been bare of trees. The history and evolution of parks is a subject on which little research has been done and remains a fascinating subject, awaiting the attention of field historians. Meanwhile, those unaware of the historic dimension of the familiar countryside should note that Palladian temples, obelisks and limpid lakes, may sometimes overlie a landscape of far greater antiquity than their presence indicates.

The end of Arcadia

Brown died in 1783. Five years later Humphrey Repton decided that he was equipped to set up as Brown's successor and was immediately successful. He was trained in botany, entomology, gardening and drawing, was competent in administration and mathematics, and had the ability to rationalise his (and Brown's) approach into theories of design, which he published. Literary warfare followed in the 1790s when Sir Uvedale Price and Richard Payne Knight launched attacks on Brown's landscapes as being at variance with all the principles of landscape painting. Kent, too, was dismissed as mean and perverse. Price believed that the surroundings of a house should appear arranged by Nature, with thick undergrowth and uneven groups of trees covered with ivy, drives should be rough and winding lanes, deeply rutted and overhung with thickets of trees and bounded by furze bushes and large stones. The effect should be savage, wild and melancholy. The approach was pictorial, literary and emotional, looking back to the paintings of Salvator Rosa, Shaftesbury's 'passion for things of a natural kind' and Burke's 'Sublime'. Price and Payne Knight stood firmly in the English landscape tradition, submerged for a generation beneath the Brown package which they found mannered and essentially dull. But it was on the work of painters that they had most influence or with whom their approach concurred [12].

The attacks put Repton on his mettle, but he made certain concessions in the interests of function and to meet the increasing eclecticism and romanticism of his age. The terrace and flower garden returned to the surroundings of the house [13] and occasionally the avenue was seen to have merits. Farms and pheasanteries, which Brown had banished out of sight, were allowed to return, and even arable farming. Pavilions were now often Gothick or Oriental in style. Brown's overall approach remained despite Repton's modifications, but Arcadia was fast fading.

This was inevitable. The belief in the superiority of the civilisation of Rome that had been the corner-stone of Shaftesbury's philosophy and of Gibbon's interpretation of history was no longer tenable except for a few devoted classicists. British science and technology had far exceeded the achievement of the Ancient World and Britain was building an overseas empire the equal of Rome. Attention turned to the Middle Ages, which suited the romanticism of the times and a genuine revival of Gothic forms in architecture replaced the sentimental 'Gothick' of the eighteenth century. In 1836 a Gothic design (in detail and appearance) was thought appropriate for the rebuilding of the Houses of Parliament.

The range of choice in architectural styles was matched by that of garden design and ornament. J. C. Loudon (1783–1843), a prolific writer on gardening who had published the collected works of Repton, wrote:

12. Uvedale Price and Payne Knight's view recalls Shaftesbury: 'wild nature has a magnificence beyond the mockery of princely gardens', and can be seen as a swing of the pendulum of taste away from Burke's Beautiful towards the Sublime. This coincided with a rise of interest by patrons (and consequently a market) for native landscape painting which became firmly established in the early nineteenth century. It tended towards the wild and picturesque, the mountainous and rocky, and in the lowlands, the landscapes of heath and common. In general, the landscape of husbandry was avoided.

Previously, the Old Masters had been admired (Poussin, Rubens, Rosa, Claude), but there was no market for contemporary landscapes and a painter such as Gainsborough painted landscapes for his own pleasure and kept them in his private gallery, while he earned his living painting fashionable portraits. Richard Wilson (1714–82), a fine painter of the Landscape of Fact, often illuminated by a golden Claudean light, died poor and neglected; recognition and admiration had to wait 20 years. In 1801 Fuseli wrote: 'He is now numbered with the classics of the art though little more than the fifth part of a century has elapsed since death relieved him from the apathy of cognoscenti, the envy of rivals, and the neglect of a tasteless public.'

One of the finest British achievements in depicting the Landscape of Fact is *Cornard Wood* by Thomas Gainsborough (1727–88), painted by the artist at the age of 21. But he received no encouragement and his later landscapes are imaginary and stylised, and beautiful though they are, bear little resemblance to the real world: the trees are botanically unidentifiable and husbandry only enters in the form of rough grazing.

A real landscape on the lines suggested by Uvedale Price and Payne Knight was created at Hafod, Cardiganshire, by their friend Thomas Johnes, who exploited the rocky scene to create a wooded wilderness containing romantic walks, waterfalls, a cave, an Alpine bridge, Druid temple and a miniature Garden of Eden. It was admired and painted by many artists including Turner.

13. Kenwood, Highgate, is a small but delightful landscape that contains the essential elements of Repton's landscape: wooded backcloth, lake with artificial classical bridge, sweeping grass sward below the house and formal gardens to the side. It is owned by the GLC and open to the public.

The modern architect may build a house in the Classic or in the Gothic style; or he may adopt the historical and geographical variations of these styles, as exhibited in the Hindoo, Elizabethan, Italian, English, and other manners of building. In like manner, the landscape gardener, who would lay out grounds at the present day, may adopt either the oldest, or geometrical style or he may adopt the modern or irregular style in which the forms of nature are brought into immediate contrast with the forms of art; and he may, further, combine the two styles in such a manner as to join regularity and irregularity in one design'.

Loudon himself had a degree of style and taste, but the demands of his time acted against both qualities, for in addition to the choice in style there was a bewildering range of new plant material available.

The introduction and cultivation of exotics and their adaptation to English gardens and parks were not new. It had begun with Romans, and the Crusaders are said to have brought back roses from the Levant (or, more likely, from Spain or Sicily). With the rise of botany, scientific collections of many different species were established in botanic gardens, of which the garden at Oxford, adorned with gateways by Inigo Jones, was the first and is still the most beautiful. In the seventeenth century, horticulture and the collection of plants became a passion and an industry of nurserymen flourished, selecting and cross-breeding for variety and size. A reaction set in during Brown's pre-eminence, but with the decline of his influence the floodgates opened and the nursery business boomed. Meanwhile, the range of trees, shrubs and flowers available had greatly increased through the travels of collectors and botanists in the Orient and the Americas, and these now became available on the market; the result was akin to the end of prohibition in America – the age of the cocktail. Strong and gifted personalities were to master the new material and produce great gardens, but this was later in the century and perhaps the finest designer of the early-middle years was Sir Charles Barry, an architect in the tradition of the Renaissance, who used a formal architectural framework for his gardens and limited flowers to parterres. By this time the landscape tradition was in eclipse, but the best of the new arboreta were grafted on to older landscapes, as at Kew and Westonbirt, and here one still finds a distinct paradisal echo.

It is unfashionable to criticise the mid-Victorians for a lack of taste while possessing an excess of wealth, but these qualities were as evident in their garden designs as in the furnishings of their churches. Seen from our reduced times, the opulence of the ornamental grounds of their great houses seems incredible: the armies of gardeners required to maintain the parterres of bedding plants and rake acres of gravel, the collections of every exotic tree and shrub that could be induced to survive, and the stonework of terraces, stairs and ornaments. But it was the glasshouses which were the original contribution of the age, in which the microclimate of the tropical forests could be re-created in steamy interiors, often in an architectural frame of considerable elegance and distinction owing little to the styles of the past and everything to the technological achievement of the times. In the Palm House at Kew the structure achieves greatness with an organic quality that seems to relate to the fronds of the palms inside, an uncanny unity of form and content that had not been known since the

Middle Ages. It has the quality of an unchanging oasis, taken from its desert context to the English climate to provide the paradox by which one can step out of a snowstorm into the warm shelter of Arabian palms.

Late in the eighteenth century the influence of Brown and Repton was felt in the urban scene through introduction of the informal garden compound of forest trees over shrubs and lawns into the squares of London, Bath and Edinburgh. Access was limited to the immediate householders, as is sometimes still the case, and the garden represented a shared amenity of a size sufficient to balance the ordered and rectilinear terraces around and give a sense of the presence of Nature in the heart of the town; the antithesis of the formal avenue, or boulevard, for England rarely requires shade and the qualities of the climate, mildness and high rainfall, encourage luxuriant grass and trees. It was a development in the spirit of Whiggery, distrusting the great avenues and set pieces beloved by despots and giving, in miniature, a breath of parkland to the town. It was blessed, by good fortune, with the appearance of the noblest of urban trees, the London plane, a sport that thrives in sooty conditions by shedding its bark and has leaves and fruit of exceptional beauty. Today, it is all too often taken for granted and this good-natured tree, which accommodates judicious pruning and lopping, is often removed to make way for 'more suitable' species: usually plebeian maples which will not grow to a size which will cause anxiety to borough arboriculturalists. Our forefathers knew better and we still benefit from their foresight.

The communal garden of the London square remained a part of urban design into the middle years of the nineteenth century, when the new developments of Kensington and Pimlico were carried out, and was still apparent in the later Cadogan Estate. Meanwhile, in the poorer areas, urban parks were being created for the enjoyment of townsfolk, a concept that has a pedigree dating back to the Assyrians and Greeks and beginning in England with the opening of the royal parks of the West End to the populace as London expanded. Hundreds of new parks followed to serve industrial cities and the new suburbs of Victorian England and one regrets that they followed the pattern of the gardens of the time rather than the Reptonian tradition of the London squares or the larger-scale landscape of Nash's Regent's Park. Too often the urban park has a lack of unity stemming from a fragmentation of function and the lack of underlying philosophy of design that is still apparent today. Detailed attention appears reserved for the garish patterns of bedding plants and the immaculate turf of bowling greens. Nevertheless, one should not dismiss the traditional parterre, for there are some to be found that are constructed with a fine eye for colour and contrasts, as in front of the Palm House at Kew, and the knot garden may yet surprise us in the late twentieth century.

Although the Brown/Repton tradition died in Britain, it was to influence profoundly the development of landscape design in North America. The reason, it seems, being the response of Americans to their superb natural scenery, some of it true wilderness, which led in due course to the establishment of the national parks and forest areas and also to an appreciation of natural qualities in landscapes planned for recreation. Andrew Jackson Downing (1815–52) of New York advocated the English or natural style through his editorials in the *Hor-*

ticulturalist and treatise on *Landscape Gardening* (1841). Downing stood firmly in the Reptonian tradition and his writings proved highly influential on the East Coast. He was followed by Frederick Law Olmsted (1822–1903) who designed and constructed many parks including Central Park, Manhattan (advocated earlier by Downing), and through his practice and associates founded a school of landscape architects that came to dominate American design.

Olmsted's method was to preserve the natural scenery and if necessary restore and emphasise it, to use native trees and shrubs, to keep open lawns and meadows in large central areas, and to avoid formal design except in very limited areas close to buildings. Thus the English parkland tradition continued across the Atlantic, purged of its cultural trappings, invigorated by fresh minds, its principles rethought and open to all to enjoy.

Virgilian painters

The early nineteenth century saw the rise of a native school of painting in which landscape was pre-eminent and English patrons were no longer limited to the works of Italian, French and Dutch artists. The school was extraordinarily diverse, including topographical painters in the tradition of the Landscape of Fact, romantic painters of remote and fantastic landscapes such as John Martin and, ultimately, the masters of light, skies and atmosphere: Turner and Constable [14]. But here we are concerned with a briefly flourishing vision of earlier concepts, which were reinterpreted in conscious opposition to the age and its basic uncertainties. The years that followed the Napoleonic Wars were a period of fear and mistrust, of extremes of wealth and poverty, of social unrest and agitation for reforms which was countered by draconian laws, deportations and the occasional massacre. The new proletariat of industrial towns was becoming a separate race from the traditional inhabitants of the countryside, though here too there was impoverishment following parliamentary enclosure and a growing rift between farmers and their men. Many people sought security in religion and bizarre and fanatic sects flourished, with visions and prophecies of coming doom – the world of Joanna Southcott and Edward Irving.

The best of the apocalyptic and visionary spirit of the times was expressed in the paintings and poetic works of the mystic and genius

Fig. 6.7 William Blake. Wood engraving for edition of Virgil's *Eclogues*.

14. The Landscape of Fact tended to be avoided by artists, even such masters as Cotman eschewing the landscape of husbandry. The Midland countryside, newly established at this time, must have appeared boring and unsuitable as a subject; on the other hand, one suspects a bad conscience on the part of patrons following the dispossession of the cottagers.

William Blake. In his old age a group of young artists gathered to learn from him, among them Samuel Palmer for whom Blake printed and signed a set of his wood engravings for an edition of Virgil's *Eclogues*. The engravings show images of the countryside that recurred in Blake's vision and are familiar from his *Dante* and *Job*, but here shown with extraordinary directness and force: shepherds with their flocks, fields of ripe corn, ancient oaks with knotted roots and branches, and enormous crescent moons illuminating the scene with white light. Palmer described them as . . .

> . . . visions of little dells, and nooks, and corners of Paradise; models of the exquisitest pitch of intense poetry. I thought of their light and shade, and looking upon them I found no word to describe it. Intense depth, solemnity, and vivid brilliancy only coldly and partially describe them. There is in all such a mistic and dreamy glimmer as penetrates and kindles the inmost soul, and give complete and unreserved delight, unlike the gaudy daylight of this world.

To Palmer and others of the group they were a revelation, Blake's greatness and nobility of nature drew out what was latent in the young man and gave him new insights and set the direction he was to follow.

In 1826 he went to live in Shoreham in Kent, a village set in a rich and hilly landscape of woods and orchards, pasture and crops, with the interest and irregularities characteristic of ancient enclosure; a landscape that had evolved through the centuries as gradually but as surely as its sunken lanes. Palmer constantly walked, sketched and studied this landscape, day and night, at twilight and dawn, experiencing the elements and observing everything, down to the minutiae of mosses and lichens. The knowledge and skill he acquired give a bedrock of conviction to the most visionary of his paintings; like Virgil, and Clare, he knew the countryside from the inside and saw it for itself as an ideal landscape, rather than the idealised landscape seen by the observer from outside.

Fortunately, we know a good deal about Palmer; his letters of the time survive as do those of his friends who joined him at Shoreham, a like-minded group from the Blake circle. They called themselves 'The Ancients' and puzzled the villagers by their walking in the twilight and watching the approach of dawn. From his letters, we know of the poets who influenced him, particularly Milton, whose imagery appears to have moved him above all, as it had Blake and Fuseli, also an idol of the young Palmer. An early experience had affected him deeply. His mother had died young and her place had been taken by his nurse:

> A Tonson's *Milton*, which I cherish to this day was her present. When less than four years old, as I was standing with her, watching the shadows on the wall from the branches of an elm behind which the moon had risen, she transferred and fixed the fleeting image in my memory by repeating the couplet:
>
> Vain man, the vision of a moment made
> Dream of a dream and shadow of a shade. . . .
> I never forgot these shadows and am often trying to paint them [15].

15. At the beginning of an edition of Milton's works he inserted a list of all the lines referring to the moon and its light and these recur in his letters:

> *. . .now reigns*
> *Full-orb'd the moon and with more pleasing light*
> *Shadowy sets off the face of things.*

and:

> *. . .there does a sable cloud*
> *Turn forth her silver lining on the night*
> *And casts a gleam over the tufted grove. . .*

A favourite spot for Palmer was Lullingstone Park, where he made studies of the ancient oak pollards. But, he writes:

> Milton, by one epithet, draws an oak of the largest girth I ever saw, 'Pine and monumental oak': I have just been trying to draw a large one at Lullingstone; but the poet's tree is larger than any in the park: there, the moss, and rifts, and barky furrows, and the mouldering grey (tho' that adds majesty to the lord of the forests) mostly catch the eye, before the grasp and grapple of the roots, the muscular belly and shoulders, the twisting sinews.

Although his imagination was fed and inspired by literature, it must be stressed that he was not in any way a literary painter, in the anecdotal sense. His landscapes of the time reflect divine order, expressed through the union of nature with productive husbandry; it is the vision of the seasons and the *Georgics*, set briefly in the English scene. And brief it was, for by 1835, when he was 30, the visionary quality of his art was fading and 2 years later it was gone. But during the 9 years at Shoreham his genius was as productive and fruitful as the landscape he depicted, reaching its peak, perhaps, around 1830 with such paintings as the *Harvest Moon*: a golden landscape of stooks against a background of wooded hills flooded with light from a crescent moon, and with the mysterious depth of *Evening: A Church among Trees*, where a winding lane leads to a church nestling in a valley and almost hidden by great trees. The last light of the sun catches the spire and glows on three figures driving sheep along the lane and on a field filled with sheaves in the foreground. The foliage of the trees is richly gemmed and textured in the light or silhouetted against the sky; all is fruitful and abundant, expressing the harmony of the countryman with the natural world. There is a sense of stability and continuity: the settlement is ancient and rooted and the painting conveys the quality of such a site, as mysterious as the deep shadows cast by the trees.

His moons of this time are often huge, far beyond reality (as in *Full Moon and Deer* and *Shepherds under the Full Moon*). Yet they are right: the moon affects the birth and fertility of living organisms and causes the tides, and its influence is out of proportion to the small globe we see in the sky. Seen from within the natural order it is a ruling force, and Palmer instinctively felt its power and showed it as such. In his own words: 'the moon opening her golden eye, or walking in the brightness among innumerable islands of light, not only thrill the optic nerve, but shed a mild, a grateful, an unearthly lustre into the inmost spirits, and seem the interchanging twilight of that peaceful country, where there is no sorrow and no night'. Shepherds are the guardian spirits of the place in these paintings; not bucolic rustics but the noble figures of Bunyan's Delectable Mountains, who tend the land for their owner Immanuel and comfort and advise souls on their pilgrimage through life:

> Thus by Shepherds secrets are revealed,
> Which for all other men are kept concealed;
> Come to the Shepherds then, If you would see
> Things deep, things hid, and that mysterious be.

Palmer's vision did not, perhaps could not, last. He felt the despair of a Tory losing his rural world of social balance to the new realities of the Industrial Revolution, radicalism and materialism. He married a dull girl and moved to a prim Surrey villa with its conifers and begonias. Blake, his mentor, was dead. In middle age he became just one of many competent landscape painters and there remained little in his pictures to suggest the brilliance of his visionary years. By 1840 the brief and brilliant flowering of the Virgilian vision in England was over.

Palmer's work of this period remained forgotten until its rediscovery between the wars, when it acted like champagne on the empty stomachs of many young painters. It is still early to say whether his influ-

Fig. 6.8 Samuel Palmer. *A rustic scene.* On the original mount, Palmer added verses from Virgil's *Georgics* (I, 208–11) (Ashmolean Museum, Oxford).

ence was productive, for his forms were often superficially imitated as a ready-made vision, but Paul Nash's paintings of the 1930s have an awareness of the historic and poetic dimensions of the English landscape which must owe something to Palmer, and the young Sutherland produced a series of engravings of the Kentish countryside that have more than a reflective glow of Palmer's vision.

The Age of Gardens

The later years of the nineteenth century and of the early twentieth in Britain were a time of vigorous and inventive architecture, exuberant, confident and frequently eclectic. The legacy is still to be seen in those centres of our cities and market towns that have escaped redevelopment, where we find buildings of an interest, intricacy and quality apparently beyond the capacity of our own age to erect. Amid this talented age an original school, centred around the figures of Webb and Lethaby and expressed in the work of the Arts and Crafts Movement and of the early LCC architect's department, rethought the first principles of architecture in form, function and use of materials [16]. Probably this was the true Modern Movement rather than the arid International Style which is now disliked by all who are not

16. The central figure of the Arts and Crafts Movement was William Morris. The Middle Ages were his inspiration, but he was too shrewd a designer and artist to imitate. Instead he sought the sources of medieval design, and the quest brought him to the Persian tradition and to fabrics woven in fifteenth- and sixteenth-century Italy, designed under Eastern influence. The Persian flowery mead, love of the forms of vegetation, and the tendency to ambiguity are all present in Morris's designs for wallpapers, and woven and printed fabrics. Many of the sources were studied in the Victoria and Albert Museum, then rapidly building up its remarkable collection of the applied arts, and to which Morris acted as adviser on acquisitions.

architects or developers. A comparison of a London school of 1910 with a system-built school of 1970 makes the point without further use of words.

It is hardly surprising that the age made its own distinct and original contribution to the history of planned landscapes, although these were usually on the scale of gardens rather than the parks of the past. Designers now emerged with the capacity to assimilate and use the range of plant material that had been introduced by botanists and explorers. First and foremost was William Robinson whose *English Flower Garden* (1883) is still a standard reference book. He trained as a practical gardener and in due course became responsible for the Royal Botanic Society's collection of British wild flowers, through which he came to have a first-hand knowledge and regard for the countryside and for cottage gardens. A cantankerous character who thrived on controversy, he waged war on the formal gardens of the mid-Victorian, denouncing 'pastry-work gardening' and the works of 'fountain mongers', advocating instead a 'natural' approach, which he described in *The Wild Garden* (1870). Here he sought to introduce appropriate specimens from other continents into English woodlands, heaths and pastures, enriching the native flora with plants growing apparently in natural conditions rather than in the formal context of the collection or botanic garden. It is an approach with paradisal echoes which seeks to expunge the effects of the Ice Ages and introduce the richness of the flora of China or southern Africa which might have been ours had not the glaciers and subsequent island geography intervened. Nevertheless, Robinson's 'nature' could not be natural, for vigorous species such as the sycamore colonise and destroy the native communities, while the less vigorous species require constant tending and protection. Moreover, exotics are of little value to the dependent fauna of insects which live on the long-established native flora, forming an essential element in food chains. Hence, today we should be wary of Robinson's 'wild garden' beyond the confines of controlled and managed areas, for the hedgerows, coppices and pastures of his own day are now considerably reduced in a countryside of intensive agriculture and alien forestry.

Such ecological reservations arising from hindsight on Robinson's approach should not detract from our regard for this great, original and practical gardener. In his own day he dominated the scene and liberated the art of gardening from the narrow parameters in which it had become confined and so contributed directly to the superb gardens that are the legacy of his age.

Gertrude Jekyll (1843–1932) was a greater master of the art than Robinson, though less of a protagonist. She agreed with his approach and wrote articles in his magazines, while embarking on her own practical career of landscape gardening, founded on her local observation of the heaths and woodlands of Surrey and her knowledge of the tradition of cottage gardens. She came of a secure and cultured middle-class family, familiar with music, painting and the sciences, and a love of vernacular architecture which led her to commission the youthful Edwin Lutyens to design her house at Munstead Wood in 1896. Lutyens was already a designer of formal gardens, attracted by their architectural possibilities, for the inevitable reaction had already begun against the freedom of Robinson, and architects who now favoured the styles of the sixteenth and seventeenth centuries were advocating a revival of the gardens of those times. The fusion of the talents of Jekyll and Lutyens produced a true breakthrough that made the efforts of their contemporaries seem limited and pedantic; the competing trends to formality and Robinsonian 'wildness' were creatively resolved at Munstead Wood where the elements of later gardens of the partnership were forged. The house was built in local stone and clad with climbing plants rising from a plinth of shrubs; the same stone extended the architecture of the house outwards forming terraces, stairs and pools, offset by informal planting, often profuse and abundant, in contrast to the geometry and order of the built forms. The site was surrounded by birch woods and chestnut coppice through which grass paths penetrated and a raised gazebo or Thunder House gave views over the surrounding country and a place to watch the progress of approaching storms. As in their subsequent gardens, the design was a counterpoint of plants growing freely into their architectural framework, making the most of the moderate English climate in which vegetation thrives naturally, in contrast to the Moorish and Italian gardens in which flowers and herbs must be supported by irrigation.

In subsequent gardens the ideas were extended and developed and in many Lutyens achieved ravishingly beautiful garden architecture. At the Deanery, Sonning, and at Hestercombe, Somerset [17], he developed his own version of the traditional water garden in which tanks of water lilies are linked by miniature canals or rills filled with lush foliage of aquatics, and the spirit of the place appears as the water source in the form of a carved head set as the keystone of an arch over the spring, formalised as a circular pool, with a jet of water falling from its mouth. It is deceptively simple and satisfying in its sure geometry and use of the plant material which our climate allows – an English contribution to the ancient tradition of the nymphaeum. Later in his life Lutyens created the last but one of the finest gardens of the Mogul tradition for his Viceroy's house at New Delhi. Here, on a monumental scale, fountains rise in the form of great lilies, but wholly geometrical in their detail and finally achieving the quest for pure forms in conjunction with water and vegetation which seems to underly his garden architecture.

Two very different gardens by other designers stand firmly in the paradise tradition. The later, begun in 1930 by Harold Nicolson and Victoria Sackville-West at Sissinghurst in Kent, relates to the work of Jekyll and Lutyens; the other, begun at Inverewe in Ross and Cromarty in 1865, is truly Robinsonian. Sissinghurst began as the ruined site of a Tudor mansion of which the gatehouse, a wing and some walls remained. From this nucleus they created a formal garden of outdoor rooms, formed by great walls of clipped yew, divided within into rectilinear beds edged with neat box hedges. Here the connection with the Tudor tradition ends, for the planting makes full use of the exotic material available, selected and governed by Sackville-West's judgement, as she herself wrote: 'There should be the strictest formality of design, with the maximum informality in the planting . . . profusion, even extravagance and exuberance, within the confines of the utmost linear severity.' The exuberance is everywhere: in the climbers enveloping the ancient walls, in the aged apple trees of the orchard over which white roses clamber in counterpoint with clematis, and in the great clumps of 'old-fashioned' and species roses in the Rose

17. The gardens of Hestercombe have been carefully restored by Somerset County Council. The house forms the headquarters of the County Fire Service.

Garden. The garden has a historic dimension that belies its youth and it is difficult to believe that the yew hedges were only planted in the 1930s, for they seem an integral part with the Tudor tower and walls. It is as though all that is best in the English garden tradition from the Middle Ages onwards is gathered into one garden, under the eye of a poet as sure in her understanding of plants as in her mastery of words [18].

Inverewe, Sissinghurst's senior by nearly 70 years, is best described as an oasis; but instead of a desert context it stands on a wind-scoured peninsula on the north-west coast of Scotland, surrounded by a land-scape of stunted heather and crowberry growing on shallow peat and soused by the salt sprays of Atlantic gales. Seen from across the sea loch it seems an enchanted woodland, protected by the spell of a be-nevolent spirit, while all round, mountains, rocky hills and bleak strands seem inimical to the art of the gardener or husbandman. How-ever, the maker of Inverewe, Osgood Mackenzie, perceived the ben-efits inherent in its situation: a high and steady rainfall, the warmth afforded by the Gulf Stream and an almost complete lack of frosts; given shelter, plants would grow in the open which at Kew required glass. He set out to create the required microclimate, fencing the peninsula securely against deer and rabbits and planting a thick perimeter belt of pine and fir, which, as it rose upwards from the 'thicket' stage, he underplanted with *Rhododendron ponticum*. Within 15 years it was established and he could begin to develop the garden within (around 1880) and today we have his mature legacy: a wild and exotic Elysium of trees and shrubs gathered from all corners of the globe that include the Californian redwoods and New Zealand tree ferns, the rhododendrons of Sri Lanka, the Himalayas and China, the twining creepers of Tasmania. Inverewe is perhaps an ultimate de-velopment of the tradition of collecting plants within a park begun by the Assyrian kings and has something of the magic of the mountain visited by the heroes in the *Epic of Gilgamash*; it seems a place apart from the ordinary restrictions of geography and subject to its own rules and climate. To enter its 'pale' is akin to the experience of en-tering the Palm House of Kew on a winter's day, but it is a pale founded on horticulture rather than glass and cast iron.

Examples have been described of the great gardens of these years: the work of Jekyll and Lutyens, Mackenzie, Nicolson and Sackville-West; but there were many others: Bodnant, Tresco, Great Dixter and Hidcote, that one can compare with the finest gardens of other ages. But they were the work of creative individuals who had mastered the vast resources of plant material now available, and it must be em-phasised that they were outstanding in their time and not typical. The point is important, for in the reduced circumstances of our times the masterpieces should be recognised and preserved, lest the dross sur-vives while the gardens of genius decline and are overrun by weeds or worse. Most gardens fell far below the standard of the best; un-adventurous historicism became a backwater for some and others, unable, one suspects, to handle the new resources, escaped into the inviting culs-de-sac of Japanese and Alpine gardens. Japanese gardens in Britain are imitations of a sophisticated but alien art form and can-not, for historical and social reasons, be anything but poor copies. Alpine gardens often seem even more bizarre and out of place in low-land Britain, and although at Kew and Wisley they have a certain

18. Informal planting within the strict rectilinear dis-cipline of the overall design as practised at Sissing-hurst accords with the Persian tradition. It is the antithesis of the parterre and formal French tradition in which all elements are ordered geometrically, with a consequent loss of contrast.

magnificence deriving from the tonnage of imported rock and the horticultural care expended, one may well wonder if the result justifies the effort and perhaps conclude that mountain scenery just 'does not travel'. At Sissinghurst, Sackville-West used Alpine plants without recourse to rocky simulations and they fuse successfully into the overall scene; in the rock garden at Inverewe they do not, and the reason is probably that they are treated in the manner of the Kew rock garden and form an 'anywhere' element within the garden, alien to its spirit and the manner in which other exotics are adapted to its woodland character.

Notwithstanding the later gardens of Sissinghurst and Hidcote, which were exceptions to their time, the great age ended effectively with the First World War. The financial resources were considerably reduced with the resulting problems of upkeep. At Sissinghurst in the 1930s Sackville-West found economies in labour through using shrubs in areas which two generations earlier would have been planted with herbaceous borders. Inverewe is maintained by two full-time and one part-time gardeners. Today even those resources seem considerable for any but a benevolent public body by which both gardens are now owned. It remains to be seen whether massive public access will erode the intensely personal nature of these gardens and whether inevitable replanting will accord with their creators' vision. There seems a strong case that they should be botanically 'fossilised' and maintained strictly as bequeathed by their designers, for any deviation will inevitably be the work of lesser men (a genius will be elsewhere making his or her own gardens) and a respect should be shown similar to that given to the form and details of buildings deemed to be masterpieces.

But economics were not the only factor in the decline of invention and confidence that had produced the great gardens. With the holocaust of the First World War the heart, it seems, went out of the native school of architecture; the architectural dearth of the 1920s had its counterpart in a general lack of invention in garden design and when young architects in the late 1930s welcomed the International style, there was no tradition or philosophy of garden and landscape design to accompany it. Le Corbusier extolled the informal landscapes of the English parkland tradition (via the Bois de Boulogne) but had no understanding of their origin, logic or necessary maintenance – he probably believed them to be 'natural'. As a result, he set his projects in bosky surroundings which in practice would become arid patches of mud and tarmac.

While the parkland tradition lingers on forgetful of its origins, the garden tradition has become democratised, the weekend hobby of every family lucky enough to own a few square yards of space around their houses. The nursery industry of earlier centuries has swelled to a boom time for garden centres, a vast publishing industry of magazines purporting to advise and, for those without taste or time, a service industry of firms who undertake 'instant' garden creation has appeared. These developments are largely outside the concern of this book, but it is fair to note that a few creative designers still plant magnificent gardens on a limited scale, the little known equals, perhaps, of Lutyens and Jekyll, but the majority seem wholly adrift, clutching at any straws their magazines can extend to them. Generally, the world of commercial and private horticulture seems without guiding values of quality, taste or usefulness and the average result reflects the lack of guidelines and underlying beliefs. The atavistic urges of the urbanite to cultivate living and rewarding plants, reaping their fruits or enjoying their flowers, deserves something better than the exploitation that masquerades as the art of gardening today. Perhaps the answer lies in the traditional cottage gardens one still sometimes finds, where a combination of productive gardening with flowers grown for cutting or delight, preserves an echo of the integrated gardens of earlier times.

Chapter 7

Modern landscapes

New and old concepts

A theme of this book has been the persistence and reinterpretation through the ages of certain concepts and the recurrence of symbols. The main concepts that we have followed, Paradise and the Golden Age, effectively died as beliefs in the course of the nineteenth century. Although a few fundamentalists may still believe in the literal truth of the Genesis account of Eden, they must be very few on this side of the Atlantic and it is generally regarded as a useful myth to explain man's arrival at a state of self-knowledge. It would seem unlikely that anyone now believes in the Golden Age as described by the classical writers.

While the ancient concepts of Paradise and the Golden Age appear effectively dead, attitudes to the natural world attended them, and it remains to consider whether these can offer insights to our own age or contribute to the evolution of new concepts. We must also consider new and fundamental developments that must affect our present attitudes to the land and, indeed, our hope of survival as a species.

First, there is the newly acquired ability of man to destroy his civilisation, and perhaps the biosphere, in the course of warfare. Bruegel in the *Triumph of Death* showed the destruction of the human race by powers outside its control. But the twentieth-century landscapes of death are man-made, the deserts of mud and broken trees of the Western Front recorded by Nash and Nevinson, whose art and geometry lent a dignity to the frightful scene of bombardment and poison gas, seeking order, as painters will, where disorder and destruction are permanent, and unable to depict the stench of putrefaction and the din of guns. Later scenes are preserved on film: the corpses of Belsen and Buchenwald, the shadows etched on the walls of Hiroshima, the poisoning of productive lands and forests in Vietnam. Bosch and Bruegel left something of human dignity beneath the assaults of demons and skeletal battalions, but little is left in the warfare of today – the work of man for which no god or demon may be surrogate. And over all hangs the ultimate threat and symbol of death, the mushroom cloud.

We have, of course, come to terms with the threat of extinction; human nature insists that life continues. The prospect of eternal torment as the reward for lust and self-indulgence did not, it seems, deter medieval man from the enjoyments of adultery, gluttony or other mortal sins. So, today, the prospect of nuclear annihilation is ignored for practical purposes. At the same time a slower, more insidious and more relentless Apocalypse may be apparent in the growth of population, production and the concomitant pollution, and the use of non-renewable resources. A vast literature now exists on the subject which is mostly pessimistic but the general, and perhaps, natural, reaction is to set the problems on one side and look to science and technology to find solutions for the future. Maybe they will, but so far the impact of man the technologist on the natural scene is not always encouraging. Problems apparently solved are found to beget new problems, usually because solutions are not considered in the context of the whole. Natural ecological systems are inherently stable and fortunately there is increasing recognition that it is dangerous to interfere with them; like the decapitated hydra, several venomous heads may sprout in the place of one.

Sometimes wrong conclusions have been drawn from schemes in themselves highly successful and this is particularly true of landscape planning. A project that caught the imagination in the 1930s and 1940s was the work of the Tennessee Valley Authority (TVA), established by Congress in 1933 on the crest of the New Deal. In a decade a land surface was remodelled on a scale that made Versailles appear parochial; new lakes held by dams of noble, indeed heroic, architecture fed hydroelectric power to agriculture and new industries; the hills around were planted with forests. Farming, forestry, industry and recreation were all considered and well served by the plan which brought new life to a degraded area. As a project it seemed to promise much: the technologist, engineer and planner might raise the quality of life by similar means elsewhere in the world. Yet subsequent dams in Africa and Asia do not appear to have achieved similar results, and the reason is that the wrong lessons were learnt. The TVA was dealing with a fundamentally derelict landscape, ruined and degraded by man, where the designers could hardly fail to produce spectacular results, whereas the designers of the later dams were altering complex existing systems which they did not stop to analyse and understand.

Another example of man's intervention in the natural world to create new planned landscapes, which rightly catch the imagination, is the more recent work of the Dutch on polders reclaimed from the Zuider Zee. Rectilinear geometry is offset by the irregular patterns of crops, trees cluster around the fine barns of the farmsteads and great belts of hardwoods stretch for kilometres through this flat, man-made, and already beautiful landscape. There is a sense of rightness born of centuries of experience which allows the Dutch to allocate large areas of hard-won productive land to recreation, amenity and natural habitats. Yet this is a landscape that began with nothing except silt.

Both the TVA and the polders make heady draughts for landscape architects and planners longing for a 'broad canvas' and their real lesson is missed, which is the need to meet a variety of demands: food and timber production, wildlife conservation, recreation and amenity, all of which are common to landscapes that are truly productive and integrated. In existing long-established landscapes a far subtler approach is necessary that begins with an understanding of their evolution and evaluation of the patterns and features already there; with such knowledge, the legacy of the past, often irreplaceable in biological and historical terms, can enrich the landscapes of today in a process of adaptation and carefully considered change.

If, on one hand, we have the evidence that man the technologist is not the master that he seemed perhaps a generation ago, on the other science has brought increased knowledge and perception of the unity and interdependence of the biosphere and man's relations with his environment. The development of systems theory and the science of ecology have countered the increasing trend to specialisation and professionalism which tend, through lack of interdisciplinary communication, to act as though in isolation – be they highway engineers, aircraft designers, or chemists plotting the elimination of agricultural pests and weeds. An interesting analysis and summary of work and observation carried out under the conditions of scientific method is contained in Lyall Watson's *Supernature*, a work that treads ruthlessly across the 'professional' barriers of scientific disciplines. Watson describes the effect of cyclical patterns, the rhythms of night and day, the moon, the influence of the sun and other cosmic factors.

> Cycles of light and dark, of heat and cold, of magnetism,
> radioactivity, and gravity all provide vital guides and life learns
> to respond to even their most subtle signs. The emergence of a
> fruit fly is tuned by a spark lasting one thousandth of a second;
> the breeding of a bristle worm is co-ordinated on the ocean floor
> by a glimmer of light reflected from the moon; the development
> of the eggs of a quail is synchronised by a soft conversation
> between the embryos; conception in a woman waits for that
> phase of the moon under which she was born. Nothing happens
> in isolation.

While life responds to the cyclical patterns and forces of the cosmos, Watson shows that it is itself a unity with continuous communication not only between living things and their environment, but among all things living in that environment. Evidence for this unity lies in the sensitivity of plants to other life in distress. This view of the natural world in which plants are regarded as living entities with some degree of awareness, rather than just as machines for producing cellulose, has something in common with the attitude of Antiquity. As we have seen earlier, Cato uttered an appropriate prayer and sacrificed a pig before thinning a grove, to propitiate the attendant spirit, the personified life force of the trees. To Cato, the farmer must work with and respect nature, not in his case because of ethical consideration, but because he believed it necessary for survival; legends abound in classical mythology of frightful punishment following the unwitting destruction of a grove or tree sacred to some fell being. Cato's caution did not seem to include domestic animals (the pig no doubt had its own view of the sacrifice) nor his fellow humans – perhaps in the latter case because his world was not anthropocentric. A broader view of earth and cosmos was expressed by Virgil in which man achieved unity with the divine by good husbandry in a well-ordered land; a vision rediscovered in the Middle Ages and expressed clearly and economically in the *Très Riches Heures*. Lyall Watson's view of the unity of life would, I think, with certain reservations imposed by time, be understandable to Virgil and, indeed, even to St Francis: 'There is life on earth – one life, which embraces every animal and plant on the planet. Time has divided it up into several million parts, but each is an integral part of the whole. A rose is a rose, but it is also a robin and a rabbit. We are all of one flesh, drawn from the same crucible.' [1]

A respect for nature on ethical grounds as well as those required by a long-term view of the conservation of resources is propounded by the late Dr E. F. Schumacher [2]. He argues against contemporary economic and governmental pressures on the farmer to regard the land and creatures on it as nothing but factors for production. He compares a man-made thing such as a car, which a man may run to ruin, with animals such as a calf or hen – living, sensitive creatures – which it is fundamentally wrong to treat as nothing but utilities. 'Man has not made them, and cannot recreate once he has spoilt them in the manner and spirit as he is entitled to treat things of his own making.' The argument is metaphysical, not scientific, and he returns to the hallowed statements of religion: the Judaic–Christian tradition refers to God's injunction to Adam to 'dress and keep' the garden, giving him dominion over the beasts . . .

> . . . not the right to tyrannise, to ruin and exterminate. For man to put himself into a wrongful relationship with animals, and particularly those long domesticated by him, has always, in all traditions, been considered a horrible and infinitely dangerous thing to do. There have been no sages or holy men in our or in anybody else's history who were cruel to animals or who looked upon them as nothing but utilities, and innumerable are the legends and stories which link sanctity as well as happiness with a loving kindness towards lower creation.

Schumacher goes on to quote a report on Buddhist attitudes in Burma (a people with far longer experience of civilisation than ourselves in the West):

> To him [the Burmese] men are men, and animals are animals, and men are far the higher. But he does not deduce from this that man's superiority gives him permission to illtreat and kill animals. It is just the reverse. It is because man is so much higher than the animal that he can and must observe towards animals the very greatest care, feel for them the very greatest compassion, be good to them in every way he can.

One suspects that the traditional husbandman has usually known and worked with such precepts. But now the farmer has been positively encouraged to embark on cruel enterprises such as the caging of hens in overcrowded, battery conditions, de-beaked because frustration and stress impel them to attack their own species – the ultimate use of an animal as a utility today [3].

Schumacher considers the 'economic' attitude to the land itself, and here he may be unduly pessimistic since farmers tend to be conservative. He cites the Mansholt Plan, which advocates the merging of small family farms into large agricultural units, operated as if they were factories, as the likely course if economic attitudes derived from industry are allowed to dictate farming ownership and patterns. He suggests alternatively a wider role for agriculture in fulfilling three tasks: 'To keep man in touch with living nature, of which he is and remains a highly vulnerable part; to humanise and enoble man's wider habitat; and to bring forth the foodstuffs and other materials which

1. The unity of life and universe was expressed a century earlier by John Muir in his journal: 'When we try to pick out anything by itself, we find that it is bound fast by a thousand invisible cords that cannot be broken to everything in the universe. I fancy I can hear a heart beating in every crystal, in every grain of sand and see a wise plan in the making and shaping and placing of every one of them. All seems to be dancing in time to divine music.'

2. E. F. Schumacher: *Small is Beautiful*. Abacus (1974).

3. In Britain, pressure from the intensive farming lobby prevented the application to battery-kept fowls of regulations which protected other caged birds.

are needed for a becoming life.' Schumacher concludes that no civilisation that recognises only the third of these tasks 'and which pur-
sues it with such ruthlessness and violence that the other two tasks
are not merely neglected but systematically counteracted, has any
chance of long-term survival'. Fortunately French and German conservatism has tended to ensure rejection of Mansholt's attitudes.

While his approach is ethical, relating to the Judaic–Christian tradition of paradise with the concomitant responsibility to the 'beasts
of the field', he believes it to be the only practical course if we are not
to turn our environment into a wasteland. Thus attitudes attending
the wider paradise tradition can be seen to have relevance to the landscape of today if Schumacher's analysis is accepted, or accepted in
part.

The relevance of the tradition of the Golden Age is more difficult
to assess. The animism of Antiquity, as far as plants and animals were
concerned, and the concept of nature as a unity has similarities to the
approach and conclusions of Lyall Watson. Perhaps the Golden Age
is a legend that embodies distant memories of man's earlier life, when
he lived as a part of the animal kingdom and his senses were tuned
to signals from other species of which he is now unaware. His emergence from this state is, perhaps, the true meaning of the Fall and of
the corruption by men formed of baser metals, which followed the Age
of Saturn. A longing for return to Arcadia and to the garden recur in
Western literature as we have seen, and while it may seem unlikely
that a time will come when the lion eats straw with the bullock and
the wolf lies down with the lamb, knowledge and awareness of the
complexity and unity of the natural world just could bring man to the
sense of stewardship implicit in God's injunction to Adam to 'dress
and to keep'.

Reduction and synthesis

The problem is to bring this awareness of complexity and unity into
practical action. I have referred to the trend to specialisation and professionalism, and these problems have been summarised by Dr Lee
M. Talbot, formerly the Director of Conservation and Special Scientific Adviser to the World Wildlife Fund, with a clarity that it would
be impertinent to paraphrase.

> The glorious photographs of earth taken from space brought
> some recognition that we have 'only one earth' (the motto of the
> Stockholm Conference), and that it and the resources on it are
> indeed finite. There has been growing scientific recognition of
> this fact, and the concurrent one that everything is interrelated,
> so that we need to approach the management of our environment
> from a holistic point of view.
>
> Yet to date, most of our endeavours are fragmented, dealing
> with one or another problem in a largely isolated and
> consequently simplistic way, in the assumption that somehow one
> part of the environment was separate from, and could be dealt
> with apart from, the rest.
>
> Nowhere is this better illustrated than in a recent study
> undertaken by the United States Government. The study was to
> examine the probable change in the earth's population, resources

and environment to the year 2000. It was intended that it would not simply project present trends forward, each in isolation from the others, but that it should consider the synergistic interactions between the different factors. Clearly, deforestation and land clearance affects watersheds and local water regimes, which in turn affect downstream agricultural lands and food production, and so on. However, after three years of effort, the study concluded that within the government there was not the capability to deal effectively with interrelationships between such different but clearly related factors.

At first thought, this appears incredible. On further consideration, however, it is totally consistent with our cultural and scientific development. Western science operates largely on the basis of reductionism: a complex whole is divided into its simpler components, on the theory that they are individually easier to understand, and once the components are understood, they can be reassembled to comprehend the whole. The problem is that the emphasis and effort is devoted to the first part of the process, the reduction, not on the reassembly, the synthesis. The consequence is the proliferation of specialities and specialists, not on synthesis and synthesisers.

This process is further exacerbated by the traditional academic divisions by disciplines, expressed in educational institutions divided into virtually watertight compartments, which make elegant sense from a classical disciplinary point of view, but which bear little relation to the real world. The system of academic advancement and awards is based on these disciplinary divisions and specialities. One result is that if a scientist emerges from such an educational system with the capability to synthesise with scientific rigour, i.e. to deal with a holistic environment in a realistic way, it is usually in spite of the system rather than because of it.

Where this is true with science, it is equally true with other academic endeavours and social aspects of life, including government [4].

The experience of Dr Talbot in America is true of Britain and, one suspects, of every developed country. One example among many in Britain is the huge planting programme that has accompanied the construction of motorways. Its purpose is scenic, to relieve the tedium of motorists on roads essentially boring due to the gradients required by the engineers: taking valleys on embankment and hills in cutting. A landscape architect designs the scenic panorama which then goes to a different section of horticulturalists for the selection of species and implementation. Trees and shrubs are consequently selected for their suitability to soils rather than their environment or regard to the presence of native species in the surrounding countryside. The policy bears no regard for nature conservation and the presence of hovering hawks is due to small mammals living on a relatively undisturbed tract of land, rather than any conscious policy of planning for wildlife conservation. No regard is paid to the future prospect of harvesting these millions of trees for a practical and useful purpose [5].

Similar reductionist attitudes have attended agricultural improvement in Britain. The Agriculture Act 1947 provided the framework

4. 'The need for an holistic approach', *World Conservation Strategy*. Inaugural American Exchange Lecture to the Royal Society of Arts, London, 19 March 1980.
5. The terms of reference were set by the Motorways Landscape Advisory Committee some time in the 1960s. If devised today, one would hope that a multiplicity of factors would be taken into account in addition to scenic effect and suitability to soil types; these would include a respect for the historical and local cover of the land through which the motorway passes, a regard for a future harvest as the world runs short of timber, and the establishment of tree, shrub and herb cover that would support wildlife populations reduced by farming changes, development and the destructive action of building the motorway itself. As it is, a unique opportunity for synthesis has been lost.

Fig. 7.1 The type of landscape that many conservationists fear will be the logical result of government policies. Permanent vegetation in the form of hedgerows has vanished leaving arable farming and wirescape. Fortunately it is a relatively rare landscape and in this case the prospect of a dual-carriageway bypass has blighted its immediate future.

for a massive programme of change within terms of reference that solely considered raising agricultural productivity, irrespective of the goals of other government departments and agencies [6]. The destruction of rich and long-established wildlife habitats, and important archaeological sites, was largely unnecessary, as recent studies and exercises have shown. Yet it was done because the brief, terms of reference and the fiscal incentives were essentially reductionist. The process still continues at the time of writing, although the pressure for change has now moved to marginal land.

Similarly, many ancient woodlands were converted into modern plantations and the funds to do so made available by government. Some 10,000 years of continuity with ecosystems of great complexity and stability were destroyed at a stroke in the interests of a marginal gain in productivity and in ignorance of the methods by which oak regeneration has been secured in historical times [7]. The process has still not ended [8].

Planning authorities during the 1950s and 1960s did little better, with no landscape planners to advise them. A low value was placed on the importance for the future of preserving good quality land in the interest of our future sustenance. The bizarre, and wholly reductionist, situation occurred in which the Ministry of Agriculture encouraged the destruction of ancient woodlands and wetlands in the interests of greater food production, while another arm of government, the local authorities and development corporations, destroyed good farmland at an alarming rate [9].

6. The requirement for ministers, government departments and public bodies to 'have regard to the desirability of conserving the natural beauty and amenity of the countryside' came as late as 1968 with the Countryside Act (Section 11).

7. See O. Rackham: *Ancient Woodland: Its History Vegetation and Uses in England*, E. Arnold (1980), pp. 295–7.

8. The Nature Conservancy Council (NCC) has estimated that between 30 and 50 per cent of ancient woodland has been lost since 1947, mostly to conifer plantations or unmanaged grazing. This compares with the similar loss which took 400 years to complete prior to 1947.

9. The success of Green Belt legislation should be noted. This, however, had its origins in recreational planning in which the need was seen for green areas as a relief and escape for urban dwellers.

Reactions to the degradation and destruction of the environment began in the 1950s and found popular support in the mid 1960s, notably in response to the destruction of historic town centres, to the sheer ugliness of new development, and to the threats of urban motorways and other works of traffic engineers. Essentially the conservation movement in Britain at that time was concerned with buildings and settlements. Concern for the landscape tended to be limited to the effects of urban sprawl, the ugliness imposed by statutory undertakers, and the effects of conifer monoculture on the uplands.

A philosophy of synthesis was first expounded to a wide audience in Britain by Sir Frank Fraser Darling in his Reith Lectures *Wilderness and Plenty* (1969), the holistic view of an eminent ecologist. Eleven years later, many of his points of concern on global destruction of habitats and pollution find a place in Talbot's *World Conservation Strategy*, but Fraser Darling was also concerned with the ecological effects on mankind, particularly children, of growing up in degraded urban landscapes and land ruined by industrial and mining exploitation: 'derelict landscapes remain to foster psychosomatic disease by their primary violation of the eye'. He drew attention to the work of Ian McHarg [10], a Scotsman who had found the freedom to work and develop as a landscape planner in America, essentially a synthesiser who managed to steer specialist interests into a respect for the land and a broadly ecological solution. Both men shared a dislike for the Judaic–Christian concept of world resources as the right of man to exploit and to ruin in his own interests, the other and contradictory concept to that of the Garden of Eden. The latter accords with the view of the American ecologist Aldo Leopold whom Fraser Darling quotes as the clearest exponent of an emergent ethic of the land: 'That land is a community is the basic concept of ecology, but that land is to be loved and respected is an extension of ethics. We abuse land because we regard it as a commodity belonging to us. When we see land as a community to which we belong, we may begin to use it with love and respect.'

It is not surprising that Fraser Darling quoted American ecologists in his lectures and referred to American achievements, for in the conservation of natural resources, as opposed to buildings and man-made environment, American thinking and actions were virtually a century ahead of Britain and Europe. There are clear historical and geographical reasons why this should be so, and a comparison between Britain and the USA is interesting [11].

Conservation in the USA and Britain

Historically in Britain and over much of Europe, a tradition of good husbandry was maintained; for survival within restricted geographical confines, it was essential to conserve soils and keep the land in good heart. The remaining forests, woodlands and commons were carefully managed with respect for natural regeneration and renewal. The alternative was starvation. We have noted the decline of customary rights during the eighteenth century, but it has been essentially in the years following the Second World War that the traditional systems of land management have been altered or come under threat. The ethic of respect for nature was carried from ancient Rome into the Christian tradition and expressed in the life and work of St Francis, the Berry

10. Ian McHarg *Design with Nature*. Natural History Press (1969).
11. This comparison has been made possible by Stephen Fox's survey of the American achievement: *John Muir and his Legacy: The American Conservation Movement* (1981).

Hours and Bruegel *Seasons* [12]. The legacy of many thousand years of husbandry is a very varied fabric of historic landscapes that were conserved and adapted until assault by reductionist programmes in the last 30 years.

By contrast, confronted with a vast land of seemingly infinite resources, settlers in North America felt no incentive to conserve; when the land was ruined they moved on. There are no historic landscapes in North America, except perhaps for certain very small areas where the native races practised settled agriculture. As the settlers moved westward they encountered natural landscapes of a grandeur and richness unknown in Europe, and these promised quick rewards in lumbering, grazing and mining. An ethic to justify exploitation was found in Genesis, by which man was authorised to 'subdue the Earth', its land and creatures being created solely for man's benefit and use, the antithesis of the injunction to 'dress and to keep'. Essentially Protestant, this ethic began in Europe where the accumulation of wealth was seen as a mark of God's favour, irrespective of the means used to acquire it. The tradition remains alive in the USA and still exerts considerable political pressure [13].

Faced with this violent concept, which justifies any assault on the natural environment in the interests of a totally man-centred creation, many American conservationists individually rethought the ethical basis of their position, tending away from Christian beliefs into animism, Buddhism and a new respect for Amerindian attitudes to nature. Eventually ecology provided a broad base within which attitudes other than stewardship were untenable, whether one began from an atheist, deist or Judaic–Christian standpoint. With prescience John Muir, himself a deist, had written in 1867: 'Why ought man to value himself as more than an infinitely small composing unit of the one great unit of creation, and what creature of all that the Lord has taken the pains to make is less essential to the grand completeness of that unit? [11]'

The reaction to exploitation and the early growth of a conservation movement was a response to several factors. A deep-rooted love of the wild and dislike of towns was characteristic of the American pioneering spirit; an attitude intensified in the face of massive immigration which tended to degrade urban life. Early settlement and historic buildings were limited to the eastern states, but these were of relatively recent origin by European standards and their value was barely appreciated in the nineteenth century. The American heritage, extolled by travellers and writers such as Thoreau, Twain and Muir lay in the wild areas, and a belief in the right of access with freedom to explore and hunt engendered a powerful (and paradoxically largely urban) counter-attack against destructive agencies and interests. Strange alliances arose of hunting organisations, backed by the gun manufacturers, with conservationists – both alarmed by the rapid decline in game and the shocking assaults on the natural forests. A century of struggle of epic proportions ensued between exploiters and conservers which still continues. To European eyes, the conservers would appear to have won; beginning with Yellowstone in 1872, many millions of hectares were acquired as national parks and wilderness areas, and these together with the national and state forests are managed for their biological as well as recreational value. This is a particular American contribution to world culture, mostly achieved

12. The Church exercised a degree of tolerance to earlier practices. Gregory the Great had advised his missionaries to the heathen English to adopt and sanctify existing feasts and shrines rather in the manner that the Church had already adopted in bestowing the attributes of former gods and goddesses on selected saints. Customs that did not threaten the established order survived, for example: morris and sword dancing – survivors of fertility rituals attending the folk play; the maypole, a manifestation of the World Tree, unfortunately killed off by the Puritans in the mid seventeenth century; the weaving of 'corn dollies'; and the practice of leaving holly trees untouched when a hedgerow is coppiced or cut.

13. Mr James Watt (until 1983 President Reagan's Interior Secretary) ascribes to this tradition: 'We don't know how many generations we can count on before Jesus returns, my responsibility is to follow the Scriptures, which call upon us to occupy the land until he does.' The land includes America's coastline, some 770 million acres of government-owned land and a national park system that runs from Cape Cod to California, which he hoped to open up to developers, oil companies and mining, logging and grazing interests. Mr Watt leads daily morning prayer sessions at work (report in *The Observer*, 7.3. 81).

during a time of complacency in the Old World, and of particular relevance to the conservation of global resources and remaining wilderness areas today.

In 1872, the British lowland landscape on the eve of the agricultural depressions presented an appearance of ordered husbandry, a palimpsest of use over centuries. The uplands appeared wild, but this was largely a man-made wilderness. All land was owned, most of it private property, with public access limited to rights of way and the remaining areas of common land. Rights to hunt, fish and shoot went with ownership of land and were jealously protected. This landscape became virtually fossilised with the depression and apart from brief periods of prosperity brought by the siege economy of the World Wars, remained so until the Agriculture Act 1947. Apart from the threat (and the reality) of urban development the countryside appeared stable, indeed immutable – public concern lay with the slums and decayed towns rather than the decaying countryside.

One attitude, however, common to both countries was an appreciation of the value of natural scenery, in particular forest, mountain and moorland, as an antidote to urban life. 'Thousands of tired, nerve-shaken, over-civilized people', wrote John Muir, 'are beginning to find out that going to the mountains is going home; that wildness is a necessity, and that mountain parks and reservations are useful not only as fountains of timber and irrigating rivers, but as fountains of life' [11]. Later, F. D. Roosevelt said: 'There is nothing so American as our national parks, the scenery and wildlife are native and the fundamental idea behind the parks is native. It is, in brief, that the country belongs to the people [11].'

In Britain, with the shift of population to the towns, the enclosures and the loss of customary rights, very little land still belonged to the people. The founding in 1865 of the Commons, Open Spaces and Footpaths Preservation Society created an effective force, often allied with the remaining commoners, first to prevent the enclosure and urban development of the surviving commons and heaths around London, and later extending the fight across the country. Of the many battles, that over Epping Forest is perhaps the most celebrated, with the strange alliance of City aldermen with local loppers and graziers who were losing their rights to enclosing landlords [14]. The movement to preserve access to the countryside has a noble history, but it did not prevent and indeed tended to overlook, the considerable changes to the fabric of the countryside carried out on reductionist principles that began in the 1950s. As late as 1968, the Countryside Act was primarily concerned with access and recreation, establishing a duty on local authorities to create picnic sites and country parks to accommodate the expected outflow of urban travellers, enfranchised in terms of personal mobility by the rise in car ownership, and so to prevent them from settling down anywhere, trespassing and causing damage to farming. It was to take several more years for landscape and ecological matters to become national rather than local issues.

British lowland landscapes

Fraser Darling's broadcast provided a framework and a respectability for a British conservation movement: 'every acre, not only of Britain but of the globe, demands thought before its biological and visual re-

14. For a full account, see Sir William Addison: *Portrait of Epping Forest*. Robert Hale (1977).

lations are altered' – a requirement that was impossible to fulfil in the climate of reductionism which pertained at the time of his broadcast (1969), but now just possible to envisage in the future countryside and in fact, already achieved on many farms. In spite of crazy fiscal disincentives there is a new stability in the British lowland landscape and the 1980s could see a trend towards creative synthesis. While, at the time of writing, pressure for change continues on lowland wetlands and remaining heaths, largely due to the availability of government grants, it is in the moorlands and uplands – mostly National Parks or Areas of Outstanding Natural Beauty – that real conflict remains. This has been well covered by other writers [15].

The late 1970s saw the growth of widespread interest and concern for the countryside, expressed particularly in the long (and ultimately unsuccessful) battle over the financial provisions of the Wildlife and Countryside Act (1981) [16]. The national headquarters of the Council for the Protection of Rural England (CPRE) emerged as an effective and expert body, comparable with similar organisations in the USA, to lead rational conservation interests [17].

The growing concern for the conservation of the natural environment and its wildlife is evident in the remarkable growth of county trusts and conservation volunteers. At the national level, membership of the Royal Society for the Protection of Birds (RSPB) stood at 14,000 in 1961, in 1971 it had reached 71,000 and in 1982 stood at 352,000. As in the case of CPRE, the RSPB now has the expertise and muscle to enter the national arena as an effective force for conservation. The

Fig. 7.2 British lowland landscapes fall into two main types: planned and ancient. This illustrates a late enclosure surveyor's road in Gloucestershire. In the Midland zone, open-field farming remained the norm until the parliamentary enclosure acts of the eighteenth and early nineteenth centuries replanned the landscape, dividing the land into tenant farms with small rectilinear fields, neatly hedged with quickthorn. Although the pattern sometimes followed the old shots and furlongs, there is often a sense of imposition on topography by the surveyor's rule and set-square.

15. Ann and Malcolm MacEwen: *National Parks: Conservation or Cosmetics?*. Allen and Unwin (1982). The Council for National Parks: *What Future for the Uplands?* (1982). Malcolm MacEwen and Geoffrey Sinclair: *New Life for the Hills*. Council for National Parks (1983).

16. For a summary see Catherine Caufield: 'Wildlife Bill: bad law, good lobbying', *New Scientist*, Vol. 91, No. 1264 (30 July 1981).

It is noteworthy that the national farmer's and landowner' organisation were willing to compromise on the most controversial part of the bill which concerned the legal protection of Sites of Special Scientific Interest. 'The sticking point was the secret cabinet committee dealing with the bill which was headed by William Whitelaw and included Francis Pym, both substantial landowners. A source close to the committee stated, "it's the landowners on the cabinet committee, especially Pym, who are sticking on this point; they're more protective of farmers than NFU is"'.

Fig. 7.3 Ancient countryside near Finchingfield, characteristic of the coastal counties – Essex, Suffolk, Kent, Devon and Dorset. The lanes wind and are sunken on hillsides and like the hedgerows, often rich in age and species, fit the topography and define soil types. It is a landscape which has evolved over millennia in sympathy with natural forces and the land.

rise in membership of such bodies is a symptom of a strong undercurrent of interest and goodwill towards the countryside, its managers and custodians, engendered by weekend trips from the cities, holidays on farms and expressed in the evident desire of many people with the means and choice to live in villages and commute to work, and ultimately to retire to live somewhere in or close to the countryside.

But there is another side to this coin. The degraded environment of the inner city, perhaps inevitably, engenders envy – a mood expressed succinctly by Hugh Clayton, agricultural correspondent, of *The Times* discussing a conference of country landowners: 'they [the landowners] do not realise that thousands of families in towns and suburbs must be content with enough land for a dustbin, a bicycle and a concrete slab. In such conditions the mere possession of space and peace appears a privilege beyond price and sometimes beyond justification.' Envy may be one of the factors that lies behind the mindless and destructive vandalism characteristic of the urban fringe and the often irrational opposition and interference with traditional field sports [18].

Parallel with the growing conservation movement has been a widespread change of attitude among many farmers and landowners, away from the single-minded emphasis on 'improvement' which gripped the industry during the 1950s and 1960s. This mood is towards a recognition of other claims on the countryside and the concept of stewardship. Direct experience suggests that a large number of farmers are now actively concerned with conservation issues, another, larger, sec-

17. Unfortunately other elements received widespread publicity; absurd projections were used to suggest that little of landscape value would be left by the year 2000 and these chimerical notions received wide media coverage, particularly television which chose to depict the actions of maverick farmers and ignore the responsible ones.

18. Organised disruption occurs mainly when animals are hunted, particularly foxes and hares. Angling clubs with their vast, mainly urban working class, membership are not harassed, although angling competitions are certainly cruel.

tion of the farming community are concerned for their public image to counter the threat of legislation, and there remains the maverick fringe who care for nothing but direct profit from the land and vex the farming and landowning organisations who see them as the enemies who attract adverse and newsworthy publicity. A leading conservationist farmer admits that in the bad days of the 1960s, his workers used to push straw into the hedgerow ditches before burning – a memory that now fills him with horror. But this attitude was consistent with the environmental climate to that time which was all for 'improvement' and the fact that we still have a hedged and wooded countryside owes much to the innate conservatism and good sense of the farming community in the face of the advice and funds offered by their ministry. It must be remembered that farm improvement and the production of food was regarded as a patriotic duty both during the Second World War and long afterwards, and had public support irrespective of the damage to the environment [19]. The extent to which the lowland landscape survives is a tribute to farmers' caution – it could easily have evolved into vast open fields spotted by occasional conifer plantations.

Unease at the consequences of change brought farmers and wildlife organisations together at the Silsoe conference in 1968. Farmers and naturalists met on a Hertfordshire farm to work out a compromise plan that allowed for both productivity and nature conservation. As a result the Farming and Wildlife Advisory Group (FWAG) was formed. Subsequent exercises brought in other countryside interests – sporting, forestry, archaeology, landscape design and history – and the group now has an impressive track record, with local groups in most counties achieving 'grass roots' co-operation and achieving an influence far beyond direct membership. The Silsoe conference, it should be remembered, was a farmers' initiative taken well before Fraser Darling's broadcasts awakened a response in wider audiences.

Towards the goal of synthesis in the countryside we shall consider first the principal demands on the working landscape and secondly the contribution which the landscape planner may make within a holistic approach.

Nature conservation

Of the factors to be considered by the landscape planner nature conservation must take priority, for although some species of wildlife apparently adapt to changing habitats, others do not. If species are lost or exterminated we may not yet know their value or understand the ecology and habitat that has nurtured them. For both practical and ethical reasons, long-established habitats with their plants and creatures should be preserved, for we cannot re-create them.

The practical arguments for conservation have been lucidly expressed in *Nature Conservation and Agriculture* [20]:

> . . . the greater the diversity of genetic material the greater are the opportunities for evolution and the deliberate breeding of plants and animals by man. Generally speaking, therefore, it is wise to ensure the survival of as many species as possible. This is what conservation is about – maintaining biological diversity and so keeping the options open as wide as possible for our own and

19. The vagaries of government policy and public opinion were succinctly described in a letter to *The Times* by Mr George Marten (15.11.80).

He described being reported by a member of the public in 1952 for having failed to bring into full production six acres of steep north-east-facing downland covered with anthills. Under the threat of compulsory purchase he felt obliged to plant what turned out predictably to be one of the most uneconomical plantations in Dorset.

Mr Marten referred to the nature of governmental and public opinion 20 to 40 years ago, when politicians spoke disparagingly of farmers who failed to clear and plough land for higher production. The Inland Revenue were urged to investigate farmers who failed to make reasonable profits and agricultural education was geared to the same ends. 'All this had the evident support of the public. The only voices I remember being raised against the excess of this policy were those of landowners themselves.'

Mr Marten pointed out that public opinion has now done a U-turn and 'conservation not productivity is all the rage'. But capital taxation regularly drains the land of the resources essential to its proper care and conservation, and he hoped that societies and individuals would appreciate this point and lend their efforts to assist the landowners.

It should be noted that the areas of steep downland which now often degenerate into scrub were singled out as 'ecological corridors' in certain books of the late 1960s (usually the same photograph). In fact these are often rare habitats for chalkland plants dependent on a grazing regime for which scrub invasion is inimical. The priority for the synthesist should be to restore grazing and secure sufficient support financially if this is economically necessary from NCC. However, national funds for conservation are a minute fraction of those available for capital work and 'reclamation'.
20. Appraisal and proposals by the NCC (1977).

future generations. The value of maintaining wild stocks of domesticated species has been demonstrated by plant breeders on many occasions in the past. The need for genetic material for such purposes and for domesticating other plant and animal species is likely to grow as fossil fuels become exhausted and fertilisers and pesticides based on them become increasingly expensive [21].

There is also the cultural argument: millions derive pleasure from their contact with nature and many of the rare, spectacular forms of wildlife are valuable for cultural reasons. 'Losses of the rarer species would greatly impoverish the cultural life of man, and losses of many abundant ones would put our survival in jeopardy.'

The ethical argument is clear and concerns man's role as custodian, so clearly expressed by Dr Schumacher. But ethics also require that one practises at home what one preaches to others; it is hypocritical to deplore the clearance of rain forests in underdeveloped countries when primary woodland is still being lost in this country and other rare and non-renewable habitats are still under threat – usually from government agencies; many species, unspectacular compared with whales or rhino, are now regionally extinct in Britain and some may have been lost for ever. To paraphrase John Donne, no man is an island and the loss of a species or rare habitat diminishes him in ethical, cultural and practical terms [22].

Nature reserves cover only 0.8 per cent of the land surface of Britain. This is inadequate to preserve the existing flora and fauna, and many plants and animals in nature reserves require support from outside populations to remain viable. Therefore, since about 80 per cent of Britain is in some form of agricultural use, conservation on the farm is vital to wildlife conservation over the country as a whole: 142 species of plants and ferns are confined to the woods, hedges, ditches, grassland and ponds which occur on ordinary farmland. If all farms were to be totally modernised to consist only of arable, grass leys, treated ditches and all cover removed, about 80 per cent of the bird and about 95 per cent of the butterfly species would be lost to the productive landscape. Fortunately, outside Fenland such farms are comparatively rare.

The conclusion to draw is that wildlife conservation and habitat management must form a positive component in the farm or estate plan. Setting aside an ancient woodland or wetland as a 'conservation area' is not enough if its linkages to the world at large are severed by a hinterland of intensive farming. The variety of species in an island tends to dwindle if the channels that could replenish it are cut. A fallacy frequently encountered is that wildlife will adapt to newly created features and consequently there is little harm in eradicating long-established ones; this is only true of certain species, many of the more interesting ones will survive only within the complex ecosystems of 'ancient' features and colonise very slowly, if at all – a modern hedge is no substitute for a Saxon one, nor a plantation for ancient woodland. Both new features have a value, but they will not re-create what is lost.

Hedgerows form valuable links between isolated sites, particularly when they are thick and well managed, and have ditches and grass brews. Many species of herbaceous plants, insects, birds, mammals

21. The scientific value of preserving genetic diversity applies also to cultivars and domestic breeds which are a living gene bank on which we may wish to draw in the future. For example, the Soay (which survived on the islands of Soay and Hirta) appears to be the sheep whose bones have been collected on Neolithic sites and has claims to be the first domesticated sheep. It is small, very hardy, agile and alert, and can live off very little and does not need the constant attention to its feet and fleece which later breeds require. There may come a time when these qualities are required again.

22. The practical, cultural and ethical arguments are considered here in the context of Britain. On the global scale, Paul and Anne Ehrlichs' *Extinction – the Causes and Consequences of the Disappearance of Species* (1981) is essential reading. This survey of the world conservation scene goes far beyond the limits of its title.

and deer are denizens of woodland edges and a good hedge will act in effect as a linear nature reserve. Many indeed originated as relic woodland margins, left as the land was cleared for farming. Even on arable farms demanding large field sizes, it is usually possible to devise a hedgerow network that will allow efficient use of the land.

While it is argued that there is a new stability in the lowland farmed landscape of Britain, serious threats to nature conservation now occur on the marginal lands: wetlands, moorlands and the remaining heaths and broad-leaved woodlands – all areas of great importance for wildlife and containing most of the areas designated by the Nature Conservancy Council (NCC) as Sites of Special Scientific Interest. The threats arise mainly for historical reasons: the powers, huge budgets, limited aims and non-accountability of ministries and government agencies, notably the Ministry of Agriculture, Fisheries and Food (MAFF) and the drainage authorities. These bodies survived the stormy passage of the Wildlife and Countryside Act, but their activities came under scrutiny and some hard evidence was produced.

It was found, for example, that Britain's moorlands were being enclosed and reclaimed at an average rate of 5,000 hectares (12,355 acres) a year, and that this included primary moorland – uplands which had never been ploughed [23]. Previously the figure had been thought to be 100 hectares. When the future of 2,430 hectares of grazing marshes in the Norfolk Broads became a major conservation issue, the role and nature of the Internal Drainage Boards were exposed, organisations whose characteristics recall the days of rotten boroughs [24].

These issues revealed the fundamental reductionism in the mechanics of government on environmental issues. On moorland, landowners are compensated for not taking advantage of subsidies to plough up marginal land. In the case of the Broads vast sums were to be paid by the taxpayer first to finance drainage and then to compensate farmers for not availing themselves of the financial advantages of converting the land to cereal production which would destroy the incomparable value of the land for wildlife conservation. 'If money was spent in this way in industry, first to drain and then to pay people not to drain, the situation would be considered a shambles and the managing director would be sacked. Surely a handful of people cannot be allowed to squander public money and this country's landscape assets when the benefits for the nation have not been assessed?' [25] The shambles, however, appears deeply entrenched and self-perpetuating.

Positive work for nature conservation has been achieved by NCC with their meagre funds, by individuals who have gifted land to the National Trust or supported their county naturalists' trusts and other conservation bodies such as the RSPB, and by certain county and district councils. But as has already been noted, public awareness of environmental issues is recent and naturalists themselves are still frequently reductionist in their own attitudes, finding it difficult to see beyond their speciality, be it birds, insects, tetrapods, plants or lichens. This myopia tends to find expression in making lists of species and concentrating on nature reserves rather than coming to terms with the world outside the 'pale' – too often the farmer has been seen as the enemy and contact avoided. It is relatively recent for the importance of management to have become accepted and most im-

23. *Moorland Change Project.* Birmingham University (1981).

24. Internal Drainage Boards are the country's only independent rating authorities. Numbering 214 virtually autonomous units, they have become self-appointing 'private clubs for farmers with the power to levy rates', although farmers pay only 7 per cent of the rate raised. See 'The anatomy of the wetlands scandal', *New Scientist*, **91**, No. 1269 (3 September 1981).

25. Lord Buxton: Letter in *The Times* (12.8.81).

Simon Jenkins ('Paying the Price of Rural Ruin?' *The Times*, 1.9.83) has pointed out the parallel between countryside conservation in the 1980s and historic buildings in the 1930s in terms of the costs demanded of and obtained from the community.

The irony for the conservationist is that we have seen this all before. The argument of the farming lobby today for 'laissez-faire plus subsidy' is precisely that of the urban landowner (including public authorities) for unfettered development rights in the 1930s and 1940s. Indeed, when desperate efforts were made between the wars to save important historic buildings from demolition, developers demanded (and for a while obtained) compensation for loss of value. This compensation was a devastating constraint. Had it not been ended after the last war – and had the concept of protection without compensation not been extended by Duncan Sandys to conservation areas – the face of English towns today would be wholly different. It is doubtful if any of the buildings of Georgian London would have survived.

Last year's legislation on sites of special scientific interest, granting compensation to any landowner who even threatens environmental destruction, is a carbon copy of a 1932 planning act on historic buildings. It was passed by a farmer-dominated cabinet – rather like giving a group of landlords free rain with the Rent Act. It is half a century since we thought of paying the Duke of Westminster annual 'rent' for not demolishing Belgrave Square.

portantly, that management on long-established sites must follow traditional practice. This is partly an explanation for the time-lag in legislation to protect scientific sites compared with that for historic buildings and towns. But the ecological view has steadily grown since Fraser Darling gave his Reith Lectures and this has been aided by the work of historical biologists and archaeologists who have given increasing attention to the study of landscapes. The correlation between age and scientific interest, or history and natural history has been firmly established and the information is available.

Farming

Over the years roughly spanning 1955–75, changes in farming practice and the consequent face of the countryside took place on a scale that has been termed the Second Agricultural Revolution – the first being the introduction of the Norfolk rotation and enclosure of open fields and commons over parts of England in the eighteenth century. In fact there have been many agricultural revolutions as there have been in ownership and methods of tenure, but the last is notable for its extent and its speed. There are now indications that the dust, as it were, is beginning to settle and stock can be taken. The problems of change now mostly concern woodlands and the marginal lands previously discussed.

The prosperity or otherwise of farmers is closely tied to government policy. In the 1880s farming collapsed in the face of competition from cheap foreign grain; no tariffs were raised and deep depression followed. In 1914 the industry revived through wartime necessity, only to be cast aside when the war ended. The 1920s were the darkest time for British farmers, when the price of their grain could be lower than that of the seed corn, the farmworkers left for the dreaded workhouse, farms became derelict and were often sold for their shooting value. Some older Essex farmers regard the cricket bat willow with affection, for at times it was virtually their sole source of income. In 1939, farming again became a patriotic duty and the Agriculture Act 1947 provided a new framework with guaranteed prices, assured markets and grants for most agricultural operations in order to raise productivity and assure food supplies in the event of a siege economy brought by another conventional war [26]. Unfortunately no time-limit was set for this programme, which had generally achieved its objective by 1970, and it became self-perpetuating. The incomes of the chemical and tractor industries, the spending status of MAFF and the natural reluctance of the farming unions to forgo support led to the White Paper *Farming and the Nation* (1979) which concluded:

> This White Paper sets out no precise targets . . . rather it is a statement of interest and of determination of the Government's settled conclusion that the continued expansion of agricultural net production is in the national interest, and of their determination so to frame their policies as to enable a progressive and efficient industry to make an ever-increasing contribution to the well-being of the nation.

Thus reductionism in action; the programme intended by the 1949 Act had already achieved its objectives within reasonable limits, and the assault on the river valleys and the remaining semi-natural landscapes

26. Compared with industry, capital development and improvement on farms and horticultural enterprises are heavily subsidised by grant assistance. Virtually all improvements – buildings, drainage, fencing, irrigation, and farm roads – are eligible. In addition there is virtual freedom from planning control, and farm buildings are not subject to rating.

on marginal lands was assured. As has been noted earlier, the terms of reference of the Agriculture Act solely concerned agricultural productivity, irrespective of the goals of other government departments and agencies, and this stance was followed in the White Paper. While the situation has been complicated by EEC membership, at the time of writing, the government have refused to implement the Less Favoured Areas Directive which would support small farmers and traditional management in areas where this is appropriate [27], and secured the defeat of the Sandford Amendment to the Wildlife and Countryside Act which would have enabled MAFF grants to be paid on similar lines. As it is, surpluses accrue, the rich farmers become richer while the small farmers often find it hard to make a living, and whether this contributes to the well-being of the nation is questionable [28]. It is a situation which can hardly continue and many farmers see its absurdity and would welcome change. It is difficult to see any justification for the continuing of development grants other than in the terms of the Less Favoured Areas Directive.

Modern farming is specialised, and EEC directives, such as subsidies to limit dairying to certain areas, encourage further specialisation. Over much of western England, where animal husbandry predominates, the landscape has changed relatively little although farming has become more efficient and animals are mostly wintered under cover, to their greater comfort. On chalk downland arable has replaced grassland and although the damage to archaeological sites has been considerable, the landscape has changed little except in texture. It is on the good corn-growing lands of eastern England that the changes are most marked, as the old system of mixed husbandry has generally given way to solely arable farming. This relies on large machines and extensive use of chemical fertilisers and pesticides, possibly a fragile situation, for it depends on fossil fuels, but the high yields together with the high cost of materials and machines compel the farmer to accept it although he is often uneasy. Basically it is a substitution of energy for man (and horse) power, although the labour force previously employed on the farm was probably equivalent to that now engaged in the packaging and distribution of food and the agricultural service industry. The present systems of cost controls have tended to force the farmer to maximise his productivity and deter him from experimenting with alternative systems less demanding in energy and toxins. The present system of support has also given rise to and maintained what may be termed the unacceptable face of modern farming in what is termed intensive animal husbandry. Millions of chickens are kept in conditions of considerable cruelty [29], and there is concern for the welfare of sows and of calves, although farmers themselves have now found humane methods to raise the latter. The farmer will argue that at present he has no economic alternative.

The specialisation of farming accords with the trend of the last 200 years away from a countryside in which everything was used – often for a multiplicity of uses – and nothing was wasted. Today hedgerows, for example, are retained for amenity and game cover and, in stock-keeping country, for shelter. In the past, a hedge had many uses, as has been described earlier.

The principle of multiple use controlled most of the elements which made up the mosaic of the former countryside: woodland, wood-pasture, meads and fens, commons, greens and roadside verges [30]. This

27. Described by Lord Melchett in evidence to the House of Commons Agricultural Committee considering the financial policy of the EEC (20.5.82).

28. The sums spent on subsidies and their consequences are described by Richard Body in Agriculture: the Triumph and the Shame. Temple Smith (1983).

29. Overt confirmation of cruelty was given by none other than D. Parnell, Secretary of the National Egg Producers Retailers Association, reported by The Times (18.2.80). Apparently two old ladies visited a poultry farm to buy a few old hens to produce their own eggs. Within 48 hours of them leaving the farm, photographs of the hens had been presented to the RSPCA who sent down swarms of inspectors. Mr Parnell advised his members to 'make sure that no one is allowed to wander round once they have been served, and to be suspicious of anyone wanting to buy live birds ... it is not their necks they are after – it is yours'.

30. J. M. Hunter: 'The pre-industrial countryside of lowland England – its appearance and management', Landscape Design, May 1979.

has now virtually vanished, the elements usually have a single use – sometimes almost no use at all. Highway verges are wastefully grazed by grass cutters and the cuttings left to rot; these verges have high amenity value and provide a strip for laying services, but they are rarely productive. Deer, once confined to parks, now range freely over the land unperturbed by the machines which have replaced the inhabitants of the countryside who would formerly have frightened and deterred them. Yields of crops have risen spectacularly, but the waste elsewhere would appal the countryman of the past, in particular the annual burning of the straw harvest on arable farms; customary rights linger in the network of public rights of way, often underused or not used at all.

Similar to the decline in multiple use governed by customary rights, the trend (over 250 years) has been noted to the private and exclusive ownership of land. The cottagers were dispossessed by the parliamentary enclosures which drove them to the towns or, if they remained, to live as landless labourers, and the rights which existed over many commons, greens and heaths were extinguished. A hierarchy became generally established of landowner, tenant farmer and labourer. Following the First World War, many of the large estates declined and fragmented, and in the years of prosperity following 1945, tenancies have declined with the growth of freehold. Economies of scale have led to amalgamations of farms – the old 40-hectare farm being barely viable today, although such farms exist and thrive in Germany [31].

Changes in ownership and tenure have been as considerable as the changes in farming technology. Seen in historical perspective we may look back to the Norman Conquest and the Dissolution – both achieved for political reasons without regard for the health of the countryside or the countryman. The first probably made little difference, as one remote landlord was exchanged for another, the second possibly more serious as the social services maintained by the monasteries were abolished at a stroke at a time of considerable suffering due to evictions of farmers and cottagers to make way for sheep. Today the ownership of land is subject to no policy for the well-being of farming or the countryside. Experience, however, suggests that the public interest is best maintained by the resident freehold farmer or secure tenant, particularly if he has a family to continue the holding; he is usually sensitive to public opinion, often sits on his parish council and is tolerant and helpful with regard to public rights of way. Purchase of land by remote investment companies or non-resident foreigners are a growing threat to a delicate balance [32].

An emotive issue of the last two decades has been the removal of hedgerows in the predominantly arable counties, but observation suggests that this is comparatively unusual now. Sturrock and Cathie [33] have shown that on an arable farm of 200 hectares there are considerable economic advantages in enlarging field sizes from 10 to 20 hectares, and on a large farm of 800 hectares, with capital to invest in larger machinery, there is much to gain by increasing field sizes to 40 hectares. Even in the latter case, however, an increase from 10 hectares should only require the removal of approximately 50 per cent of the total length of hedgerow. But there are many other limiting factors that in practice must be taken into account, as the authors point out. Particularly on the productive soils left by glacial drift, there are

31. Schumacher would probably argue that the German farms are viable and useful to society. There is certainly a case that these small farms maintain a good standard of living for their owners who also have jobs in local light industry. This preserves the community structure and avoids the divorce between farming and the urban community characteristic of Britain. British propaganda on the subject of 'inefficient' European farming needs to be looked at carefully in terms of social and community goals and benefits.

32. The benefits to the landscape and wildlife of the frequent instinctive awareness of the owner-occupier is remarked on by Sturrock and Cathie (see below) who describe the results of a survey of hedgerows in the MAFF eastern region, carried out by Dr J. Rossiter in 1971. No environmental restraints were evident on farms that were financed through sale and lease-back arrangements or those owned by large financial institutions and run by managers without hereditary connection with the farm or estate. Efficient production was the sole aim and interest.

33. F. Sturrock and J. Cathie: *Farm Modernisation and the Countryside: the Impact of Increasing Field Size and Hedge Removal on Arable Farms*. University of Cambridge, Department of Land Economy, Occasional Paper No. 12 (1980).

frequent changes in soil type and structure that can cause uneven ripening of crops, there are frequent springs and watercourses, and these factors suggest that in these areas the 20-hectare field may be the optimum size [34], whereas the 40-hectare field is more suitable for fenland and chalk downland. Discussion between farmers at an Essex FWAG meeting concluded that 16 to 20 hectares was the optimum field size; on the basis that any of the various jobs – ploughing, drilling, spraying, combining, etc. – could be completed in a day, and this was good for morale. My own observation in Essex is that fields of 40 hectares are usually broken into smaller units for cropping purposes, which brings this discussion back to the point that it is relatively unusual now to see hedgerows being removed for the basic reason that most fields have been increased to economic sizes [35]. There is a new stability.

Whether this stability will be maintained is debatable due to the policies of central government. Grant assistance for 'improvement' and reorganisation of farms remains an inducement for change for its own sake – almost inevitably at the expense of natural habitats. Nevertheless, the apparent stability of the present and an awareness that improved technology may have reached the watershed of diminishing returns, seems to have generated the new interest in the non-agricultural elements of the landscape that has been referred to earlier. A strong factor has been the ravages of the strain of elm disease, introduced in the late 1960s as untreated deck cargo, which has shown the fragility of the existing scene over those areas of Britain where the standing tree cover of the hedgerows was mostly elm. The true extent of agricultural change was often concealed by the lines of trees, giving, in perspective, the impression of a wooded countryside; stripped by disease and death, the new lineaments have been revealed in their frequent bareness. Another factor is the elderly character of hedgerow trees which reflects a long lapse in the tradition of promoting 'maidens' – a practice now being revived.

An increasing number of farmers and landowners have become interested in planting on their land for a variety of motives: game cover, conservation, a desire to 'put something back' and also for quality in their working environment. The movement has steadily grown with the backing of the Countryside Commission and many county councils. Advice on planting gives the landscape planner the opportunity to advise on the landscape generally and to point out the value of existing features, and the management appropriate to them, and it is generally found that the advice is welcomed and acted on. This point is of importance as it is all too easy to see planting as a general panacea which excuses the removal of remaining areas of wetland and old pasture which have less obvious value and appeal than trees, spinneys and ponds.

The problem that vexes the farming organisations is the threat of an extension of planning controls to cover farm operations such as tree and hedgerow removal, the infilling of ponds and the ploughing of heath and moorland. They argue that most of their members are responsible people and if not invariably sensitive to the countryside are aware of the strength of public concern. But there remains the maverick element, so beloved by sensation seekers, whose actions are solely motivated by agribusiness and who do not respond to, and may not belong to, the farming organisations. To these one must add in-

34. Another limiting factor is the unpredictability of the British weather which may mean that the smaller field unit is more easily worked before the weather breaks and therefore avoids uneven ripening of a crop.

35. The form of management followed for hedgerows is critical for their value to wildlife. Neglected hedges that have become thin and leggy have little value, nor have those cut too low. Where permanent hedges are required to contain stock, the A-shape is the most satisfactory: the narrow top encourages growth at the base which makes it stockproof for sheep, at the same time allows the wind to filter, thus making a better windbreak. Differently shaped sections are considered by Sturrock and Cathie.

The difference in cost between fencing, which has to be replaced and maintained, and hedgerows which are only maintained, has been discussed (E. Pollard, M. Hooper and N. W. Moore: *Hedges* (1974) and British Trust for Conservation Volunteers: *Hedging* (1975)) with the conclusion that an established hedgerow was more cost effective than a fence.

On arable farms an economic and traditional form of management, which is a good compromise between farming, wildlife and amenity interests, is to treat the hedge as coppice and cut the trees and shrubs back to their stools every 10 to 15 years. This can be done on a rotation around the farm, so that only a small proportion of hedgerows are cut right back at the same time. Pollards, which often occur in the older hedgerows, can be pollarded when the hedgerow is cut, but this is best done at 20 to 25 year intervals, so they should be missed on alternate cuttings. Good stem of oak, elm or ash can be selected and left uncut to produce long-term timber.

vestment companies who run their farms by remote control through managers and expect their 6 per cent return. Some degree of control seems necessary, and while it might be appropriate to bring farm buildings under the jurisdiction of planning authorities [36] who at present can also control woodland clearance by means of tree preservation orders, it is doubtful if these are the appropriate bodies to administer detailed controls which would affect the practical working of an industry in a manner no other industry has to contend with. To extend planning powers to the extent that has been suggested is a recipe for conflict which could undermine the good work and co-operation achieved over the past decade [37].

We have noted earlier that the 1980s might just see the movement towards creative synthesis already achieved on certain farms and estates spread across the countryside as a whole. It is also possible that the reverse could apply, a countryside of specialisation and conflict, brought about by insensitive legislation beside which the ineptitudes of the Wildlife and Countryside Act would appear unimportant. At the time of writing, the landscape planner can only hope that the former prognosis will prevail.

Silviculture

The term 'silviculture' is chosen to include woodmanship, forestry, the growing of farm timber and the potential within urban areas and derelict land. It is a field bedevilled by fiscal intervention as crazy as that affecting the farmed landscape, and threatening further destruction of the national heritage of ancient broad-leaved woodland and the upland wilderness.

Silviculture is also burdened with a false mythology. We still read that England was largely wooded in 1066; villages were supported by fields in forest clearings and much of England was Royal Forest; in subsequent centuries a long history of neglect and mismanagement degraded the forests, imperilling the fleet, and wooded areas were cleared improvidently to provide charcoal for smelting. The truth is very different: England was largely cleared of forest in prehistoric and Roman times, and by 1066 the wooded area of most counties averaged only 15 per cent. *Forest* was a legal term covering large tracts of country, often arable, over which the King's deer had special protection. The charcoal woods were self-renewing coppice which declined in the face of agricultural expansion and in the case of the Scottish Highlands, sheep browsing which destroyed the stools. The mythology resembles that of hedges (all planted in the 18th and 19th century) and ships' timbers in medieval oak-framed structures. From early times, the fertile soils of England have limited its woodland to a small proportion of its land area, and intensive and prudent management followed to supply the timbers for cathedral roofs, Westminster Hall, Ely Octagon and the frames of countless manor houses and farms. Our pre-plantation history is the record of the means and efficiency by which a very limited resource was managed to the best effect. The resource itself was self-renewing. The cobwebs have now been blown away and a fresh understanding and assessment is possible of the role of silviculture in the landscape and the economy.

There are two distinct traditions of productive woodland management in Britain; the first is woodmanship and the second, forestry

36. Under present legislation planning controls apply only to farm buildings exceeding 12 metres in height and 465 square metres in area.

37. A solution presents itself which would bring a measure of restraint and might be acceptable to farmers and landowners as an alternative to planning control. This is to build on the Strutt Report, *Agriculture and the Countryside* (1978). Sir Nigel Strutt and his colleagues argued that landscape considerations and wildlife conservation should go further than the vague injunction of Section II of the Countryside Act 1968 [6] and that criteria on these lines should be built into schemes grant-aided by MAFF. They saw the divisional and regional staff of the Agricultural Development and Advisory Service (ADAS) of MAFF as uniquely fitted to this role and recommended that they be trained to give advice on conservation matters, and while complying with the confidentiality required for MAFF grants, could consult with other bodies. It would seem feasible to bring in a system of notification by which ADAS officers could consider proposals which might be damaging to the landscape and wildlife, and if they believed this to be the case, to have the power of veto. This might be seen as a *quid pro quo* for continuing fiscal support and of a possible further measure which has been proposed, of extending the Capital Transfer Tax exemptions, which presently apply to Sites of Special Scientific Interest to farms operating an agreed management plan which conserves landscape features, wildlife habitats and archaeological sites.

Veto might in certain cases justify a claim for compensation which would best be settled on a once and for all basis, similar to capital improvement grants. This, however, would require enabling legislation on the lines of the Sandford Amendment.

However, it must be remembered that an early measure of the Thatcher government was to remove the requirement for prior consent for grant-aided schemes. This effectively undermined the purpose of Strutt's recommendations and seems astonishingly feckless in the control of public funds, particularly as the National Farmers' Union favoured prior consent. By 1983 it had become clear that £30 million had been overspent on agricultural development grants as a direct result.

Fig. 7.4 The Forest of Bellême. The French tradition of growing oaks of the quality that once produced the timbers for cathedral roofs.

[38]. Woodmanship is the management of a self-renewing resource, obtaining the produce of the wood without destroying its existing vegetation; it exploits the capacity of most native broad-leaved trees to renew their growth, with increased vigour, when coppiced. These woods were traditionally managed as coppice with standards; the coppice or underwood was regularly cut on rotation, leaving the standards to grow on to form timber trees. The system was fully developed in England by the thirteenth century and remained the method of woodland management until decline began in the nineteenth. In the twentieth century the market for the products of underwood was superseded by cheap energy and fuel, factory-made building materials and metal fencing, and during the depressions the timber trees were felled as a cash crop and the management which would encourage their replacement was discontinued. Now there is a revival in coppice management with a market for pulpwood and wood-burning stoves, and the old woods are beginning to resound to the sound of the chainsaws which will renew their youth. But still lacking is the incentive to bring on the standards which will provide the future timber.

38. The definitions are those of Dr Rackham.

Forestry is the practice of growing trees in plantations: the land is cleared, planted and eventually harvested, and then either reverts to some other use or is replanted. It makes no use of the self-renewing capacity of broad-leaved species and relies predominantly on conifers whose stumps die when the tree is felled. Examples of planting as opposed to managing woods are rare before 1700 [39]. Forestry makes its appearance in the eighteenth century and develops in the nineteenth, with increasing reliance on a limited mix and emphasis on conifers. In 1919, as a result of the First World War, the Forestry Commission was established in order to build up a home-grown timber resource for the event of a siege economy. Huge tracks of marginal land in the uplands and heaths elsewhere were acquired by purchase or lease and in addition, fiscal incentives were given to landowners to plant and manage woodlands with the Commission's advice. The area covered by plantation had risen from 24,000 hectares in 1920 to 720,000 hectares in 1972. Initially the Commission acted solely with forestry objectives without regard for environmental factors other than soil and climate; however, as the effects became visible and large areas of upland were seen covered by a blanket of monotonous conifers, the force of criticism compelled the Commission to make some concessions. A landscape consultant was employed to guide them in softening the outlines of plantations, by fitting them sensitively to topography and by leaving stands of broad-leaved trees. In the more attractive areas of rough or rocky land, beside water, or in areas of established native trees, camping and picnic sites have been established which are justly popular and have added considerably to the nation's recreational resources. But these areas are few, and the character of many forests is that of gloomy and monotonous monoculture which as they mature become seemingly lifeless with a dank, dead floor and bird-song heard only in the rides and firebreaks. Kielder Forest on a dull and misty day has a nightmare quality reminiscent of the paintings of Grunwald.

The monoculture favoured by the Commission is justified on the grounds of cost effectiveness and mechanisation – machines are cheaper than their equivalent in labour, and demand single-species even-aged plantations. This is similar to the trend in arable farming, but whereas a corn or leguminous crop is harvested in less than a year, conifers will require up to 75 years, depending on conditions and species. This makes them vulnerable to diseases and pests whose existence may be unknown at the time of planning the plantation. An arable farmer may write off a crop due to an outbreak of aphid or disease, a similar occurrence for the forester may mean 60 years' investment wasted. For example, the Commission have sprayed their extensive Scottish plantations of lodgepole pine for 3 years in succession with an insecticide, fenitrothian, in order to control the ravages of an insect with the delightful name of pine beauty moth. The cost in environmental damage as well as sterling must make these plantations extremely costly. The solution of 'hedging one's bets' and planting with a variety of species, harvested at selected stages, does not yet appeal to the Commission except where public pressure demands such a programme on grounds of amenity. The private sector has always tended to be more catholic and experimental, preferring mixed plantations on grounds of amenity, game cover, interest of many owners in arboriculture, and an instinct among experienced

39. A third tradition which lies between the two is practised in the oak forests of France. This is a monoculture raised to form high forest over a rotation of 200 to 220 years. The final fellings are spread over 12 to 18 years to allow copious seeding to form the next rotation. The principles were laid down by Colbert, but medieval miniature paintings suggest that the tradition was older. The French experience has been virtually ignored in Britain, which is unfortunate as it would seem to have much to teach us. For a guide to French forests and their management, see J. L. Reed: *Forests of France*. Faber and Faber (1954).

landowners to diversify their planted assets. Tax subsidies and substantial grants have fostered this valuable national asset. With his subsidies, the private owner may indulge his own interests in silviculture, whereas the state forester is always conscious of Treasury scrutiny as to whether his plantation will meet the returns required from public funds [40].

A bid to expand the forest industry has been made in a report: *Strategy for the United Kingdom Forest Industry* [41]. Predictably the report refers to our reliance on imports and the unlikelihood of these being forthcoming in the context of a world timber shortage in the 1990s; it concludes that the area under plantation should be increased by an additional 1,800,000 hectares by the year 2005, most of which would be in the Scottish Highlands. This could involve the virtual nationalisation of the uplands, destroy the 'green lungs' for the inhabitants of the Clyde and have a disastrous effect on the moorland ecology and sites of scientific interest. The last great area of wilderness in Europe would be destroyed in the interests of what might prove an expensive will-o'-the-wisp.

Maintenance of the present improvident level of wood consumption seems unlikely. Micro-electronics and the silicon chip may replace newsprint, recycling of paper waste will become necessary and commonplace while deer farming and hay production may be more attractive to highland owners than the long wait for conifer maturity. If projections are revised, the Commission's case collapses; but if there remains a case for further afforestation it must also combine with other land uses and achieve shared goals – the alternative is vast public expenditure on a single aim of dubious validity. The private sector has always understood this principle; forestry has served the purpose of providing game cover, amenity, shelter and a tax haven.

Undoubtedly all timber will be at a premium in the year 2000 and a case does exist for expanding the industry without the destruction of wilderness. There are three options; first the integration of forestry with farming on the upland margins which would extend the farmed landscape into the moorland purlieus without destroying the former. Planting in belts and blocks, and as peripheral shelter to buildings could extend the areas of both sheep and cattle husbandry, with shared costs for made-up tracks, roads and fencing. Such a solution invites the analysis that a landscape planner can give, but is difficult at present given the reductionist attitudes of both the Forestry Commission and MAFF. It could be achieved by a large estate or a development commission. Such an integrated approach could include recreation and give the added income that caravanning and farm holidays bring. A new type of skilled countryman could emerge – a farmer and forester who also understands the public and recreational needs [42].

The second option lies in the afforestation of derelict land, the legacy of industrial spoil heaps and mineral extraction. Even with careful and planned restoration, success for future agricultural production of any value depends on the existence of a substantial overburden that will provide both top- and subsoil. Most sites lack this. On valley floors extracted areas may turn into lagoons for water sports and angling, but elsewhere after-use tends to be sub-agricultural with fragmentation and 'horsiculture' which extends the air of dereliction into permanency. Similarly sites are often restored with a minimum of

40. The demands of the Treasury are partly responsible for the quick returns sought by the Commission. The French Forestry Service is able to take a different view, thinking in terms of centuries rather than decades and regarding it as short-sighted to plant conifers on land capable of growing oak and beech.
41. Compiled by the University of Reading's Centre for Agricultural Studies (1980).
42. *Ad hoc* acquisition of upland sites for forestry can have the effect of making existing farms uneconomical. Landscape planning is essential if farms are to remain viable with contiguous fields and a mixture of sown and rough pasture. The reader is referred to the *Biennial Report 1979–81*, pp. 122–44, of the Hill Farming Research Organisation, Midlothian, and to T. J. Maxwell, A. R. Sibbald and J. Eadie: 'Integration of forestry and agriculture – a model', *Agricultural Systems* (1979).
A degree of integration can be seen in Penmachno Forest in Snowdonia with good agricultural land retained on the lower slopes and valley bottoms, with access to hill grazing on unplantable land at high elevation. This is an attractive forest where a balance seems to have been kept between different uses, and the exotic plantations well fitted to the landscape.

cover and prone to subsidence. The alternative to a return to agriculture is woodland planting; trees will grow on poor ground and traditionally, ancient woodland has survived on the land least suitable for farming. It has been found that nitrogen-fixing trees such as alder will grow well on sites that would prove inimical to other species; in due course their leaf-litter will enrich the soil – earthworms and microorganisms will enter and the arid, ruined land will develop into a living and fibrous floor. In 100 years the decision could arise as to whether the land, by then enriched, should return to agriculture. In the meantime, successive coppice crops will have been harvested and a wider range of woodland trees introduced as the micro-climate and subsoil improve.

A third option lies in the development of poplar and willow hybrids with spectacular growth rates which can be converted to fuel. Valley floors converted to arable are liable to flooding and with high water tables could become the energy forests of the future. Swedish experiments have been made with densely planted willow hybrids which are coppiced on a two-year rotation. Certain dangers, however, are inherent if economic considerations were to put pressure on wetlands of high importance to wildlife – essentially it will be a question of balance and synthesis.

The growing of trees and use of their products appear to have reached a new point of departure which, on one hand, looks back to woodmanship and on the other, forward to new techniques and uses. In the next two decades the art of silviculture may change radically and make a major contribution to the landscape, provided that this is with a framework of synthesis which considers other demands. Farm and estate timber, grown in hedges and small spinneys, undoubtedly has a future. In the meantime, conflicting fiscal incentives require resolution on the lines suggested by a working party of the House of Lords, which predictably has foundered on the ministerial rocks of sectional empires [43].

The role of the landscape planner

Landscape planning is the art of knitting together the competing demands on the landscape, of finding ways by which its components can at worst coexist and at best form an harmonious synthesis. It is similar to urban design – the art of integrating and reconciling differing demands and in doing so, seeking to create an urban environment which transcends functional requirements and enhances the quality of life. Both skills have acquired a degree of recognition in the wake of the destruction caused by sectional interests and narrow professional goals. A landscape architect is not a landscape planner any more than an architect is an urban designer, although both professions provide a useful training from which to step into the wider context of applied planning.

Planning requires a framework and this is provided in the structure, local and subject plans prepared by planning authorities, which should include both protective and prescriptive policies. Protective policies may be concerned with the preservation of good agricultural land, landscape quality, and sites and features important for nature conservation. Prescriptive policies are concerned with initiatives which arise from particular problems of the locality, for example landscape

43. Select Committee on Science and Technology: *Scientific Aspects of Forestry*. House of Lords session 1979–80.

restoration following mining or mineral extraction, the restoration of tree cover, the resolution of conflicts due to recreational use or reduction of wildlife habitats, or the particular problems of the urban fringe, to name a few.

The landscape planner puts the policies into effect, largely through negotiation and the establishment of goodwill. He will rarely have a broad canvas to work with such as that offered by the Dutch polders, and in Britain will work in the context of a landscape that has evolved over millennia; however ruined an area may have become, its past must be studied and taken into consideration. If the potential landscape planner harbours delusions that he will be a le Nôtre or Lancelot Brown, it would be better for himself and the landscape if he decides to follow some other calling. In the late twentieth century humility is called for in the spirit of Fraser Darling's dictum on 'every acre'.

The interest of many farmers in planting on their land in the wake of elm disease and field alterations, and the scope this gives the landscape planner, has been referred to. The creation of new features provides the opportunity to consider what already exists in the landscape, how it should be evaluated and maintained. On most farms this will be the framework within which additional planting and conservation measures can be planned, and for this it is essential that the historical dimension is understood – today's alterations and additions are but one phase in a landscape with a very long history of management. Historically, useful and valuable features have always been adapted and retained although farming methods have evolved and improved; the problem now is to identify these features which can so easily be destroyed in ignorance and haste; it is a matter of knowing the difference between a Saxon hedge and an eighteenth-century one, between an ancient wood and a nineteenth-century spinney, of recognising old pasture and sites of archaeological interest. With this knowledge, the farm plan can take such features into account.

Tree and shrub planting on farmland should pay strict regard not only to the range of native species, but to those present locally. There are good reasons for this; first, historical continuity: farmland was carved from the woodlands and sometimes hedgerows are former woodland margins. Although doubts have been cast on the origin of the suckering elms and sycamore occasionally invades, the basic species used traditionally for hedgerows were native and local. Spinneys of spruce look as alien as flat-roofed buildings in historic villages. The second reason is aesthetic and concerns the spectrum of tree species which gives both contrast and identity to the landscape; amid the native cover of farmland, ornamental species such as horse chestnut mark a farmstead or village edge, cedars a country house or manor. There are good traditional trees for village and town to choose from, leaving total personal choice for the private garden. Tree species are as important to an area's identity as dialect and architectural style and building materials; if too much variety is attempted, the result is a loss of all variety. The third reason is nature conservation: many native trees and shrubs have a considerable dependent fauna, particularly of insects, and with the depletions of the last 30 years it is important to restore this cover. The fourth and last reason is establishment: countryside planting cannot expect the quality of maintenance expended in a garden and the local hedgerows are a guide to

Fig. 7.5 The parish boundary of Saffron Walden, Essex, rich in tree and shrub species, and in existence before the Norman Conquest. This is an example of the type of landscape feature which it is the duty of the landscape planner to identify, evaluate and seek to preserve.

what species will flourish on particular soils and in particular climatic conditions.

The restoration of tree cover is but one aspect of the landscape planner's role, but an important one. Many county councils now have specialist teams working on both this and its wider aspects and consequences. Essex, the first, has evolved techniques that suit small-scale planning and achieve rapid growth without the traditional forestry method of using alien nurse species.

A parallel development of great interest is emerging in urban landscape design, notably at Warrington and Runcorn, where wildlife is recognised as part of the habitat area of the urban community and contact with nature is seen to enrich urban life. The degraded tradition of ornamental planting is fundamentally rejected and an ecological base sought for parkland and urban design. It is a logical development; the natural flora of waste areas and bomb sites was generally far more interesting and beautiful than new landscaped areas, and it is to be hoped that parks and gardens departments will recognise the merits of rethinking traditional viewpoints. The ecological design movement is very purist at present, but many garden escapes and unintentionally imported species play an important part in urban wildernesses, for example the buddleia, and one hopes the range of species chosen will not be too restricted as the method evolves [44].

Two fields of work which concern the landscape planner have been touched on above. Fifteen years ago such work did not exist, at least in Britain. Now with growing concern for the conservation of natural resources and recognition of the need for a holistic approach, landscape planning is coming to be accepted. It is an exciting time of developing techniques and ideas and the scope is immense.

44. On ecological design and the urban environment, see Ian G. Laurie: *Nature in Cities – the Natural Environment in the Design and Development of Urban Green Space*. Wiley (1979) and Department of Town and Country Planning, University of Manchester: Occasional Paper No. 8 (1982).

Chapter 8

The historical dimension

The correlation between age and scientific interest, or history and natural history, has been noted and the need for humility when altering or adapting ancient landscapes has been stressed; but the past need not be a burden and it often points the way to a synthesis between differing demands and requirements on the landscape. Three examples are described below. The first is Epping Forest.

Epping Forest is a surviving part of the Royal Forest of Waltham. The term 'forest' described land over which the Crown had particular rights to protect the royal deer and other beasts of the chase or warren; it could include heathland and farmland and should not be confused with the use of the term today to describe large tracts of land put down to the single purpose of growing timber. Medieval forests embraced many uses with both customary and manorial rights. By 1300, Waltham Forest had shrunk to an area in South-west Essex, much of which was grazing land with scattered hamlets and greens. The remaining wooded areas were Epping and Wintry which survive today and Hainault which was destroyed in 1851; the Crown was the landowner of Hainault where there were few customary rights, but in Epping and Wintry fragmented manorial ownership of the soil and the tenacious fight of the commoners saved the forest until purchase by Act of Parliament in 1878, by which the land was vested in the ownership of the Corporation of the City of London 'for the enjoyment in perpetuity by the citizens of London'. It is a stirring and extraordinary tale of an unlikely alliance between commoners with rights to lop and graze ranged with City aldermen against enclosing landlords. Today, it seems incredible that the citadel of commerce should have intervened so effectively in the interests of conservation and recreation.

Epping Forest is a landscape of wood-pasture with its trees managed mainly as pollards. Chapman and André's *Map of Essex* (1777) also shows wide areas of open grassland or plains. In ancient times the forest may have been more open since two Iron Age forts lie under the present tree cover but from the late Middle Ages to Victorian times it seems to have been remarkably stable both in its management and boundaries.

The Corporation was faced with the problem of devising management principles which were incorporated in the Act of 1878. Today,

Fig. 8.1 Beech pollards in Epping Forest, magnificent relics of an ancient form of management and recalling the tree shepherds of Tolkien's *Two Towers*.

we can view the last 100 years as a case study of the management of a historic landscape with its successes and failures. Light has been shed by recent research and study on landscapes of this type which has only become available in the last 10 to 15 years. This information, together with an appreciation of the historic dimension in landscape was not available in 1878; thus the subsequent history of the forest is of particular interest to both the landscape historian and landscape planner.

In 1878 many people probably thought of the forest as a 'natural' environment – certainly many do now – but then it was no more natural than the surrounding farmed countryside having been managed for centuries, perhaps thousands of years, for a variety of uses: grazing for cattle, horses, pigs and sheep, the production of timber and under-wood, and in the Middle Ages, supply of venison to the court; it was the functional landscape of wood-pasture. Since 1878 the cutting of timber and firewood has ceased and the grazing declined (although one can still meet cows happily blocking traffic in Woodford) and the overriding management practices have been in the interests of amenity and recreation for which the principles were laid down in 1878.

Fortunately the early conservators sought the advice of Edward North Buxton, a man of perception and sensitivity, and he described the principles and reasoning behind them in his classic handbook to the forest, first published in 1885. These were: (1) variety; (2) the preservation of natural features; (3) restoration of a natural aspect; (4) reproduction with a view to the future. In (4) Buxton was very advanced, advocating native species only and natural regeneration where possible – this was a time when William Robinson was advocating his wild garden with exotics naturalised, and we must be thankful that park designers and 'improvers' did not get their hands on the forest which could easily have happened.

With (1) and (2) there can be little disagreement, but (3) is highly problematic (and Buxton found it so) as it involved the removal of 'artificial' features – to be precise, the beech, hornbeam and oak pollards that formed much of the tree cover of the forest. Pollarding should not be confused with crude lopping or mutilation – it was the practice of regularly cutting a tree for underwood at a height of 6–12 feet (2 to 4 metres) above the ground. Underwood provided fuel and material for fencing, stakes, hurdles and a variety of other uses, similar to coppice which is cut at ground level, but where there are grazing animals it must be cut above the point which the animals can reach, otherwise they will browse the regenerating shoots eventually killing the tree.

Pollards develop into strange, fantastic shapes and provided that cutting continues are virtually immortal for, paradoxically (to a human), the regular pruning invigorates the tree and halts the process of natural ageing – there are pollards in the forest which must be many hundreds of years old. To the forester trained to think in terms of straight lengths of timber, preferably conifer, pollards have little appeal, but to those with minds open to other considerations they may be seen to have historical and archaeological interest as relics of a past form of management, considerable importance for nature conservation, and a romantic quality in their strange, sometimes grotesque, forms. In the context of Epping Forest their importance lies in their numbers and the peculiar character the forest still essentially derives from them – in some glades one feels as though surrounded by an Ent army straight from the pages of Tolkien – and without them the forest would be little different from many other large stretches of pleasant but ordinary woodland [1].

To Buxton the restoration of 'a natural aspect' was of paramount importance and the background to this view of his must lie in the appearance of the countryside in the 1880s [2]. Compared with the landscape of today it would have appeared highly managed and organised; small fields bounded by neat hedges with timber trees at regular intervals, trunks 'shrouded' to make straight stems, the

Fig. 8.2 The traditional management of pollards in Waltham Forest – the bole belonged to the lord of the manor, the upper branches to the commoners and the lower to the king, to provide shelter and browsing for his deer.

1. Against pollards Buxton quoted an observer writing in 1864: *They are not, strictly speaking, trees at all, but strange, fantastic vegetable abortions. Their trunks, seldom more than a foot or eighteen inches in diameter, are gnarled, writhed, and contorted, and at about six feet from the ground, just within reach of the axe, they spread into huge overhanging crowns, from which spring branches which are cut every other year or so, and never long escape the spoiler; then baffled in their natural instinct to grow into branches, the trees throw up spurs and whips from their roots, and every pollard stump – more or less rotten at the core – is surrounded with a belt of suckers and of sprew. It is no more nature's notion of primeval woodland than are closely-cropped hair and shaven lip and chin her intention for the real expression of the human face.*

Dr Rackham, in a letter to the author, put a very different view of the value of pollards:

Pollards are often of great age and of archaeological interest as survivors of an ancient form of tree management. With other very old trees, their bizarre shapes and enormous girth are part of the romantic delight of the countryside. They are an important habitat for hole-nesting birds and certain insects and lichens: their dry hollow interiors are particularly important as bat roosts because other sites are fast being lost to bats. Fascinating plant communities – including other trees – often grow in their crowns. Ancient trees should be treated with the respect due to historical monuments: the action needed (if any) will vary widely with the importance and condition of individual trees. Most pollards, though hollow, are stable and have a long future life.

2. Buxton admired the forests of Eastern Europe. He disliked tidyness and in making the case for the retention of dead, decaying and fallen trees referred to 'fallen giants, gorgeous with moss and lichen, and telling a story of mighty hurricanes and snowstorms that we should miss if they were removed'.

Fig. 8.3 Hornbeam pollards at the density that Buxton found and recommended thinning.

woodlands in regular coppice rotation, a labour-intensive farm economy; everything was used. Today the fields are larger, but the hedgerows and woods are generally unmanaged and have a wild, rather scruffy appearance; the people have virtually vanished from the landscape and the fuel and fruits are mostly wasted. To see a woodland today in full traditional working order is a memorable experience, in Buxton's day such a sight would have been commonplace. In this context his view is understandable and he notes his dislike of trim parklands – Lancelot Brown, it should be recalled, was as denigrated then as he is over-praised today.

Buxton came to the conclusion that the pollards must be drastically thinned to allow the lateral growth of the branches (lopping had by then ceased) and to permit light to reach the floor to stimulate undergrowth and seedlings. But he was unhappy: elsewhere he refers to 'old oak pollards and the venerable air their ancient boles give to this wood' and he expressed his admiration for the great hornbeam pollards at Hatfield Forest. Nevertheless, thousands of pollards were removed to allow the remainder to grow up to form 'high forest'.

The result, however, can now be seen to be ultimately self-defeating, for the canopies of the thinned pollards have met and the floor appears virtually dead over very large areas. Interest is still given by the shapes of the pollards themselves – many have thrown out great buttresses to support the weight of the 'groves' of upward-growing branches springing from their overloaded crowns. But soon they will split, many have blown over, and their end is now in sight. Variety, principle (1), has not been achieved. Elsewhere variety has been lost through the decline in grazing – a trend already under way in Buxton's time but hastened particularly after the Second World War. The

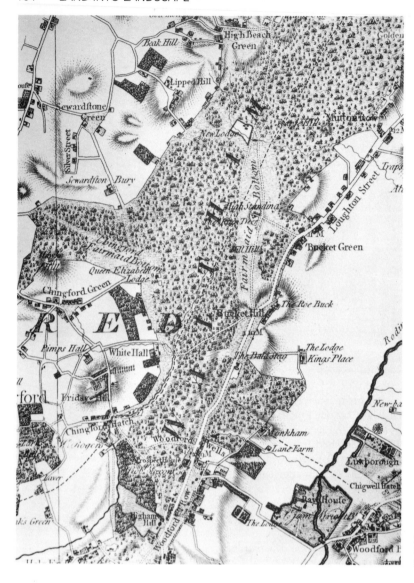

Fig. 8.4 An extract from Chapman and André's *Map of Essex* (1777) showing the areas of pasture within the pollard forest.

tracts of grassland have consequently become areas of scrub, highly vulnerable to summer fires.

Three facts were not available to Buxton at the time that he was writing and formulating the principles. First, the longevity of pollards provided that this form of management is continued; second, their importance for nature conservation; third, the elusive nature of the 'natural aspect'. No woodlands in Britain are natural, as all have been profoundly affected by man since the advent of the first farmers in the Neolithic age. Many woodlands, including Epping Forest, are 'primary' – meaning that the land has always been wooded and has direct biological links with the primeval forest – but even primary woodlands have been altered by their long history of management going back at least 1,000 years, possibly 5,000. It is not possible to re-create the primeval wild wood, it is gone for ever, and 'natural' neglect will only result in the conversion of woodlands and wood-pasture, historically interesting and biologically rich, into rather ordinary woodlands of the type that can be found on established wasteland anywhere. In the 1880s there was virtually no awareness of the importance of historic landscapes – although Buxton, ahead of his time, suggested retention of some pollards for their historical interest. Epping Forest is truly historic in the sense of 12,000 years of continuity, profoundly influenced and managed by man for probably nearly half that span – to the landscape historian its value is comparable to a medieval cathedral for the architectural historian; it is an historic monument, albeit living, that merits a similar respect.

If Buxton were alive today, one could feel reasonably sure that he would appreciate the changing context of the forest and his views might be very different from those he wrote down nearly 100 years ago. No doubt he would be dismayed to find that the policies he set out had become inflexible and apparently incapable of change, although patently they were not achieving the aims intended. Meanwhile the present conservators face a monumental problem left by their predecessors who adopted a *laissez-faire* policy. The floor of the forest is virtually dead, the great trees are aged and prone to windblow, the variety has almost disappeared, and the unique quality of this pollard forest is unlikely to last longer than a couple of generations. The solution to the problem can only lie in a revival of historic management: the resumption of pollarding on the scale in which it operated 150 years ago and the restoration of the open plains; pollarding should be self-financing and the grasslands should yield a hay crop. The benefits for nature conservation would be considerable as the forest floor would once more come to life and there would be the aesthetic delight of witnessing the restoration to working order of what is essentially a functional landscape.

From the 2,500 hectares of Royal Forest we turn to the comparatively tiny site of High Wood, Chigwell, covering some 18 hectares of which approximately 9.5 hectares were covered by woodland and scrub contained within an area of poor-quality boggy pasture. The site is undulating land above the Roding valley and commands long views in the Essex countryside and also towards London – the Post Office Tower is visible on clear days. It lies on the fringe of London, and walkers and joggers regularly use the public right of way along the south of the site. In 1975 a proposal for refuse tipping led to angry local reaction and lengthy petitions to have it refused.

In 1978 new owners who were dairy and stock farmers were concerned at the rapid annual increase of scrub cover and while the optimum farming solution would have been almost total clearance and drainage, they felt that the prominence of the wood in the landscape and its proximity to the urban area called for a compromise solution – if it were possible to reach one – in order to give a reasonable return from land now out of control, from a farming viewpoint, while preserving the amenities.

Much of the wooded area consisted of old, overgrown attenuated thorn trees, giving a dense canopy and dead floor, while the surrounding hedges of thorn and dogrose were rapidly invading the grassland beyond. The scrub area contained many young self-sown trees as well as mysterious pits. The general impression was of a Neolithic landscape of shifting agriculture followed by recolonisation. One small area (1.7 hectares) had a recognisable coppice structure of hornbeam.

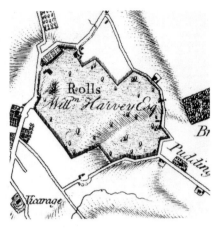

Fig. 8.5 Chapman and André's *Map of Essex* showing Rolls Park in 1777 with no woodland and an indication of wood-pasture.

Several fine oaks stood in the grassland area, two of great age and magnificence.

The site had considerable value for nature conservation, in particular the areas of new scrub which provided nesting for areas for migrant birds. Natural ponds, spring fed, lay on the higher ground. If managed as a nature reserve, scrub clearance would have been achieved by hand tools and the old thorn areas coppiced, the ponds cleared gently and then left – a labour-intensive operation impossible for a farmer and difficult for a naturalist's trust without extensive volunteer support.

Without such management the farmer was left with a situation in which every year his grassland shrank, and the scrub areas expanded to form a dense canopied thorn woodland useless to both farmer and wildlife.

A compromise was sought and initially the history of the site was examined for guidance to present management. Cartographical evidence revealed the historical sequence: Chapman and Andre's *Map of Essex* (1777) showed the area as forming the southern extent of Rolls Park and depicted it as parkland rather than woodland. The public footpath along the south edge of the site was then a road and inspection of an earthwork beside it showed the bank and internal ditch characteristic of the enclosing pale of a medieval deer park. The Tithe Map of 1843 showed three enclosed woodland areas established and the area disparked. The coppice must have been established at this time and the hawthorn hedges planted, while many old oaks remained as relics of the park. These were pulled out during the First World War (hence the pits) but had meanwhile set seed which, protected and drawn up by the thorn, had become fine young trees with straight stems.

Fig. 8.6 Unmanageable scrub in 1978, useless for man, grazing animal and wildlife – no songbirds and no mammals.

Fig. 8.7 The clue to future management – mature oaks surviving from Rolls Park, providing biological links with the Middle Ages and beyond.

The compromise solution between the farming, amenity and conservation interest of the site, took account of its history, returning it to wood-pasture, with the coppice area alone being fenced and retained as woodland. The hedges, although recent in origin have been generally retained as a nesting habitat for migrating birds as well as shelter for cattle, but they can now be kept under control by occasional maintenance. Many good young oaks have been retained, together with some hornbeam and isolated whitethorn of good shape. The two principal ponds have been carefully preserved and fenced.

By autumn 1980 the scars of change had healed and High Wood had become a bewitching landscape of a type now very rare: youthful wood-pasture. The land is productive for all purposes – the grassland cleared and grazed, the coppice fenced for future management, and continuity assured of the local strain of oak thus maintaining links to the earlier wood-pasture landscape and beyond that to the primeval forest cover. A landscape has been brought into a stable balance meeting the separate demands of conservation and productivity.

The third example is the Bovingdon Hall estate which lies on the fertile glacial soils of the East Anglian till. The land-form is dissected plateau crowned by ancient woodlands on the highest and flattest areas, with a multitude of springs filling meandering ditches and courses which bring the spring and rain-water down from the heavy clays into the River Pant which winds through the estate. The topography is gentle and all the land can be cultivated without difficulty, providing a considerable choice and flexibility for farming patterns. Constraints are present in roads, rights of way, major watercourses and changes of soil type, but even so, a prairie method of farming could be seen as possible and logical to an owner without concern for other demands on the land's surface.

The landscape has characteristic features deriving from early and piecemeal enclosure of woodland and waste into fields. Hedges are

Fig. 8.8 1979 – a new landscape of youthful wood-pasture.

botanically rich and sinuous, winding lanes link scattered farms, and the pattern of fields appears to have grown from the land rather than having been imposed upon it. It seems unlikely that open-field farming was ever practised to any extent. The diversity of the glacial soils, with their gravel caps and frequent areas of silty clays beside watercourses, favoured the retention of areas as woodland and mead, while the many springs encouraged a dispersed settlement pattern of small farms, based on an economy of mixed husbandry.

The age of the estate's hedgerows have been analysed using the Hooper dating method and from this it was clear that the main structure of land use and access tracks are defined by Saxon and medieval hedgerows. Approximately one-third of the hedgerows appeared of Saxon or early medieval date, one-third late medieval or Tudor, and the remainder modern or undatable.

The earliest evidence of settlement is Roman: a scatter of sherds and debris not far from Bocking Hall, the capital manor of a Saxon estate given to the monks of Canterbury in 978 and described in the Domesday Survey. Expansion followed on to all land with natural drainage, further manors were built (Fennes and Bovingdon) and five outlying farmsteads. By the Black Death (mid-14th century) land clearance was virtually complete, except for the remaining woodlands and the monk's park which occupied a large area (194 hectares) of flat and ill-drained land. The park was gradually cleared in succeeding centuries and with the application of modern drainage became high-quality arable land and now includes the most open area of the estate.

The Tabor family make their appearance in records of the seventeenth century and by 1803 owned virtually all the land included in the present Bovingdon Hall estate which comprises some 691 hectares (1,706 acres). Long-established ownership by a resident and active family usually brings a feeling for the history of the land and its main features, and in the climate of improvement during the 1950s and 1960s when fields were rationalised and the land drained, the amenities were kept in mind and the extent of surviving woodlands and hedgerows is a testimony to John Tabor's care. The term 'amenity' is particularly relevant in this context, as in those decades the value in historical and wildlife terms of such features and their importance as a resource that cannot be recreated, were unknown except to a handful of historian-biologists who were then embarking on the research which would bring new dimensions to landscape management in the 1970s.

In 1972, following a conference, Landscape in Decline, Essex County Council set aside funds for the advice and grant assistance of farmers in restoring tree and shrub cover to the countryside. Alarmed by the loss of elms, John Tabor sought advice, so beginning a long collaboration with the County's landscape staff which still continues. In the summer of 1972 the first field corner spinneys were planned, prototypes for many hundreds to follow across Essex, and the first appraisal of major hedgerows forming linkages and corridors across the estate.

When in 1975 the Countryside Commission came to establish the Demonstration Farms Project, the Bovingdon Hall estate was the obvious candidate for farms on the chalky boulder clays of East Anglia, Hertfordshire and Essex [3]. The purpose of the project was to investigate and then demonstrate how conservation interests could be

Fig. 8.9 Bovingdon Hall – a Saxon trackway surviving as a farm road and public footpath today.
Fig. 8.10 A parish boundary on the Bovingdon Estate.
Fig. 8.11 Bovingdon: narrow lanes open up views to arable landscapes.

3. The Countryside Commission's Demonstration Farms Project consists of ten commercially run farms in England and Wales selected from a variety of landscapes and farming systems as well as size and ownership. They have all shown that modern farming and conservation need not be incompatible. Each farm hosts a series of demonstrations during the year, primarily for farming audiences. Over 2,500 farmers, landowners, advisers, land agents, agricultural students and others visited project farms during 1982.

Fig. 8.12 Small-leaved lime recently coppiced.
Fig. 8.13 View of part of the Bovingdon Hall estate as it appeared in about 1950 before agricultural improvement.
Fig. 8.14 1974. Except for Fennes (the area in the middle distance) which is still a dairy farm, the estate has gone over to arable farming. The emphasis of the past 20 years has been on improvement with drainage and enlargement of field sizes. The landscape is starting to appear somewhat threadbare in places.
Fig. 8.15 1984. Some further field rationalisation has taken place but there is now an emphasis on amenity and cover. Spinneys have been planted and hedgerow trees either planted or promoted by good management. These are depicted as they will appear in 10–15 years.

combined with commercial farming. This enabled very detailed studies to be made by specialist interests: farming, forestry, sporting, recreation, wildlife conservation and landscape conservation, which then led to the preparation of a multi-purpose plan. It was noteworthy that the only clash of interest which could not be reconciled concerned

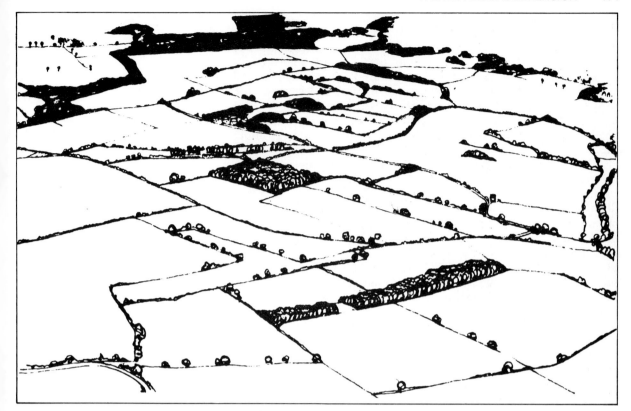

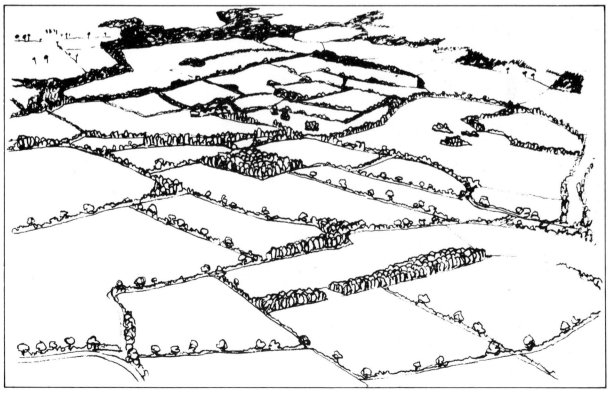

woodland management, and that otherwise a harmonious compromise proved possible between commercial and other interests, although this did not differ to any marked degree from the management already favoured on the estate. However, from 1975 onwards management became extremely positive with every feature examined and treated with care. The great moat at Fennes was drained and cleaned, and then each spring and pond was cleared of debris and scrub to let in light and sometimes be enlarged; hedgerows were brought into coppice rotation with 'maidens' selected to be brought on to form future timber trees and redress the rather elderly balance of tree cover, a characteristic of much farmland where traditional practices lapsed in the agricultural depressions. New farm buildings and grain stores are painted with bitumen and harmonise with the landscape, and new plantings are implemented each year on crooked headlands and areas of land awkward to cultivate. Two former farmstead sites are now managed as nature reserves by the Essex Trust. Agricultural improvement has continued, but always in the knowledge of what is valuable to preserve or possible to create. The public are well served by clearly marked footpaths, hedged farmtracks and ancient lanes, and there is little evidence of the vandalism that besets farmers near to urban areas.

The conflict of views on woodland management has been mentioned and illustrates perfectly the clash between the aims of the Forestry Commission and those of other parties. The estate contains a complex of primary woodlands comprising 71 hectares of oak standards, with an understorey mainly of small-leaved lime and hornbeam. The oak is approaching maturity which presents the problem of restocking and the coppice was found to be uncommercial to the extent that cutting made a loss to the estate. The Forestry Plan proposed the conversion of a substantial area to a conifer–broadleaf plantation, a proposal that was wholly unacceptable on grounds of nature conservation, historic continuity, amenity and sporting interest. Once destroyed the long-established ecosystem could not be re-created, and this seemed unethical – the equivalent of the replacement of a Grade I building of national significance with a modern structure, the process enabled by a substantial government grant. The proposal was not implemented and by 1981 the demands of the log market had made coppicing once more a source of small profit. It now seems likely that the woodlands will return to their traditional management.

The lesson of Bovingdon Hall is that management on conservation principles can become a part of the farm plan. It is no longer a question of compromise, a synthesis has been achieved which gives a sense of rightness, apparent to the many visitors on spring and summer demonstrations. It shows the beauty attainable by the functional landscape when the historic dimension is appreciated and recalls the early eighteenth-century vision of Addison, Switzer and Shenstone, while looking sideways to the twentieth-century awareness of ecology and diminishing resources. Addison had suggested 'Why may not a whole estate be thrown into a kind of garden by frequent plantations?' and this has been done at Bovingdon, although within the parameters of efficient arable farming and not the meadow landscape which Addison loved – although some meadows have been retained in spite of economic incentives to remove them. For Switzer at Grimsthorpe, the surrounding countryside which included cornfields and woodlands was more important than the formal areas around the house, and one imagines that he would approve if transported through time to Bovingdon. Shenstone, the inventor of the farm trail, devised a winding path with seats carefully devised to admire scenes and prospects, without interfering with the practical conduct of his farm. On Bovingdon demonstrations with their regular stops, I have wondered if this is our contemporary version of Shenstone's trail; visitors consider new spinneys, sensitive field amalgamations, a newly created pond, old coppice restored, farm buildings made handsome by a coat of bitumen, a grove of wild service trees and a restored moat. Shenstone's visitors admired a temple of Pan, a cataract and a ruined priory as well as farming scenes, and he set urns and obelisks engraved with verses for contemplation along his route. Is this really so different? The eighteenth- and twentieth-century ideas of total landscape and the pursuit of synthesis may differ in their details and in the pressures and priorities perceived in these different times, but an element of shared vision remains. Bovingdon stands in an English tradition; not that of Brown and Repton, but one more relevant to the needs of our times.

Earlier I quoted Schumacher's three tasks for agriculture: 'To keep man in touch with living nature, of which he is and remains a highly vulnerable part; to humanise and enoble man's wider habitat; and to bring forth the foodstuffs and other materials which are needed for a becoming life'. It would seem that the Bovingdon Hall estate fulfils these tasks and that all farmland could do so if the will is there and the right advice is available. John Tabor is a pioneer in applying conservation principles, but fortunately he is not alone and an increasing number of farmers are coming to regard the concept of stewardship as a far wider requirement than the needs of agriculture alone.

Bibliography

Chapters 1 to 4

Boethius, A. and Ward-Perkins, J. B., *Etruscan and Roman Architecture.* Penguin (1970).

Clark, K., *Landscape into Art.* Murray (1949).

Creswell, K. A. C., *Early Muslim Architecture.* Penguin (1958).

Crisp, F., *Medieval Gardens.* Bodley Head (1924).

Combe, J., *Theronimus Bosch.* Batsford (1946).

Ghirshman, R., *Iran.* Penguin (1978).

Gibson, N. S., *Bruegel.* Thames and Hudson (1977).

Gothein, M. L., *A History of Garden Art* (from the German). Dent (1928).

Grant, M., *The Climax of Rome.* Weidenfeld and Nicolson (1968).

Gray, B., *Persian Painting.* Ernest Benn (1930).

Harvey, J., *The Medieval Architect.* Wayland (1972).

Harvey, J., *Medieval Gardens.* Batsford (1981).

Lethaby, W. R., *Architecture, Nature and Magic.* Duckworth (1956).

Macdougall, E. B. and Ettinghausen, R. (eds), *The Islamic Garden.* Dumbarton Oaks (1976).

Masson, G., *Italian Villas and Palaces.* Thames and Hudson (1959).

Masson, G., *Italian Gardens.* Thames and Hudson (1961).

Norwich, J. J., *The Kingdom in the Sun.* Faber and Faber (1976).

Pearsall, D. and Salter, E. *The Landscapes and the Seasons of the Medieval World.* Elek (1973).

Pevsner, N., *The Leaves of Southwell.* King Penguin (1945).

Pliny (the Younger), *Letters.* Translated by B. Radice. Penguin (1963).

Virgil, *The Eclogues, Georgics and Aeneid.* Translated by C. Day Lewis. Oxford (1966).

Vogt, J., *The Decline of Rome.* Weidenfeld and Nicolson (1965).

Ward-Perkins, J., *Pompeii A.D. 79.* Royal Academy of Arts (1976).

Chapters 5 and 6

Barrell, J., *The Dark Side of the Landscape – the Rural Poor in English Painting, 1730-1840.* Cambridge (1980).

Dutton, R., *The English Garden.* Batsford (1937).

Grigson, G., *Samuel Palmer*. Kegan Paul (1947).

Hadfield, M., *A History of British Gardening*. Spring Books (1960).

Hoskins, W. G., *Midland England*. Batsford (1949).

Hoskins, W. G., *The Making of the English Landscape*. Hodder and Stoughton (1955).

Hoskins, W. G., *English Landscapes*. BBC (1973).

Hunt, J. D. and Willis, P., *The Genius of the Place*. Elek (1975).

Hussey, C., *English Gardens and Landscapes, 1700-1750*. London (1967).

Jellicoe, G. and S., *The Landscape of Man*. Thames and Hudson (1975).

Jourdain, M., *The Work of William Kent*. Country Life (1948).

Malins, E., *English Landscaping and Literature, 1660-1840*. London (1966).

Parris, L., *Landscape in Britain c. 1750-1850*. The Tate Gallery (1973).

Piper, J., *British Romantic Artists*. Collins (1946).

Robinson, W., *The Wild Garden*. London (1870).

Stroud, D., *Capability Brown*. London (1950).

Stroud, D., *Humphry Repton*. London (1962).

Watkin, D., *The English Vision*. John Murray (1982).

Williams, J. D., *Audley End: The Restoration of 1762-1797*. Essex County Council (1966).

Willis, P. (ed.), *Furor Hortensis*. Elsium Press Ltd, Edinburgh (1974).

Chapters 7 and 8

Ehrlich, P. and A., *Extinction – the Causes and Consequences of the Disappearance of Species*. Victor Gollancz (1982).

Fox, S., *John Muir and his Legacy – The American Conservation Movement*. Little, Brown and Company, Boston and Toronto (1981).

Fraser Darling, F., *Wilderness and Plenty*. BBC (1970).

Green, B., *Countryside Conservation*. Allen and Unwin (1981).

Grove, D., *The Future for Forestry*. British Association of Nature Conservationists (1983).

Lords Select Committee on Science and Technology, *Scientific Aspects of Forestry*. HMSO (1980).

McHarg, I., *Design with Nature*. Natural History Press (1969).

O'Riordan, T., *Earth's Survival – A Conservation and Development Programme for the U.K.* Report No. 7, 'Putting trust in the countryside'. World Conservation Strategy (1982).

Peterken, G. F., *Woodland Conservation and Management*. Chapman and Hall (1981).

Pollard, E., Hooper, M. and Moore, N. W., *Hedges*. Collins (1974).

Rackham, O., *Trees and Woodland in the British Landscape*. Dent (1976).

Schumacher, E. F., *Small is Beautiful*. Abacus (1974).

Sturdy R. G., Allen, R. H., Rackham O. and Ranson, C. E., *Epping Forest – The Natural Aspect?* The Essex Field Club (1978).

Sturrock, F. and Cathie, J., *Farm Modernisation and the Countryside*. University of Cambridge Department of Land Economy. Occasional Paper No. 12 (1980).

Watson, L., *Supernature – The Natural History of the Supernatural*. Hodder and Stoughton (1973).

Paintings referred to but not illustrated in text

Geertgen tot Sint Jans, *St John the Baptist in the Wilderness*. Pearsall and
    Salter, Plate VII.
Benozzo Gozzoli, *Adoration of the Magi*. Pearsall and Salter, Fig. 60;
    Clark, Fig. 10.
Sandro Botticelli, *Birth of Venus*. Berenson, Plates 204-5.
    Primavera (Spring). Berenson, Plates 203 and 206.
    Adoration of the Magi. Berenson, Plate 212.
Grunewald, *Isenheim Altar*. Clark, Figs. 34 and 35.
Bruegel, *Allegory of Lust*. Gibson, Fig. 21.
    The Triumph of Death. Mettra, Plate and three details.
    February (The Gloomy Day). Mettra, called *The Dull Day*.
    July (Corn Harvest). Mettra, Plate.
    October (Return of the Herd). Mettra, Plate.
Leonardo da Vinci, *Virgin and Child with St Anne*. Clark, Fig. 46b; Gold-
    scheider, Fig. 87.
    Mona Lisa. Goldscheider, Plate and Figs. 26 and 27.
    Madonna of the Rocks. Goldscheider, Plate and Figs. 83 and 84.
Giovanni Bellini, *Madonna of the Meadows*. Hendy and Goldscheider,
    Figs. 94 and 95; Clark, Fig. 23.
St Francis in the Wilderness. Hendy and Goldscheider, Figs. 47 and 48;
    Clark, Fig. 25.
Giorgione, *Fête Champêtre*. Clark, Fig. 54.
Titian, *Bacchus and Ariadne*. Berenson, Plates 43–5
Claude Lorraine, *Ascanius and the Stag*. Clark, Fig. 59.
    The Temple of Apollo. Clark, Fig. 61.
Nicolas Poussin, *The Gathering of the Ashes of Phocion*. Clark, Fig. 64.
Samuel Palmer, *Harvest Moon*. Piper, page 32; Grigson, Fig. 40.
    A Church among Trees. Piper, page 31; Grigson, Fig. 39.
    Full Moon and Deer. Grigson, Fig. 37.

SOURCES

Berenson, B., *Italian Painters of the Renaissance*. Phaidon (1952).
Clark, K., *Landscape into Art*. John Murray (1949).
Gibson, W. S., *Bruegel*. Thames and Hudson (1977).
Goldscheider, L., *Leonardo da Vinci*. Phaidon (1943).
Grigson, G., *Samuel Palmer – the Visionary Years*. Kegan Paul (1947).
Hendy, P. and Goldscheider, L., *Bellini*. Phaidon (1945).
Mettra, C., *Bruegel*. Ferndale Editions (1980).
Pearsall, D. and Salter, E., *Landscapes and Seasons of the Medieval World*.
    Elek (1973).
Piper, J., *British Romantic Artists*. Collins (1946).

Index

Compiled by
County Councillor Dennis J. Nisbet, J.P.
Member of the Society of Indexers

Notes:
1. Entries in italics refer to books, documents or paintings
2. Figures in italics refer to illustrations on pages where they are not mentioned in the text.